Bio-cultural Development of Scheduled Tribes

Bio-cultural Development of Scheduled Tribes

Policies and Issues

Edited by

P.K. Misra
H.K. Bhat
K.K. Misra

Indira Gandhi Rashtriya Manav Sangrahalaya, Bhopal

Anthropological Association Mysore

RAWAT PUBLICATIONS

Jaipur • New Delhi • Bangalore • Hyderabad • Guwahati

ISBN 978-81-316-0534-9

Published by

Indira Gandhi Rashtriya Manav Sangrahalaya
Shamla Hills, Bhopal 462013 (Madhya Pradesh)
E-mail: directorigrms@gmail.com

Anthropological Association
93/12 & 94/14, Bogadi, Mysore 570026 (Karnataka)
E-mail: promodkumarmisra@gmail.com

Prem Rawat for **Rawat Publications**
Satyam Apts., Sector 3, Jawahar Nagar, Jaipur 302 004 (India)
Phone: 0141 265 1748 / 7006 Fax: 0141 265 1748
E-mail: info@rawatbooks.com
Website: www.rawatbooks.com

New Delhi Office
4858/24, Ansari Road, Daryaganj, New Delhi 110 002
Phone: 011-23263290

Also at *Bangalore, Hyderabad* and *Guwahati*

Typeset by M & M Pre Press Consultants, Trivandrum
Printed at Chaman Enterprises, New Delhi

Contents

Acknowledgements vii
Introduction ix

1. Understanding tribes and their socio-cultural ethos for a sustainable policy for their development 1
S.N. Ratha

2. Policies and issues in the bio-cultural development of Scheduled Tribes 30
P.K. Misra

3. Applied anthropology, development and cultural diversity 39
P.R.G. Mathur

4. The concept of tribe in the Indian context 62
T.B. Subba

5. Tribal development and security of land 74
P. Ishwara Bhat

6. Tribal development in north-east India vis-à-vis national integration: An overview 92
R.K. Kar

7. Genetic architecture of Indian people 101
V.R. Rao and A. Chandrasekar

8. Bio-cultural aspect of sickle-cell trait in tribal populations of India 115
R.S. Negi

9. Nutritional status based on anthropometry of tribal children of Paschim Medinipur district, West Bengal 125
Sanjib Ganguly, Argina Khatun, Samiran Bisai, Subal Das and Kaushik Bose

10. Some biological factors associated with infant mortality among the Kol of Madhya Pradesh: A multivariate analysis 134
Ajay Kumar Gharami

11. Disability among the Scheduled Tribes: Observations for policy towards the disabled 151
Udita Rathi and B.V. Sharma

12. The Betta Kuruba of Karnataka: Struggle for existence 162
B.R. Vijayendra

13. Impact of the *Velugu* programme and changes in lifestyle of the Yanadi tribe of Rayalaseema region of Andhra Pradesh 170
S.A.A. Saheb

14. Policies and issues in the education of Scheduled Tribes 184
B.V. Raviprasad

15. Medical pluralism and mainstreaming AYUSH: An anthropological analysis of health policy 198
P. Kalyan Reddy

16. Indigenous medicine and its practice among the Jaunsari 215
S.N.H. Rizvi

17. Illness and health-seeking behaviour among the Baiga tribe of Madhya Pradesh 225
Nilanjan Khatua

18. Coping with cataract blindness among tribal patients: Some case studies from Mysore district, Karnataka 244
C.K. Kantharaju and H.K. Bhat

List of Contributors 253
Index 255

Acknowledgements

Sincere thanks are due to the Director, Indira Gandhi Rashtriya Manav Sangrahalaya, Bhopal and the Director, Anthropological Survey of India, Kolkata, for their financial support in organising the national seminar on 'Policies and Issues in the Bio-cultural Development of Scheduled Tribes' during 26–28 November, 2007 at Mysore. We are also thankful to the Director, Anthropological Survey of India for allowing us to organise the event in the premises of their Southern Regional Centre.

Our thanks are also due to all the scientific and administrative staff of Anthropological Survey of India, Southern Regional Centre for their assistance in organising the seminar. We are also grateful to all the members and office bearers of Anthropological Association, Mysore for their help in organising the event. We express our special thanks to Smt. Anupama for her secretarial assistance.

Editors

Introduction

The Anthropological Association, Mysore, was established in March 1999 to promote activities related to anthropology. From a modest beginning, it has progressed well during the last thirteen years.

The Association seeks to enhance the understanding of humankind and their global concerns without borders. It perceives anthropology holistically as the study of the material, cognitive, biological, linguistic and socio-cultural dimensions of humanity. It views the anthropological method of holism as a particular kind of epistemology.

The Association advocates anthropologically informed engagement in development work, while it also acknowledges the human agency or the capacity and capability of people distanced by miles and milieus to order their lifeways. It is for critical debate to complement the intensive ethnographic and ethnological studies on which anthropology fundamentally depends, with particular concern for the voiceless people. In this context, the Association aims to innovate and develop knowledge, tools and human resources to establish linkages between studies of human groups and emergent issues for future development programmes. The Anthropological Association intends to collaborate with other eminent institutions of anthropology in India and abroad. In this direction, it became an institutional member of Indian National Confederation and Academy of Anthropologists (INCAA) so that it could initiate major collaborative ventures and enter into partnership programmes with other educational and research institutions, museums and industry.

The present volume is the outcome of the national seminar on 'Policies and Issues in the Bio-cultural Development of Scheduled Tribes' held on

26–28 November, 2007 at Southern Regional Office of Anthropological Survey of India, Mysore. About forty papers were presented in the seminar by eminent scholars, of which eighteen papers are selected for the present volume. The papers deal with themes such as nutrition and growth, health, disease and health care, tribal economy, concept of tribe and tribal development programmes. A brief introduction to the papers of this volume is presented below in chronological order:

S.N. Ratha, in his comprehensive account, traces the emergence of the term 'tribe' and then goes on to show that tribal development plans in the country have failed to deliver the promised results. The author has shown through case studies that forest and land are the integral parts of tribal culture. He pleads that rightful place should be accorded to tribal knowledge, wisdom and values which are exhibited in their art, music, dance, etc. He also argues that development plans for the tribal people should be culture-friendly and participatory.

P.K. Misra in his paper poses a relevant question as to why the Scheduled Tribes are at the bottom of human development in spite of so much attention being paid to them. He then forcefully argues that the modern development paradigm cannot address the problems of these people. In fact, he demonstrates with illustrations that the Scheduled Tribes are being progressively dispossessed of whatever resources they had under their command. According to him, there is an urgent need for an alternative development paradigm.

P.R.G. Mathur's paper is the First Ananthakrishna Iyer Memorial Lecture organised during the seminar. In this, Mathur highlights the importance of anthropological knowledge in the process of planning and development of the Scheduled Tribes. Mathur has done ethnographic and applied anthropology research in Kerala for more than four decades and exposed several instances where the benefits meant for the Scheduled Tribes, Scheduled Castes and backward communities have been usurped by economically and socially dominant castes. In the present paper he has cited several cases, with rich ethnographic data, to justify his argument. The difficulties involved in implementing the constitutional provisions for the weaker sections of the society are also highlighted in the paper with illustrations from southern India.

T.B. Subba's paper opens a debate on the concept of tribe in the Indian context. After reviewing the various ways in which the term has been defined, he comes to the conclusion that none of them is inclusive enough. However, he proposes reciprocity as the basic feature of the tribal society which is inversely related to monetisation. Further, he says that defining a tribe is problematic for a simple reason that all societies in the modern world are fast changing. Regarding the nature of reciprocity the author has given detailed explanation and illustrations. He also says that in a generalised sense, reciprocity appears to be a basic human trait.

P. Ishwara Bhat in his paper points out that conferring security to the tribal people in respect of land they occupy is essential to ensure dignified life, economic development and socio-cultural activities to this vulnerable section of Indian society. In the background of these factors, legal recognition of the rights of Forest Dwelling Scheduled Tribes emerged under the Act of 2006. He has discussed the salient features of this new Act. The special provisions under V and VI schedules are also discussed in the paper.

R.K. Kar in his paper argues for a comprehensive and holistic development of tribes keeping their culture in perspective. He points out that inadequate and inefficient development efforts and inequitable distribution of the benefits of the development are the major factors that have contributed towards the sub-national sentiments among certain ethnic groups in north-east India. The paper attempts to outline an effective alternative strategy suitable for the region.

V.R. Rao and A. Chandrasekar discuss issues relating to peopling of the Indian sub-continent. They have attempted to trace out ancient successive human migrations, peopling of India and variations in Indian gene pool. Genetic links with west Eurasians, east Eurasians and Australians are also shown in the paper. Y chromosome lineages and their typologies are described with special reference to tribal population.

R.S. Negi discusses the bio-cultural dimensions of sickle-cell trait in tribal population of India. The interactions between human biological endowment and the environmental factors and culture are brought out to explain this hereditary disease. The author traces the history of the disease and its distribution in India, with special reference to tribal population of India.

Sanjib Ganguly and associates have attempted to estimate the nutritional status of tribal children in Paschim Medinipur district of West Bengal. The authors have studied age and sex variations in height and weight, levels of stunting and underweight among 431 school children aged 8–18 years by using anthropometric method. The study showed that the prevalence of underweight is very high whereas stunting is medium among the tribal children.

Ajay Kumar Gharami has attempted to highlight the various factors associated with infant mortality among the Kol tribe of Madhya Pradesh. The author has used multivariate analysis to show that birth order, birth interval and ANM check-up are the important determinants of infant mortality among the Kol tribe.

Udita Rathi and B.V. Sharma in their paper focus on the disabled among the Scheduled Tribe population of Andhra Pradesh. The paper is based on the data generated by the 2001 census. The authors show that despite a significant number of disabled among the Scheduled Tribes, their problems are ignored. Unequal distribution of resources among them demonstrates that the major share is going to the people living in urban areas. The authors argue that disabled among the Scheduled Tribes should be specifically targeted for support so that they can lead a life of dignity and self-respect.

B.R. Vijayendra describes the struggle for survival by the Betta Kuruba tribe of Karnataka, using variables such as housing, malnutrition, unemployment, indebtedness, education, health, drinking alcohol etc.

S.A.A. Saheb outlines the impact of the 'Velugu' programme among the Yanadi tribes of Rayalseema region of Andhra Pradesh. The programme was started with the aid of World Bank in 2000 and is in operation in 22 districts of the state. The paper focuses on the impact of the programme in the fields of eradication of child labour, promotion of female education and biodiversity programmes.

B.V. Raviprasad discusses the policies and issues related to education of Scheduled Tribes. The paper is based on secondary data. Comparison between Scheduled Tribe and general population is done with respect to literacy rate, school enrolment status, time taken to secure employment etc.

P. Kalyan Reddy has done an anthropological analysis of mainstreaming AYUSH in the context of medical pluralism. National health policies of India formulated in 1983, 2000 and 2002 and the efforts made in popularising the indigenous medical systems are discussed in the paper. The reasons for integrating various medical systems are also given.

S.N.H. Rizvi discusses the nature of indigenous medicine among the Jaunsari of the Himalayas. He shows that the flora and fauna of the region is well integrated into their health culture. The traditional medical practitioners and the traditional medicines are described in the paper.

Nilanjan Khatua's paper deals with the health problems and health seeking behaviour of a small tribal population in a backward region of the state of Madhya Pradesh. The kinds of illnesses identified by the people are described well in the paper. Health status of the people is also presented, especially in terms of mortality rates.

C.K. Kantharaju and H.K. Bhat, in their paper on cataract blindness among the tribal population of Mysore district, describe the health behaviour of these people. Jenukurubas, Bettakurubas and Yeravas are covered under the present study. Accessibility of eye care services and other factors influencing their utilisation are discussed. The authors have also described the concept of blindness among the three tribal groups.

1

Understanding tribes and their socio-cultural ethos for a sustainable policy for their development

S.N. Ratha

The ancient Indian society was characterised by a four-fold division termed as *varnasrama.* The *varnas* were *Brahmana, Kshatriya, Vaisya,* and *Sudra.* Initially and ideally, these divisions were not based upon birth but on the quality and calling of the individuals in groups (*guna* and *karma: Geeta* IV.12). Down the corridors of time, the *varnas* consolidated into isogamous but functionally interdependent groups in the society. Consequently, intermarriage among the *varnas* lowered the social status of the offsprings and led to the formation of new isogamous groups called *sankara-varna.* Further intermarriage between the *varnas* and the *sankara-varnas,* and among the *sankara-varnas* led to the formation of new groups in a continuous process (Manu X). In course of time, all these groups came to be known as *jati* and the terms of *varna* and *sankara-varna* became obsolete in functional vocabulary. Manu's list includes many community names, among which some are found among the castes, some among the Scheduled Tribes, and some among the Scheduled Castes of contemporary times. Therefore, all such communities are to be regarded as socio-genetic extensions of the *varna;* the tribes therein are to be regarded, not as the antecedent stages of civilisation but its product.

By the time the Indian society was exposed to the Europeans, it was constituted of innumerable *jatis.* The Portuguese called them *casta.*

Possibly they had not intimately come across with that section of the Indian population whom the English called 'tribe'. The test census of 1872 and later the regular decennial census initiated in 1881, the Indian population was divided into two social types, namely, the tribes and the castes, by which time the term 'tribe' was already in vogue in Europe to designate non-European communities of Africa, Asia, Australia and America. The term came to be associated with social formations of allegedly less civilised status, a concept recurrent in 19th and the early 20th century anthropology parading evolutionism (Service, 1962: 110–42). The terms—caste and tribe—became handy for the colonial administrators to 'divide' the people of India. Beginning in 1918, nine orders/notifications were issued in different times till 1936 listing the 'Hill Tribes' and 'Backward Tribes'.

What emerges as an ideal tribe or tribal formation, in positive terms, from a run through of some textbook definitions, is that it is a social group of simple uncomplicated kind consisting of a collection of families of common origin or derivation or descent and custom, possessing a distinctive language or dialect and culture, a name and a definite territory and engaged in joint activities of some common purpose. Some have used negative descriptors, such as absence of any occupational specialisation (Risley, 1912: 22), lack of state organisation, absence of classes and literacy (Steward, 1955: 44), non-involvement in cash economy, little supra village political organisation, non-adherence to any great religion, limited cultural elaboration and non-existence of central regulative political organisation (Sahlins, 1968) to identify tribes. India is exposed to multiple and varied historical forces over several millennia. It is not hard to find social formations conforming fully or partially to the indicators used in circumscribing tribal societies. Anthropologists in India do not seem to project a unified view on the concept of the tribal society. While some hold tribal societies completely different from the caste society; others do not find any difference between the two (Bailey, 1961: 7–19). So whatever be the administrative compulsions, separating the Indian communities into two distinct social types begins with the European colonialism.

The constitution makers of post-British India stuck to the use of the term 'tribe' to set aside a section of India's population to be scheduled under the Article 342 of the Constitution, by the President. Article 365 (25) described 'Scheduled Tribes' (the compound term first appeared here) as "such tribes or tribal communities as are deemed under Article

342 to be scheduled for the purpose of this Constitution". Article 342 prescribes the procedure to be followed in the matter of identification of 'Scheduled Tribes'. The indicators used by the Government of India to classify communities under 'Scheduled Tribes' are "primitive traits, distinctive culture, geographical location, shy of external contact, and backwardness". These criteria do not figure in the Constitution but have come down as a British legacy coined by the 1931 census commissioner. All commissions and committees, set up from time to time by the Government of India, followed the 1931 census definition. Some of them are the report of the first Backward Classes Commission 1955 (Chairman: Kaka Kalelkar), the Advisory Committee on the revision of Scheduled Caste and Scheduled Tribe List 1965 (Lokur Committee), and the Joint Committee of the Parliament on the Scheduled Castes and Scheduled Tribes Order (Amendment) Bill 1967 and the Chanda Committee 1969.

The Government of India issued nine orders listing various communities in different states under the specified schedule of the Constitution since 6 September 1950. With the introduction of the Tribal Sub Plan (TSP) strategy for an integrated development of Scheduled Tribes in 1975, some tribes or parts thereof have been identified as Primitive Tribal Groups (PTGs). These groups are identified for their pre-agricultural level of technology, low level of literacy, small, stagnant or diminishing population, remote and isolated habitat, distinct cultural and ethnic individuality and specialised avocation, if any. These indicators were prescribed through administrative orders (GoI, 1990: 146 and 153). In a publication brought out by the Government of India in 1998 for 'official use only' 608 communities were listed as 'Scheduled Tribes' in an alphabetical order (GoI, 1998: 30–45) among whom there were 75 PTGs. This publication also includes a state-wise list. Communities which are scheduled in one state are not necessarily scheduled in another, scheduled in one district of the state not in the other and sometimes only in one part of the district. All communities, irrespective of their socio-economic status, have been declared as Scheduled Tribes in Kinnaur, Jaunsar-Bawar, Pangwal and in Ladakh (except one community). In a nation-wide study of community situation undertaken by the Anthropological Survey of India, it is noticed that 11.80 per cent among the tribal communities claim their place in the *varna* system. Among them 8.30 per cent claim *Kshatriya* status, 0.90 per cent *Brahman* status, 7.50 per cent *Sudra* status. These include the Gaddi and Pangwala of Himachal

Pradesh and Kagaty of Sikkim and West Bengal positioning themselves as *Brahmans*; and the Jaunsari tribe claiming *Vaisya* status (Singh, 1994: 7). The same study reports that 171 (26.90%) tribal communities perceive their status as 'high', 298 (46.90%) as 'middle' and 161 (25.30%) as 'low'. Among the non-tribal communities, 11.20 per cent accord tribes as of 'high' social status, 39.20 per cent as 'middle' and 49.40 per cent as 'low'. Thus, in India, "tribe is an administrative and political concept" (ibid.: 1). There are recurrent newspaper reports of attempts by non-tribal communities, individually or in collectivity, claiming tribal status. No Indian language had a word in its vocabulary synonymous with the English word 'tribe'. Now, several terms, often meaning different from each other are in use. For example, in Oriya the term is *Ādivāsi* (early inhabitants), in Assamese it is Jana-jāti (the word defies translation into English), in Telugu it is *Girijana* (hill people), in Hindi it is *Adimjāti* (primordial jāti?), and in Malayalam it is *Pāttikā Vargam* (listed groups). Some also use the term *Vanavāsi* (forest dwellers). Of late, another term, 'the indigenous people' has surfaced. However, every Indian claims the indigenous status.

Those whose tribal identity is already established are innovating methods to establish their distinct identities. "In their quest for distinct identity", writes Roy Burman, "the tribal peoples created scripts for and literature in their languages. Today there are at least 10,000 publications including text books. Intellectuals among them have brought out analytical history of their social processes, language and literature. They raise their voices against display of their culture objects in museums without relating the same to their social, cultural, economic, historical and ecological contexts. There is a growing tendency to claim their religions as distinct spiritual calls. Five per cent of the tribal population returned their religions by the name of their respective tribes in 1981 census". Ten years after, in 1991 census, the percentage reached nearly ten (1995: 10). There is a perceivable rise in their awareness and inspirational levels. Some tribal communities are seen to leave no stone unturned to safeguard the privacy of their habitats, for exclusive access, control and management of their resources, to maintain their traditional role and role models within their own socio-economic set up as well as in their interaction with 'others' including government. The recent governmental step of extending the provisions of the *Panchayati Raj* to the tribal areas is looked upon as a historic landmark in the fulfilment of tribal aspirations.

II

The Constitution (Article 46) imposes the responsibility of improving the quality of life of the Scheduled Tribes on the Union and the State Governments. Initiative to development and change has come to be regarded as an urgent and pressing national responsibility. Therefore, identifying communities fit enough to be scheduled, has come to become a permanent administrative exercise; and tribal development has become a major, increasingly more important component of the nation's Five-Year Plans.

A large number of projects covering almost all aspects of tribal life are in operation. Investments including the cost of administration in these projects are massive. The achievements, however, are not proportionate to the investments. Some progress is, no doubt, made. In many cases, the differences in the level of development between the tribal areas and the remaining areas in the states are even accentuated. A Government of India document issued by the Ministry of Home Affairs (for official use only) laments, "In the name of tribal development, we have spent a lot of money during the last several Plans, but when accounting was made at the end of the last period of safeguards to the tribes in the constitution, it was found that actual benefits trickling down to the tribes have not been consistent with the promise we have made. Expenditure has not resulted in the benefit that should have accrued to this population. Unfortunately, the developmental programmes for tribal areas did not yield the desired results". It further observes that more than 75 per cent of the total benefits have not reached the tribes and cautions that "we cannot have development at this rate" (GoI, 1975: 98). The same document quotes a report, "Some responsible tribal bodies have refused to accept a larger programme in tribal areas for fear of exploitation". The organisational structure has seemingly failed to reach the benefits of the programmes to the target groups. The process only widened the psychological gap between the tribes and the non-tribes, including the government and its machinery. Such promises as "all problems of the tribes would be solved by the end of 1989" (GoI: 1977: 1–2), are frowned upon. In spite of all the strategies and efforts of years, 85 per cent of the tribal families remain below the poverty line, compared to the national average of about 38 per cent (from the performance appraisal documented by the VII Plan Working Group, quoted in Roy Burman, 1995: 67). Even the results of the often praised Tribal Sub-Plan (TSP) strategy developed during the V Plan are said to be not in proportion with the expectations and the investments (Report of the Working Group for the Scheduled Tribes in the VIII Plan). Reports of the committees and commissions appointed by the Government, from time to time, outline a dismal picture on the achievements of various programmes (ibid.: 16–18). Of late, even the X Plan document is candid enough to confess that the progress made by the Scheduled Tribes "could not bring them anywhere nearer to the mainstream society as the gap in their socio-economic status continued to prevail" (p. 451). The gap in the literacy between the ST and the total population continued to widen from 18.15 per cent in 1971 to 19.88 in 1981 and further to 22.61 in 1991. The growth in tribal literacy during the same period was from 11.30 per cent to 16.35 for 1971–81 and from 16.35 to 29 for 1981–91. Likewise, the gap between the ST female literacy and of the total female population also widened from 13.84 per cent in 1971 to 21.81 in 1981 showing a marginal respite in coming down by negligible 0.71 per cent in 1991 (ibid.: Table 4.2.5 and 4.2.6, p. 453). At the economic level too, the progress is found to be very slow. From 51.94 per cent living below the poverty line during 1993–94 to 45.86 per cent during 1999–2000 in rural sector; and from 41.14 per cent to 34.75 per cent in urban sector is not an appreciable progress (ibid.: Table 4.2.9, p. 455).

Several case studies from time to time and from different parts of the country have identified such avoidable lacunae as poor planning, non-participation and lack of awareness among the target groups (Basu, 1985: 26; Bhatt, 1982; Yadav, 1981: 13–15), indifference to or neglect of the felt needs of the target groups, rigidity of administrative procedure (Sharma, 1973: 23), vulnerability of the target groups to the exploitation and vested interest of the non-tribes (ibid.: 24) and divergence from the basic human aspirations (ibid.: 27) in developmental efforts for the Scheduled Tribes and other weaker sections. Other non-starting factors and causes of poor progress/failure can be seen in the unequal and uneasy relationship between the people and the development functionaries, and the bureaucratic tendency to downcast local knowledge and potential, as well as 'we give-you take' attitude.

Almost all case studies tend to attribute success and sustainability to culture friendly inputs/interventions, participatory approach, involved personnel, advance planning based upon reliable and adequate data, programmes based upon felt needs of the target groups, fixing achievable targets, and carried through a single line administration.

Thus, faith in the capabilities, knowledge and skill of the common man, and elimination of external vested interests (Chambers, 1994: 1253–68) and a paradigm shift from recipient to partnership, from dependency to self-reliance have come to be looked upon as indispensable tools of sustainable development.

III

Development, though popularly regarded as an economic process, equal emphasis should be placed on the qualitative aspects of human development. It should be looked upon as an organised and institutionalised activity with the aim of satisfying the basic needs of the people to psychologically orient them to adopt new skills, attitudes and lifestyles, so that they build up the inner strength to appropriately adjust their social and cultural infrastructures to stand the pressure of the changing situations; internalise benefits accrued from the development inputs to lift themselves to a higher level of life (Belshaw, 1972). Judged from this angle, development is a multidimensional process. It involves changes in structure, attitudes and institutions. It connotes acceleration of all-round growth, reduction of social and economic inequalities and eradication of absolute poverty (Todaro, 1977). Therefore, it should progressively improve the social, cultural, economic and human conditions of the people—all vital sectors necessary for a balanced growth of the society (Schneider, 1975; Basu, 1985).

The development strategy should also include ways and means to utilise latent, unused and underused human resources, skills and knowledge. It should be able to motivate the individual to produce more and better, to build capacity of a society, to define its own objectives and to carry out its programmes effectively (Belshaw, 1972). Further, it should ensure life sustenance, self-esteem, and freedom of choice for all individuals as well as for their societies (Goulet, 1971). It should also include tangible efforts to bring effective freedom to unify the people for the greater task of nation building. No wonder that development is supposed to be less technical and more emotional (Robertson, 1983: 107–9).

Effective development is, therefore, to be comprehensive, balanced and integrated. It is obviously a dynamic process signifying goal-oriented, guided and gradual change from something considered less desirable to something thought to be desirable or more desirable (Sparkman, 1961). It is also a rational process of organising and carrying out conceived and staffed programmes or projects (Esman, 1966).

Therefore, goal-oriented development should relate to transforming the entire society—economic, social and political, all-round, balanced and upward change. For the formulation of a sustainable development strategy, it is necessary to have a clear methodology of approach, not only in delimiting or defining the beneficiaries but also a clear knowledge of their socio-cultural base and their physical environment.

No single science can provide all data or the conceptual apparatus necessary to identify, analyse and understand the problems of tribes who are at different levels of technological, economic and cultural development. The anthropologists are supposed to have special skills to offer. They can provide adequate data to identify the cultural forces to steer the development wagon to avoid head-on-collision with the resistant spots of tribal life and culture. Their skill can be used to bring in people to effectively associate with and participate in the developmental programmes; instead of being indifferent or resistant (Mandelbaum, 1978).

Accordingly, an anthropologist views tribal development as a movement emphasising upon building up organisational structures, a programme emphasising certain achievable targets, a process emphasising upon what happens to people not only economically and socially but also psychologically; and institutionalisation of the newly discovered skills and procedures, so that the intended changes take place without completely breaking away from the past and without disturbing the time-honoured cultural values (Sanders, 1958: 6).

A strategy for development must be able to identify culture friendly vantage points and create a facilitating environment for initiating action. In the context of tribal development, this should initially be attempted at the micro level as plans conceived in terms of the tribal societies as a whole or even a tribe as a whole may not be useful; because the environment in which they live differ from tribe to tribe or within the same tribe, if it is large and widespread. Therefore, schemes for development should be conceived and developed within the socio-cultural norms of the target group based upon micro level parameters and need-based priorities. The approach inevitably requires an adequate assessment of the needs of the target population and a thorough understanding of its cultural base. Non-understanding or misunderstanding of the cultural background of the target population has, in the past, led to failure of many well-meaning programmes. For example, the scheme of building colonies to provide houses with farm land to some tribal groups to wean them away from nomadic habits and shifting cultivation completely failed because the colony way of life was widely divergent from the cherished cultural values of the communities involved.

Contemporary researchers on human resource development assert, "Human resource is the only resource whose upper limits are not known to the person himself or herself" (Chaudhury, 1996). Thus, human potential is limitless. To harness this potential, a clear understanding of the strength and weakness of the target group is essential. Each community has its own value and moral bases which are built by people by their own wills, of their own initiatives, over their unique paths through the endless ways of their own cultures, traditions and experiences. They are "unarguable absolutes", as Sol Tax (1959) puts it. When Elwin advised the Government of India to "approach the tribesman with the mind of the tribesman" or when Jawaharlal Nehru suggested that "the tribal people should be allowed to develop along the lines of their own genius"(1958), they were definitely converging to a point of view that the master key to tribal development lies hidden somewhere in the tribal ethos itself, because, development to be sustainable, roles and institutions it would create must be able to handle the psychological and institutional consequences of an interconnected society.

IV

The pre-condition to make all development interventions culture-friendly requires a clear understanding of the cultural moorings of more than 80 million people divided into more than 600 communities, spread over the length and breadth of the country, living in varied geo-climatic conditions and subjected to diverse administrative policies under different state governments. The task is not very easy. We have to take into consideration more than 600 culturally autonomous communities. It requires an objective and intellectually detached methodology to distinguish a culture of a tribe from the tribal culture. Students of culture tell us that a culture is time and space bound whereas the culture is universal in its coverage. It is the culture which distinguishes human beings from all other living creatures; and it is a culture that distinguishes an Indian from an American, an Oriya from a Punjabi or a Lambadi from a Saora. On this simple conceptual frame we shall have to try to conceptualize "an Indian tribal culture" distinguished from "the tribal culture of India".

V

We know that most tribal formations, all over the world, are organised around land and almost every thing they do is strongly conditioned (although perhaps not wholly determined) by the natural environment. Anthropologists, all over the world have tried and still trying to understand the relationship between nature and human behaviour. One of the important and earliest studies establishing the link between human behaviour and the habitat is Forde's *Habitat, Economy and Society* (1934). *The Nuer* by Evans-Pritchard (1940) is another important ethnographic landmark, empirically documenting man's relationship to his physical environment and so is Raymond Firth's *Human Types* (1956) outlining a four fold role of the environment in determining the course of human life. Richard B. Lee's own study of the *Bushmen of Kalahari Desert* (1969) and the volume he edited with Irven DeVore (1968), as well as the recent study of Binford (2001), have analysed the world view and the way of life of hunter gatherers' societies which lived or live closer to nature and have come to the conclusion that such people perceive themselves to be an integral part of the natural system. For example, when a plains Indian kills a buffalo, it is not a part of his plan to dominate nature and exploit it, but it is a part of his interaction with nature (Friedl, 1976: 140). Natural forests with their wide eco-diversity are repositories of a large number of plant and animal species used by man as food. For substantial part of its history, humanity looked upon forests as the only source of food supply. Till today, for pre-agricultural communities the forest acts as a granary. Marginal farmers living close to the forest are beneficiaries of a variety of free food and are nutritionally better off.

VI

In India, in spite of a steady assault on their habitats and livelihoods beginning with the British control over India's forests in 1865, many tribal communities all over the country continue their stubborn dependence on the forests. One of the early ethnographers, S.C. Roy recognised the symbiotic relationship between man and nature in his studies of the Munda, the Asurs (1915) and the Birhor (1925). A number of studies bring out the close link between economy and the immediate environment. Vidyarthi's study of the Maler (1963), Sandhwar's study of the Korwa (1973) and Roy's study of the Chotanagpur region significantly contribute to the understandings of the intimate relation between the forest, forest dwellers and their styles of life. To estimate the extent of dependence on the forest, I have chosen two Odisha cases, one is that of the Paudi Bhuyan (Mohapatra, 1992), the other is of the Oraon (Ratha, Goswami and Nesha, 1966); and from another micro-study, namely that of the Lanjia Saora, I have tried to assess the extent of attachment a community exhibits to the land around its habitat. All three communities are classified under the Primitive Tribal Groups (PTG). They live in the scheduled areas of the state.

VII

The Paudi Bhuyans are inhabitants of the Bhuyan Pidha of Kendujhar district and the Bonai subdivision of Sundargarh district, Odisha. Hills, elevated valleys and dense forests characterise the Bhuyan habitat, containing 55 Reserved Forest Blocks over an area of 1183.35 sq kms. The forest is of tropical moist deciduous type.

The data base is 100 randomly selected households from five villages in Koira and Bonai (the community is predominantly confined to 21 villages of Bonai subdivision with a population of 3055 persons: 1991 census). Because of the geographic and physiographic constraints, the area of land available for wet cultivation is meagre forcing the inhabitants to shifting cultivation. Thus, the Paudi Bhuyan agriculture is a combination of wet cultivation, shifting cultivation locally known as *biringa*, and *badi* (cultivation around the homestead).

Among the sample households, 77 per cent are cultivators and 23 per cent are landless wage earners. 52 among the cultivators primarily depend on shifting cultivation and the rest lean on it as a supplementary source of living. While 42 per cent do not own any livestock, 15 per cent own sheep or goat (Table 1). Cows and goats are not milked. Cows, bullocks and buffalos are used to pull the plough. Sheep and goats are sold for cash and occasionally slaughtered for food. The landless wage earners seasonally get engaged by the Steel Authority of India in mine-digging. The entire population, however, supplements its food and income by gathering and hunting.

Table 1 *Land Holding and Livestock Ownership*

	Land Holding %			*Livestock Ownership %*		
Name of the village	*Landless*	*1–2 AC*	*2–4 AC*	*Cows/Bullocks*	*Buffalo*	*Sheep/Goat*
Derula	70	20	10	30	10	20
Dalai Sara	20	50	30	40	5	10
Expadi	10	20	70	50	10	5
Hatisul	90	10	0	40	20	10
Patamund	70	20	10	20	20	20

The dependence on the forest is two-fold: using forest land for shifting cultivation and collection of roots, tubers, fruits, berries, oil seeds, edible leaves and flowers, etc. A total of 95 per cent of the Paudi Bhuyan are estimated to be engaged in shifting cultivation affecting 2270 sq kms of forest area. A shifting field is used for 2–3 years and left for 4–5 years (in the past it used to be 10 to 15 years). Locally the shifting field is called *biringa* or *thami* or *toila.* The cultivation is termed as *dahi* or *kaman.* The shifting fields are situated either in the lower or middle slopes of the hills. A family cultivates 3 to 5 acres. In first year, black gram (*biri)* together with a variety of legumes is cultivated. In the second year, different millets (*suan, kangu, kosala, ragi,* etc.) are grown; and in the third year paddy, mustard and turmeric are raised.

Collection of a wide variety of items used by the community for food, fodder and medicine, continue throughout the year by men, women and children alike (Table 2). Several kinds of wild fruits, berries, fig, *kendu* fruit, *kusum* fruit, wild mango, a number of tubers (local names: *pitaalu, kantaalu, goinga, kalia boinga, ramakanda, saru,* etc.) are collected and taken as food supplements in different seasons (Table 3). Wood is collected for fuel. An average family requires one cartload (about 6 quintals) every month. Each household requires 25 to 40 full-length bamboos per year for

Table 2 *Collections of Forest Products*

Name of the Product	*Month of Collection*
Sal seed (Shorea robusta)	April–May
Char seed (Buchania lanzan)	November–December
Kusum seed (Schlreicha oleorasa)	January–February
Mohua seed (Modhua latifolia/flower)	May–June/March–April
Bana tulsi (Perimela ocimodis)	February–March
Tamarind (Tamarindus indica)	April–May
Bhalia (Semecarpus anacardium)	April–May
Amla (Emblica officinalis)	April–May
Bahada (Terminalia belerica)	May–June
Harida (T. Chebula)	May–June
Bana Khajur (Phoenix sylvestris)	January–April
Dhatri (Wood wondia fruticosa)	December–January
Broom grass (14) kendu leaf (15) sal leaf	December–January

roofing. *Sabai* grass, *khejur* (date) leaves are used for thatching. Fuel wood, bamboo, non-fuel timbers are not sold. From the marketable forest produces an average family adds 30 to 40 per cent to its annual income.

Summer months, almost exclusively, are used for forest collection. While *kendu*, *kusum*, mango, jackfruit, are food supplements, *mohua* flower is converted to liquor. The date palms are used to tap toddy. From the *mohua* and *kusum* seeds oil is extracted. *Sal* seeds are sold away. From the sale of *kendu* leaves, sal seeds and *mohua* flowers, an average family makes an income of Rs 3000–3500 per season. Though the forest belongs to the state, *mohua* trees and date palms are marked and respected as private property. Other collections are free for all. Most collections involve a walk of 8 to 10 kms per day. Many items of collection, particularly *mohua* seeds and flower, char, etc., are bartered for salt, tobacco, chilly, etc. (Table 4). Different parts of a number of plants are used as medicine (Table 5). Some of these plants are defied. In worshipping the *bel* (aegel marmelos) and *aswath* (ficus religiosa), the Paudi Bhuyan shares the great tradition of the country. The *simili* (combax ceiba) tree personifies Goddess Durga and it is worshipped during Dasahara. *Kusum* (adina cordifolia) is regarded as the abode of Goddess Basari. The tree is worshipped during the month of Margasira. The *sal* (shorea robusta) personifies the presiding deity of the

Table 3 *Average Collection (in kg) Per Family: Qty consumed/Qty sold*

Village	*Fruits*			*Flower*			*Seeds*			*Leaves*		
	1	2	3	1	2	3	1	2	3	1	2	3
1	215	115	100	1585	25	133	244.5	15	229.5	77.1	4.5	72.6
2	45.5	10.5	22.7	112.3	12	89	145.7	10.5	115	21.1	11	10.7
3	200	72.8	121.9	98.8	15.8	63.2	150.6	25.5	75.5	35	5.7	29.8
4	212.5	152	45.7	500	185.6	300.2	481	50	295.5	154.5	25	77.6
5	216.6	55.5	89.8	350	23	309	559	70	391	91.6	21	73.3

1. Collection 2. Consumption 3. Selling

Table 4 *Barter Rate of Some FPs*

Item (1kg)	*Item/quantity exchanged*
Mohua flower	Salt (1.5 kg)
Mohua seeds	Salt (2 kg)
Char seeds	Salt (10 kg)
Sal resin	Chilli (0.5 kg)

Table 5 *Medicinal Herbs from the Forest*

Name of the plant	*Local name*	*Part used*	*Disease*
Adhatoda zealanica	Basanga	Leaves, roots	Cough, bronchitis
Asparagus racemusus	Satabari	Tuber	Dysentery
Antidesma diandrum	Mamuri	Leaves	Indigestion
Chloroxylon suitenia	Bhera	Branches	Malaria
Emblica officiralis	Amla	Fruits	Pyorrhoea
Erythrina variegata	Paladhua	Leaves	Lund warm
Madhucca longifolia	Mohua	Twigs	Dental pain
Phoenix sylvestris	Bana khajur	Tuber	Eye infection
Thespesea lampus	Ban kapasia	Seeds	Constipation
Vitem peduncularis	Chadelgudi	Leaf	Malaria

village. Huge *sal* trees occupy central positions of most villages symbolising man–plant coexistence.

VIII

The Oraon, one of the major tribes of the country, is found in West Bengal, Bihar, Madhya Pradesh and Odisha. In Odisha, their concentration is in Sundargarh district. The study, involving three Oraon villages, is designed to assess the contributions of the forest to the nutritional intake of the people in its proximity and to test a hypothesis that closer the community to the forest better is its nutritional intake.

The sample households for the study come from Luhuradhipa, on the fringe of the district headquarters town of Sundargarh in Western Orissa. Khutgaon, a village 15 kms away from Sundargarh, is separated from it by the river Ib. One has to cross the river to board a bus for the town. The other location is a village, Junajam by name. It is 45 kms away from Sundargarh town. The transport point to board a bus for the town is 5 kms away, negotiated on foot. The houses are scattered on hill slopes. The data base is spread over these three locations, taking 50 randomly chosen households from each (Table 6).

Table 6 *Population in and Distance from the Town of the Sample Population*

Sample area	*No. of persons*	*No. of families*	*Male*	*Female*	*Distance from Sundargarh town*
Luhuradhipa	216	50	124	92	Neighbourhood
Khutgan	281	50	156	125	15 kms
Jurajam	321	50	168	153	45 kms
Total	818	150	448	370	

The field work was carried through for a period of three months, one in each location, spread over three seasons with ten days in each. The summer data was collected in May, the winter in January and of the rainy season in July. The raw food, before cooking was weighed item-wise, twice—once in the morning and again in the evening in the sample households; and the calorie value of each item was calculated.

The nutritional status of each family and the individual average therein is determined with reference to the size and income levels of the family in each location and in relation to seasonal variations (Tables: 7, 8, 9, 10, 11). In the Luhuradhipa sample, there are 32 small and 18 medium sized families, where the average individual calorie intake is 2653.40 and 2458.53 respectively. The corresponding figures for Khutgaon are 2898.48 and 2469.91 and for Jurajam are 2950.69 and 2712.77. Luhuradhipa does not have large families. In the large sized families of Khutgaon and Jurajam, the calorie intake is 2245.78 and 2424.51 respectively. The small families are better fed than their medium and large counterparts. The calorie intake of Jurajam inhabitants is higher than those at the other two locations, for all family sizes.

Table 7 *Family Size and Average Nutritional Intake Per Individual (K Cal)*

Location	*Small (1–4)*	*Medium (5–8)*	*Large (8 and above)*
Luhuradhipa	2653.40	2458.53	—
Khutgaon	2898.48	2469.91	2245.78
Jurajam	2950.69	2712.77	2424.51

Table 8 *Income Groups and Average Individual Intake (K Cal)*

Location	*HIG: Rs 12000+/year*	*MIG: Rs 6000 to 12000/year*	*LIG: < Rs 6000/year*
Luhuradhipa	2522.05	2581.55	2653.12
Khutgaon	2561.69	2416.90	2680.68
Jurajam	2902.81	2524.14	2700.16

Table 9 *Seasonal Family Average Nutritional Intake (K Cal)*

Locations	*Summer*	*Winter*	*Rainy*	*Total Average*
Luhuradhipa	133561.68	121684.83	129156.67	128134.39
Khutgaon	136167.43	124161.15	132205.88	130844.82
Jurajam	137660.44	130313.47	133438.48	133804.13

Table 10 *Seasonal Variations in the Individual Average Nutritional Intake (K Cal)*

Locations	*Summer*	*Winter*	*Rainy*	*Total Average*
Luhuradhipa	2671.23	2433.70	2583.13	2562.69
Khutgaon	2723.35	2483.22	2644.12	2616.91
Jurajam	2753.21	2606.27	2668.77	2676.08

Table 11 *Seasonal Variation in Individual Average Calorie Intake (K Cal)*

Seasons	*Luhuradhipa*		*Khutgan*		*Jurajam*	
	Highest	*Lowest*	*Highest*	*Lowest*	*Highest*	*Lowest*
Summer	4038.41	1533.70	3688.40	1907.86	4009.98	1096.79
Winter	3718.43	1421.64	3295.27	1703.46	3345.26	1946.19
Rainy	3858.20	1581.36	3420.93	1756.74	3491.12	2105.71

Looking at the calorie intake, in terms of income groups, one can notice that lower income families are better fed in all locations, and that the lower income families of Jurajam are much better fed than their higher as well as middle income counterparts. This is because dependence on the purchased nutrition/food appears to be directly proportional to the income level. Collection of items of food from the forest and the neighbourhood is largely a domain of the poor and normally is a female job. The town influenced high income or even middle income households consider it less prestigious for their women to move around the neighbourhood to collect items for food. Thus, we notice that calories available to the inhabitants of Jurajam (where collections from the forest are substantial) are highest and dwindle down as one approaches the town (Table 13).

The calorie intake in the family (Table 9) and the average individual intake therein (Table 10) is recorded highest in summer and lowest in winter in all locations and that in both counts it is higher at Jurajam, compared to Khutgaon and Luhuradhipa. The number of best fed individuals and families is far more in Jurajam than in Khutgan or Luhuradhipa (Table 12).

Thus, the empirical data at our disposal lead us to conclude that a community living close to the forest enjoys certain nutritional advantages not available to those which are away from it.

Table 12 *Average Family and Individual Intake (K Cal)*

		Luhuradhipa	*Khutgan*	*Jurajam*
Highest	Family	20450.50	22114.17	38444.95
	Individual	3408.42	3459.42	3615.45
Lowest	Family	6565.81	9487.31	9696.85
	Individual	1617.24	1789.35	2060.64

Table 13 *Nutritional Availability per Individual in Calorie*

Locations	*Summer*	*Winter*	*Rainy*	*Total Average*
Luhuradhipa	163.75	25.83	126.95	105.44
Khutgan	161.08	104.36	154.71	140.05
Jurajam	239.94	323.74	310.40	291.43

(food includes the kitchen garden produces also)

IX

The intimate relation between the forest and the forest dependent communities can be seen through the institution of totemism. The Birjia Asur of Chotanagapur regards the totem as a relative, and salutes it when they sight it. They weep over its dead body and ceremonially dispose it off as is done to a relative (Roy, 1917). Eating, killing or destroying the clan totem is regarded as equivalent to killing a human member of the clan among the Birhor, who believe that a diminution in the number of the totem animals or plants or other objects caused by their destruction or killing will result in a corresponding decrease in the size of the clan. Violation of the totem taboo entails payment of a fine and treating the clan with a feast (Roy, 1925). The Oraon of Chotanagapur, not only abstain from hunting, killing, or using the totem, but anything that resembles it. For example, those of the tiger clan abstain from eating the squirrel as its stripped skin resembles that of a tiger (Roy, 1915). The Bhumij regard their totem as an agnate (Das, 1931). The Muria Gond of Bastar region, not only avoid injuring or eating their totem, they also worship it and mourn for the dead totem (Elwin, 1947).

X

These accounts provide fairly adequate data to look upon the forest as an integral part of culture rather than an impersonal habitat of plants and animals. A cursory glance at the sample ethnographic data (Table 14) reaffirms that harmony in man–plant–animal interaction is a universal phenomenon and the relationship is largely symbiotic. Each community inhabiting a particular geographic area seems to have consciously applied this universal principle to construct a cultural device to ensure reasonable safety to the flora and fauna in its neighbourhood.

Though the forest policies from 1894 onwards never doubted the intimate relation between the forest and the forest dwellers, the blame for the depletion of the forests has invariably been showered on the poor tribal communities. In contrast to the tribal ideology of holding all components of the environment, human as well as non-human, with almost equal respect; modern civilisation, from its very inception, has been homocentric in general and ethnocentric in particular. All discoveries and inventions have been oriented towards human welfare. The non-human part of the creation has been ruthlessly exploited to provide comforts, real as well as imaginary, to the human beings only. This is particularly so following the industrial revolution which created several man-made needs at 'others' cost. The homocentric arrogance has already taken its toll. More than half of the animal extinctions have occurred since 1900 AD. Currently, as per

Table 14 *Totems of Some Indian Tribes*

Tribes	*Reference*	*Habitats*	*Number of Clans and Totems*				*Total*
			Fish/bird/ reptile insect/ animal	*Plant/leaf/ grass/root/ flower fruit*	*Inanimate objects/ natural formation*	*Unclassified*	
Birjia Asur	Risley 1891	Bengal	10	3	***	***	13
Birjia Asur	Roy 1917	Chotanagpur	34	***	***	***	34
Birhor	Roy 1925	Chotanagpur	12	10	7	8	
Munda/ Mundari	Risley 1891	Bihar, MP, Bengal, Orissa	142	83	72	42	339
Santal	Frazer 1910	Bengal	7	3	1	1	12
Bhumij	Risley 1891	Bihar, Orissa, Bengal	11	4	***	5	20
Bhumij	Roy Chowdhury 1929	Orissa	5	3	2	5	15
Juang	Risley 1891	Orissa	12	10	1	1	24
Juang	Elwin 1948	Orissa	5	12	3	***	20
Korku	Driver 1893	MP	***	5	7	***	13
Gond	Risley 1891	Bengal	15	1	4	12	30
Gond	Ferriea 1965	MP, Bihar, AP, Orissa, MAH.	39	17	6	13	75
Muria gond	Elwin 1947	C.garh, Bihar	29	3	***	4	36
Oraon	Roy 1915, 1928	Chotanagpur	43	19	4	2	68
Kutia Kond	Niggemeyer 1964	Orissa	5	1	***	8	14
Bhil	Luard 1909	MP	19	23	15	69	122
Bhil	Ethoven 1920	Gujarat	12	5	***	***	17

the estimates of the International Union for Conservation of Nature and Natural Resources, an average of one animal species is lost every year; and about one thousand birds and mammals are now thought to be in jeopardy (Eckholm, 1980: 22–25). About 103 species of mammal, bird or reptile are known to have become extinct in between 1500–1999 (Flannery and Schouten, 2001).

After facing centuries of indifference, the forest and the forest people are now beginning to make their presence felt in the administrative agenda of our country. It is a pleasant surprise that the World Bank Group in its Revised Forest Strategy, approved by its Board of Directors on 31 October 2002, seems to have realised that the poor are not the cause of deforestation and that there is a close link between the livelihoods of the poor and the forest (P2). The report admits that the flow of funds into the forests for management and protection purposes will continue to be dwarfed by investment in activities that may have damaging impacts upon forests (P2) and cautions: the Bank must have an appreciation of how its action and investments in other sectors or at the macro-economic level, will impact on forests and forest peoples (P35).

Along with these realisations, the Government of India's belated wisdom in extending the provisions of the Panchayats to the scheduled areas (Panchayats Extension to the Scheduled Areas Act, 1996) is beginning to provide a silver lining around a primordial dark cloud. We hope that it sustains.

XI

The community base chosen to understand the culture woven around land is of the Lanjia Saora, the primitive part of the great Soara Tribe. The Saora habitat is spread over in Orissa (Rayagada, Ganjam and Gajapati districts) and in Andhra Pradesh (Srikakulam and Vizianagaram districts). The Lanjia Saora derive their name from the loin-cloth worn by their men folk, the loose ends of which hang simulating a tail (lanja in Oriya) on the both sides of the groin, the frontal part being slightly longer. A typical Lanjia Saora village/hamlet perches on a hill slope, with the houses overlooking the terraced paddy fields. The forest line on the hill begins behind the houses.

The geographical area of the database of this paper is the Lanjia Saora Development Agency in Gunpur ITDA (Integrated Tribal Development

Agency) of Rayagada district (formerly a part of undivided Koraput district). The project covers a gram panchayat containing eight revenue villages. Six of them have more than one hamlet. The inhabitants, however, call their settlements as villages. Thus, there are 21 villages under the project area. The geo-morphology of the area is hilly and forest clad. The pattern of land management and use is determined by the location of land. On the basis of location, land can be classified into homestead land, land under shifting cultivation and terraced land.

Homestead land

A few trees such as, *mohua*, mango, jack, tamarind, date palm, sago palm, are normally found on the homestead land. The space between the trees is used to cultivate vegetables, tobacco, maize, etc. Patches of banana and pineapple are also found in some household enclosures.

Land under shifting cultivation

The unterraced hill slopes and low hills are used for shifting cultivation. They are primarily forestland used for the purpose over several years. Though such land belongs to the state, the users have been enjoying usufructuary rights. The upper contours are used to cultivate minor millets and the lower slopes, which are comparatively flat, are used for maize, sorghum, finger millets, pulses, oil seeds (sesame), etc.

Terraced land

A substantial part of land on hill slopes is terraced. The terraces are built with great ingenuity and with inputs of a substantial amount of manual labour—the most important asset of the Lanjia Saora. The terraces bear testimony to the meticulous, skilful and optimum use of this asset. The magnificence of the Lanjia Saora terraces can only be compared with those of the Naga of the north-east India. The land situation restricts large plots of land in any particular level. Small plots, at different heights, are used for crops suited to their location. The upper terraces are rain-fed. The lower terraces get the benefit of irrigation from the streams nearby and yield two to three crops per year. The terraces, though largely used for paddy, plots retaining dampness after the second paddy crop are used for pulses—black and green grams.

The livelihood pattern, life skills, crops raised, food habits, gender relations in the organisation of the work force, the ritual cycle largely centre around land and forest.

Livelihood pattern and life skills

From the age of 6–7 years children accompany parents to the workplace—fields and forest, to learn associated skills. The skills constitute raising protective boulder facing to the paddy terraces, clearing forest for shifting cultivation, land preparation, sowing, transplantation, weeding, harvesting, etc. The forest-oriented skills are to recognise, locate and collect utility items including those, which are edible. Around the age of 10–12 they are capable of taking part in household activities, tending cattle, participating in agricultural operation, forest collections, etc.

Apart from the basic skills related to agriculture and forest, an important supplementary skill is preparation of wooden accessories for the agricultural implements, making doors and doorframes for the living houses. This skill and the skill of terrace-building have produced many skilled workers as carpenters and masons.

Tree crops

Single or in clusters tamarind, *mohua,* jack, mango, sago palm, are planted on *podu* land, homestead land and on any available suitable land. These trees including those in homestead land constitute an important source of income as well as providing supplementary items of food. Stray *mohua* and mango trees in the forest, public land or on the road side are treated as common property resources; whereas tamarind, *karanj, kusum,* date palm and sago palm have their owners whose rights are traditionally respected by the community. Sap tapped from the date and the sago palms is the traditional indigenous drink for all occasions—social, religious or casual. Another indigenous drink is distilled from the *mohua* flowers. Oil is extracted from *karanja, kusum* and *mohua* seeds. *Kusum* wood is exclusively used in the manufacture of agricultural implements, especially the plough. A substantial quantity of *mohua* flowers, seeds and tamarind find its way to the external market bringing in some cash income. Mango kernel and tamarind seeds are processed to render them edible in times of scarcity. People regard these trees as items of wealth. Felling of any edible or otherwise useful fruit bearing tree is regarded as a taboo, the violation of which is visited as divine wrath in the form of famine, drought, epidemics, etc.

Food habits

The items of staple food available to the community are rice, finger millet, sorghum and other millets. A family of five members normally consumes about 500 grams of rice and an equal weight of powdered finger millet per day in the form of a watery gruel. Sorghum and other millets substitute finger millets (ragi). The gruel is normally prepared in the evening and kept overnight, adding salt to taste. Its consumption begins as breakfast and continues through lunch to dinner. Children take it as many times as they feel hungry. It is also carried to the work place in bottle-gourd containers. A full rice meal is a luxury. Scarcity is met by supplementing the menu with roots and tubers, a number of edible fruits, leaves, berries, etc., collected from the forest as per their seasonal availability. Mango kernel and tamarind seeds are processed to render them edible to meet scarcity and to meet transient hunger. The latter are regarded as scarcity food.

The workforce

Men and women join the work force when they are in 10–12 years of age. In farming operations there is no discernible division of labour except that holding the plough is a taboo to women. Forest collection is largely a feminine activity. Of late young males are seen periodically going out of the village, in search of work, to places outside the state. It is noticed that they return home with a substantial amount of money earned through their skilled work as masons and carpenters.

On the backdrop of this scenario we tried to figure out the people's perceptions of wealth/poverty on the one hand and well-being/distress on the other. We also tried to make a qualitative evaluation of the impact of the institutional interventions in strengthening/weakening these perceptions. Our unit of observation was the individual household. In all, 105 pairs of men and women (oldest in the household, not necessarily husband and wife), chosen on a random basis, were interviewed with the help of structured interviews and informal group discussions. The informants were asked to spell out at least five items, they perceive as wealth in a descending order of importance. They were also asked to indicate five livelihood skills in the same manner. On the last leg of fieldwork we chose a small hamlet of 32 households *(rungrungba)* and casually asked a group of men and women to name the households which they consider as non-poor (*thila ghar*) and poor *(nathila ghar)* in their local dialect.

In the perception of the community, land emerges as the most important material expression of wealth with land types in a hierarchy positioned on the basis of their productive capacity. The "terraced land" is the best form wealth, followed by "homestead land and *dangar*" (land under shifting cultivation). Within terraced land there is a hierarchy. The terraces advantageously located to be irrigated from nearby streams yielding three crops are on the top followed by two crop land and then the one crop yielder. Next to land are the "house and the household compound". Of late the concrete/tin-roofed cement plastered houses are emerging as status symbols. Among the traditional house types the brick/stone-walled thatched ones are higher than their mud-walled counterparts. Then the trees follow among which the tamarind occupies the most exalted position followed by the *mohua,* sago palm, date palm, mango, jack, *karanj* and *kusum.* In recent post-project times, cashew plantations have emerged as the most important material expression of property.

The livelihood skills—skills associated with different stages of agriculture, hunting, collecting forest produces, skills acquired by the priest, the medicine man, communication skills in dealing with outsiders and in presenting a point of view in the village council and other intra-group/inter-group discussions, culinary skills, carpentry, masonry, thatching, plucking tamarind, setting the container to collect sap from the sago palm and the date palm, etc., are various forms, may I say, of non-material wealth/possession.

XII

Thus, the tribal cultures of India are products of human interaction with land and the forest. If culture is to be understood as a complex whole or a cluster of capabilities that encompasses "knowledge, belief, art, morals, law, custom" (Tylor, 1871); "inherited artifacts, goods, technical processes, ideas, habits and values" (Malinowski in Linton, 1936: 90), the tribal cultures of India, individually and collectively are functional wholes, within which each part is a manifestation of the capability or genius of the human aggregate that created and sustained it. Therefore, beliefs woven around them are unarguable absolutes. They need to be respected in cross-cultural situations and any policy towards any social formation, such as the tribes, to be sustainable is to be culture friendly, not only in terms of 'wholes' but if necessary, in terms of 'parts' also.

References

Bailey, F.G. 1961 "'Tribe' and 'Caste' in India", *Contributions to Indian Sociology*, V: 7–19.

Basu, A.R. 1985 *Tribal Development Programmes and Administration in India*, New Delhi: National Book Organisation.

Belshaw, C. 1972 "Development: The Contribution of Anthropology", *International Social Science Journal*, 24: 84–86.

Bhatt, V. 1977 "The Contribution of Anthropology to Development", in H.M. Mathur (ed.), *Anthropology in the Development Process*, New Delhi: Vikas Publishing Company.

——. 1982 "Tribal Sub-Plan for Koragas", *Yojana*, 26(23).

Binford, Lewis R. 2001 *Constructing Frames of Reference: An Analytical Method for Archaeological Theory Building Using Ethnographic and Environmental Data*, Berkeley: University of California Press.

Chambers, Robert 1994 "Participatory Rural Appraisal: Analysis of Experience", *World Development*, 22(9): 1253–68.

Chaudhury, S.S. 1996 "HRD: A Blend of Organisational Soft S's and Hard S's", *The Statesman*, Calcutta, April 19.

Das, T. 1931 *The Bhumijas of Saraikella*, Calcutta: University of Calcutta Press (quoted in Ferreira, 1965).

Driver, W.H. 1893 "The Korku", *Journal of Asiatic Society Bengal*, LXI: 128–32 (quoted in Ferreira, 1965).

Eckholm, E. 1980 "The Age of Extinction", *SPAN*, 21(3).

Elwin, V. 1947 *The Muria and Their Ghotul*, Bombay: Oxford University Press.

——. 1955 *The Religion of an Indian Tribe*, Bombay: Oxford University Press.

——. 1958 *Philosophy for NEFA*, 2nd Edition, Shillong: NEFA.

——. 1963 *A New Deal for Tribal India*, New Delhi: Ministry of Home Affairs, Government of India.

Evans-Pritchard, E.E. 1940 *The Nuer*, Oxford: Clarendon Press.

Esman, M.J. 1966 "The Politics of Development Administration", in J.D.

Montgomery and W.J. Siffin (eds), *Approaches to Development: Politics, Administration and Challenge*, New York: McGraw Hill.

Ferreira, J.V. 1965 *Totemism in India*, London: Oxford University Press.

Firth, Raymond 1956 *Human Types*, New York: Thomas Nelson and Sons Ltd.

Flannery, T.F. and Peter Schouten 2001 "A Gap in Nature: Discovering the World's Extinct Animals", *Nature*, Atlantic Review Press.

Forde, C.D. 1934 *Habitat, Economy and Society*, London: Methuen.

Frazer, J.G. 1910 *Totemism and Exogamy*, London: Macmillan (quoted in Ferreira, 1965).

Friedl, John 1976 *Cultural Anthropology*, New York: Harper & Row.

Goulet, D. 1971 *The Cruel Choice: A New Concept on the Theory of Development*, New York: Atenium.

Government of Andhra Pradesh 2004 Tribes and Tribal Areas of Andhra Pradesh (Basic Statistics), Tribal Cultural Research and Training Institute, Hyderabad: Tribal Welfare Department.

Government of India 1951 First Five Year Plan, Planning Commission, New Delhi.

——. 1956 Second Five Year Plan, Planning Commission, New Delhi.

——. 1957 *Report of the Study Team for the Study of Community Projects and National Extension Service* (Chairman: Balwant Roy Mehta), Planning Commission, New Delhi.

——. 1961 *Report of the Scheduled Areas and Scheduled Tribes Commission* (Chairman: U.N. Dhebar).

——. 1969 *Report of the Study Team on the Tribal Development Programmes* (Chairman: P. Shilu Ao).

——. 1975 Tribal Development in the Fifth Plan: Some Basic Policy Papers, Ministry of Home Affairs.

——. 1977 Approach to Tribal Development in the Sixth Plan: A Preliminary Perspective, Occasional Papers on Tribal Development, Ministry of Home Affairs.

——. 1990 National Conference on Problems of Scheduled Tribes (March 31), Ministry of Welfare, Tribal Development Division.

——. 1990a Compendium of Circulars: Guidelines on Tribal Development, Ministry of Welfare, Tribal Development Division.

——. 1998 Scheduled Tribes, Scheduled Areas and Tribal Areas in India, Ministry of Social Justice and Empowerment, Tribal Development Division.

——. 2003 *Annual Report*.

——. 2002–03 Ministry of Tribal Affairs, Government of Orissa.

——. 1994 *Report of the Annual Administration of Scheduled Areas in Orissa for* 1993–1994. Social Welfare Department, Bhubaneswar.

——. 1996 *Development Handbook of the Bonda*, Bhubaneswar: Scheduled Castes and Scheduled Tribes Research and Training Institute.

Lai, R.B. 1977 "Problems of Tribal Development in Gujarat", in R.S. Mann (ed.), *Tribes of India: Ongoing Challenges*, New Delhi: M.D. Publications Pvt. Ltd.

Lang, A. 1905 *The Secret of the Totem*, London: Longmans (quoted in Ferreira, 1965).

Lee, Richard B. 1969 "Eating Christmas in Kalahari", *Natural History*, 78, Dec, Reprinted in Friedl (1978: 453–57).

Lee, Richard B. and Irven DeVore (eds) 1968 *Man the Hunter*, Chicago: Aldine.

Linton, Ralph 1936 *The Study of Man*, New York: Appleton-Century.

Luard, C.E. 1909 *The Jungle Tribes of Malwa*, Lucknow: M.L. Bhargava (quoted in Ferreira, 1965).

Mandelbaum, David G. 1978 "Potentials of Anthropology", in D. Shimkin, Sol Tax and J. Morrison (eds), *Anthropology for the Future*, Urbana: University of Illinois Press.

——. 1974 "Accomplishing Ethnicity", in Roy Turner (ed.), *Ethnomethodology*, Harmondsworth: Penguin, 1975 Reprint, 54–68.

Mohapatra, Ajay 1992 "The Forest Dwellers' Dependence on Forest: A Case Study of Pauri Bhuinya Tribe of Orissa", *Journal of Rural Development*, 11(6), NIRD, Hyderabad.

Nehru, Jawaharlal 1958 "Foreword", in Verrier Elwin, *Philosophy for NEFA*, 2nd Edition, Shillong: NEFA.

Niggemeyer, H. 1933 Kutia Kond: Dechungelbauren in Orissa, Munich (quoted in Ferreira, 1965).

Radcliffe Brown, A.R. 1941 "The Definition of Totemism", *Anthropos*, IX: 622–30 (quoted in Ferreira, 1965).

Ratha, S.N., M.C. Goswami and F. Nesha 1966 "Caste and Occupation in an Assamese Village", *Man in India*, 46(3).

Risley, H.H. 1891 *The Tribes and Castes of Bengal*, Vols. I & II, Calcutta: Government Press.

——. 1912 *The People of India*, Bombay: Thacker and Co.

Robertson, A.F. 1983 *People and State: Anthropology of Planned Development*, Cambridge: Cambridge University Press.

Roy, S.C. 1915 "Probable Traces of Totem Worship among the Oraons", *Journal of Bihar and Orissa Research Society*, 1: 53–56.

——. 1917 "A Note on Totemism Amongst the Asurs", *Journal of Bihar and Orissa Research Society*, 567–71.

——. 1925 "The Birhors: A Little-known Jungle Tribe of Chotanagpur", *Man in India*, Ranchi.

——. 1928 "Oraon Religion and Customs", *Man in India*, Ranchi (1985 Reprint).

Roy Burman, B.K. 1995 "Tribal Situation and Approach to Tribal Problems in India: A Preliminary Appraisal", Discussion Paper, Rajiv Gandhi Institute for Contemporary Studies, New Delhi.

Roy Choudhury, T.C. 1929 "The Bhumij of Mayurbhanj, Orissa", *Man in India*, IX: 95–115.

Sahlins, Marshall D. 1968 *Tribesmen*, New York: Prentice Hall.

Sanders, Irwin T. 1958 "Theories of Community Development", *Rural Sociology*, 23: 1–12.

Sandhwar, A.N. 1973 "The Korwa of Palamau: A Study of their Society and Economy", Ph.D. Thesis, Ranchi University (unpublished).

Saxena, R.P. 1964 *Tribal Economy in Central India*, Calcutta: K.L. Mukhopadhyay.

Sharma, B.D. 1973 "Economic Development of Extremely Backward Tribal Regions", *Indian Anthropologist*, 3: 109–34.

——. 1982 Micro-level Planning for Full Employment in Tribal Areas, Occasional Papers on Tribal Development, Government of India, Ministry of Home Affairs, New Delhi.

Schneider, Harold K. 1975 "Economic Development and Anthropology", *Annual Review of Anthropology*, 4: 271–92.

Service, Elman R. 1962 *Primitive Social Organization: An Evolutionary Perspective*, New York: Random House.

Sinha, U.P. 1990 *Demographic Profile of Tribal Population in India* (quoted in Roy Burman, 1995).

Singh, K.S. 1994 "The Scheduled Tribes", in *People of India*, National Series–1, Vol. 3, London: Oxford University Press and New Delhi: Anthropological Survey of India.

Sparkman, John J. 1961 "Economic, Social and Political Implications of Community Development", *Community Development Review*, 6: 1–9.

Steward, Julian H. 1955 *Theory of Culture Change: The Methodology of Multilinear Evolution*, Urbana: Illinois University Press.

Tax, Sol 1959 "Action Anthropology", *Journal of Social Research*, 11: 1–9.

Todaro, M. 1977 *Economics for a Developing World*, London: Longman Group Ltd.

Tylor, E.B. 1924 (1871) *Primitive Culture*, 2 Vols., 7th Edition, New York: Brentano's. Vidyarthi, L.P. 1963 *The Maler: A Study in Nature-Man-Spirit Complex of a Hill Tribe in Bihar*, Calcutta: Bookland.

Yadav, H. 1981 "Impact of Farm Subsidies in Tribal Development", *Kurukshetra*, 29: 13–19.

2

Policies and issues in the bio-cultural development of Scheduled Tribes

P.K. Misra

Alternative development

It is still considered "at the level of ethos though not always empirically, the tribal social entities represent values of conviviality, reciprocity, sharing and caring and extension of the self to surroundings—animate or inanimate. It is the last attribute which imparts to the tribal people a sense of custodial responsibility towards the endowments of nature in the geographical space" (Roy Burman, 2003: 177). This statement may sound a bit romantic in the modern world which is moving in completely opposite direction but in any case, let us face the truth that world of the tribes indicated in Roy Burman's quotation lies shattered. The modern development is basically oriented towards meeting the physical targets rather than addressing the basic issues facing the humanity and the environment. Mahana writes: "economic betterment is the sine qua non of the mainstream development process. Ironically, it has also enhanced deprivation and destitution, increased inequality, deepened exploitation and institutionalised oppression. In the long run skewed development process ends in violation of human rights, dignity, freedom and autonomy. Globalisation, liberalisation and post-modern development have thrown away the varied cultural heritage ..." (2006: 354). There is nothing to dispute in the above statement, it is therefore imperative that alternatives to modern development are discussed, debated and adopted. There is no other better way to begin the discourse on alternatives to development with the tribes, for one, they had holistic and integrated ethos, second the tribes are most studied people in this country. The process of studying them systematically began with the establishment of colonial rule in India which got intensified after they got scheduled status in the Indian Constitution. They have been the focus of studies by the administrators, scholars, and development planners. There are government and non-government organisations exclusively focused on the research and development of tribes. Since 1950 they have been targets for planned development. Budgetary allocations for their development and the development of their region have been progressively enhanced, plan after plan. An office of the Commissioner for Scheduled Castes and Scheduled Tribes was created to independently record and report the situation among them. The Commissioner's reports are directly submitted to the parliament for discussion. Now, even a separate Ministry of Tribal Affairs has been created in the central government for quick decision and implementation of the programmes for the development of the tribes. Apart from the formal institutions, to look after the welfare of the Scheduled Tribes, innumerable reports of the commissions and committees, seminars, conferences and workshops on tribal affairs are available. In other words, there is no dearth of data for objective evaluation of what has happened to them. Thus, the situation of tribes provides splendid opportunity for a debate on development itself. For the human societies are but a part of larger system, they or any segment of them cannot be considered in isolation within or without. It is all the more necessary that we look at the tribal situation more closely because the course of modern development when looked holistically, in spite of spectacular and awesome breakthroughs in almost all fields, is causing serious concern about the very existence of life on this planet as well as of planet itself. Any systematic projection of the future indicates that the modern course of development is not sustainable. Such concerns though have not put any breaks either in the course or in the intensity of development.

Tribes at the bottom of human development

In spite of this scenario and so much investment on development of tribes in India they are at the bottom of the scale of human development. Education which is considered to be the foremost index of development is considerably low among the Scheduled Tribes. What Surajit Sinha and B.D. Sharma (1977: 4) wrote that one of the yardsticks to measure the development among the Scheduled Tribes was to bring the process of science and technology within their social control, has remained a distant dream. Although usually the tribes live close to nature, a majority of them need healthcare on account of malnutrition, lack of safe drinking water, poor hygiene, environmental sanitations and above all, poverty. A large number of members of Scheduled Tribes have been displaced on account of some mega project, reservation of forest as national parks, etc. It is however, a matter of serious concern that about 5,000 forest villages do not have minimum basic living conditions and above all face a constant threat of eviction. Further, in overall scenario the situation of 'Primitive Tribal Groups' among the Scheduled Tribes is grim. As they are small in number, in political terms they do not count for much in the regional or state political jostling. They do not have any capacity to exert any political pressure. So far they have survived because their quest for autonomy has remained strong in spite of the fact that socio-economic and political environment around them has significantly changed. Say, for instance, the Paliyans of Pallini hills, a food gathering and hunting group of Tamil Nadu, face grave threat for their existence. They are encompassed by plantation and other activities of non-tribals, their resource base has considerably shrunk, and progressively they and their region have been brought within the framework of the government administration and its laws. The new development strategies designed by the government and non-governmental agencies, on account of their own national and international compulsions have been forced upon them (Misra, 2006). Norstrom (2003) who studied them has listed 24 NGOs working for the upliftment of the Paliyans each with its own focus, understanding an agenda. This is apart from the intrusion of political parties and their agents in their region who desperately need to legitimise their concern for "backward regions and backward people". All this in spite of the fact, all that the Paliyan wants is to be left alone. The Paliyans, according to Norstrom have three social strategies to deal with these intrusions, namely avoidance, negotiation and alliance (ibid.). So far the Paliyans have been partly successful but other groups like Jenu Kuruba in Karnataka or Kadar in Kerala have not been so lucky. They have been totally devastated (Misra, 2003). The dominant society around these groups have always been interested in the resources of their habitats, their skills but never had a genuine respect for their ways of life. Thus, the point that I would like to emphasise is that the problems of the 'primitive tribes' or tribes in general can never be addressed in isolation of the wider society, its development and its dominant ethos. While some among the 'primitive groups' may have retained the ethos to be left alone, there have been a variety of responses from other groups of Scheduled Tribes. In 1972, K.S. Singh in his introduction to a landmark volume *The Tribal Situation in India* wrote: "the situation in the north-east tribal region, having remained turbulent over the past few years, gave hope. Elsewhere in the country, the tribal scene was becoming rapidly politicised and tribal unrest had turned violent at a few places. A new tribal image was emerging" (1972: XI). After a quarter of the century that statement appears to be vastly understated. There are many hot spots in the tribal map of India today. In some places they have been caught up in vice like grip between extremist and state forces. The monograph like that of Verrier Elwin, *The Muria and their Ghotul* (1947) describing the romance and leisurely life of the Muria in the district of Bastar of the modern state of Chhattisgarh would now appear like a fairy tale. The trouble is brewing up in many other places too. To repress the unrest considering them as merely law and order problem will be the greatest folly. There are genuine issues. Way back in 1949 when perhaps the condition of tribes was not as bad as it is now, Dube (1949: 34) had written: "economic rehabilitation…must have precedence over empty sermonising" and Majumdar (1949: 42) had noted in the same volume of *The Eastern Anthropologist* "in some cases prior to education and employment of tribal teachers the problem of bread must be solved" (Srivastava, 2003: 173). Much has happened since then. International and national bodies have conceded that indigenous people have the right to control their land, territories, and natural resources and to maintain their traditional ways of life. But these acceptances including the many rights guaranteed to the members of the Scheduled Tribes by the Constitution of India and the various other acts passed by the parliament have either remained on paper, or not properly implemented or openly violated. Kerala experience is instructive in this regard. In 1975, the Kerala legislature unanimously enacted the Kerala Scheduled Tribes Act, the purpose of which was to restrict the transfer of lands from the members of the Scheduled Tribes and also to restore alienated lands to them. This act was not notified for years. In the meanwhile, non-scheduled people who had occupied the lands of the Scheduled Tribes got opportunity to consolidate their position and not only that, encouraged by the attitude of the authorities they also encroached upon the land in the forest areas. The forest dwellers became daily wage earners on their own land. They were disowned. The government did not implement its own law. The members of Scheduled Tribes began direct action and also brought the land alienation cases before the Kerala High Court. Ultimately, the Kerala High Court ordered pre-emptory compliance of the provisions of the Act, that the land that has been alienated from the members of the Scheduled Tribes should be restored to them. Instead of implementing the orders of the High Court, the Kerala government brought out legislation as an amendment to the previous Act sapping its basic objective of restoring land to the members of the Scheduled Tribes both in letter and spirit. The government resorted to firing and repression when the evicted members of Scheduled Tribes tried to occupy their land. In this regard the record of the government of Andhra Pradesh is no better. The government there passed Land Transfer Regulation as early as 1959, which proscribed the transfer of tribal lands to the non-tribals and provided for retrieval of tribal lands illegally acquired by the non-tribals. After passing the regulation they did not take any steps to enforce it. In 1969 when a dispute arose, the High Court had to point out that the regulation of 1959 could not be enforced as working rules were not framed. Since then the Andhra Pradesh government has been trying to water down the provisions of the original regulation by series of action so that the land acquired by non-tribals remains with them only (Reddy, 2006). In January 2006, 12 members of the Scheduled Tribes were shot dead in Kalinganagar in Orissa because they were protesting against the acquisition of their lands for a steel plant. Nandigram which is so very much in news these days may not have involved the members of Scheduled Tribes but basically the story is the same, that is to dispossess the weak from owning the resources considered important by the powerful. It is basically the nature of relationship between have and have-nots.

Development plan and process of marginalisation

The author of the new strategy of Tribal Sub-Plans drawn in 1970s after a careful review of the tribal situation in the context of simmering discontent and growing interest so that exploitation of the members of Scheduled Tribes is eliminated, in 1995 wrote: "the special development plans proved to be most effective instrument of consolidation of 'colonial' stranglehold on the tribal areas. The state, the industrialists, the contractors, the middleman and non-descript crowd of outsiders have descended on these areas in search of new opportunities in a spirit of no holds barred" (Sharma, 1995: 21). He further elaborated that extensive forests in many areas have disappeared. The natural forests have been converted into economic plantations, knocking out the base of the subsistence tribal economy. Extensive tribal areas have been devasted as a large variety of minerals are extracted. Tribal land has been acquired for industrial use. The use of water resources for land irrigation and power project also had the shattering impact on tribal people (ibid.: 22). These and much more are the direct consequences of new economic policy in which market dominates. The tribals neither have the skills to manage market, nor required training to take advantage of the new opportunities offered by the new economic policies. The process of marginalisation of the tribes began during colonial period. Large tracts of their land were released for commercial agriculture. Their forests were penetrated for laying down road and rail links and also reserved for fulfilling colonial interests. The natural rights of the forest dwellers were openly violated. The impact of imposing various limitations on using forest resources and starting of so many activities in the forest on the life and society of people who were living there were never considered seriously. They were so to stay outside the horizon of the civilised world. They were part of the 'waste' land. Ironically, this is the period when a number of 'excellent' anthropological monographs were written on them and discussed in the 'temples of learning' across the so-called developed world!

Lofty ideals empty deeds

Today, there is much talk about the rights of the indigenous people, empowering the weak, providing them education and skills, building their capacities, maintaining biodiversity, conservation, etc. These are beautiful phrases which enshrine lofty ideals but the ground reality, to say the least, is frightening. It is not merely the tribes but a large number of non-tribes particularly the small farmers and peasants have been ruthlessly marginalised. No doubt a lot of illusion has been created but a systematic analysis will indicate that there is no prospect for them. Between 1997 and 2005, 1.5 lakh farmers have committed suicide in India (*The Hindu*, 12 September

2007). The cold statistics provided by the various studies being conducted on the farmers' suicides in the different parts of the country do not tell the grim story of the agony, sufferings, helplessness and struggle of the persons and their families before the final step of committing suicide was taken. Obviously, they saw no ray of hope at the end of the long and dark tunnel they were in. Taking one's life is the extreme step. If it was a solitary happening it is possible to dismiss them as some kind of aberration but the phenomenon is so widespread that it is clear that the situation of the marginalised people is extremely serious. The tragedy is further compounded by the fact that it is happening amidst so much development.

Bar moves up

Development itself cannot be decried but certainly its nature, thrust and its consequences should be intensively and widely discussed. No doubt, development has brought some benefits even to the weak but in the meanwhile the parameters of a reasonable good life have moved high up that a large majority cannot feel but frustrated and angry. And also it has generated cut-throat competition. It can be argued that the competition in itself is a positive development. It stirs activity, entrepreneurship, innovation and urge to do better but if at the end of all that effort, investment and risks, returns are to be determined by an invisible force called market, the control of which in the so-called free economy are located somewhere else, then there is not much hope for the weak. Thus, the food gatherers, for instance can collect gold but they will never be given enough to raise their standard of living. Second, competition is bound to aggravate inequality among people which in turn fragments communities and also aggravates environmental degradation. The environmental degradation can intensify tensions between people and can impede collective action. Third, the mutual trust between people gets diminished. Nilgiri which was enormously rich in biodiversity and was home of so many tribal groups provides enough evidence what unfettered development and market can do to the communities and the environment. The Toda, the Kota, the Kurumba and the Irula as communities are on the verge of extinction. The Nilgiri environment itself is endangered and now there is no scope for conviviality, sharing or caring. Ruthless competition has been unleashed; value-addition is the name of the game. While the tribes have been dispatched, their jewellery, cuisine, handicrafts, shelter or in short their ways of life are advertised to attract gullible tourists by the clever and enterprising investors which also includes the local and indigenous collaborators too, in the name of tribal tourism, a new venture being promoted by tourism industry in places like Nilgiris (see *The Hindu* editorial human safari's promoted by some tour operators in the Andaman Islands dated 21 June 2010).

Considering the overall scenario among the tribes in India and for that matter among the poor we need to identify the issues. Keeping those issues in view, appropriate outline of the policies have to be framed for wider discussion and understanding. Howsoever a good policy it may be, it cannot be in isolation of the larger framework as well as the instruments through which it has to be implemented. Modern society is aggressively promoting conspicuous consumption. Conspicuous consumption requires tremendous resources much of which is absolutely essential for masses. In the process, elite get away with conspicuous consumption, masses are denied basic necessities of life. Conspicuous consumption degrades environment. Thus, the basic issue is how to discourage conspicuous consumption, how to contain growing inequality. Targeting the poor and preaching them conservation, sustainability, etc., are not going to work. The biggest emitters of greenhouse gases are today's industrialised countries and rich in the developing countries. The problem is how to make the global society learn from the tribal society that the values of conviviality, reciprocity, sharing and caring, and the extension of the self to the surroundings is essential for all.

■ References

Dube, S. C. 1947 "Some Aspects of the Tribal Problem", *The Eastern Anthropologist*, Vol. 3, No. 1; 28–35.

Elwin, V. 1947 *The Muriya and Their Ghotul*, Cambridge: The Oxford University Press.

Mahana, R.K. 2006 "Culture and Development", *The Eastern Anthropologist*, Vol. 59, Nos. 3–4; 353–367.

Majumdar, D.N. 1949 "The Changing Canvas of Tribal Life", *The Eastern Anthropologst*, Vol. 3, No. 1; 40–47.

Misra, P.K. 2003 "Primitive Tribes in Southern Region: A case study", *The Eastern Anthropologist*, Vol. 56, No. 2–4; 379–389.

——. 2006 "Identity and Autonomy Among the Food Gatherers and Hunters", *The Eastern Anthropologist*, Vol. 59, Nos. 3–4; 465–469.

Norstrom, Christer 2003 *"They Call for Us": Strategies for Securing Autonomy Among the Paliyars, Hunter-gatherers of Palini Hills, South India.* Stockholm Studies in Social Anthropology.

Reddy, N. Subba 2006 "Development Through Dismemberment of the Weak: Threat of Polavaram Project", *Economic and Political Weekly*, April 15.

Roy Burman, B.K. 2003 "Tribal Identity, Globalisation and Planned Development", *The Eastern Anthropologist*, Vol. 56, Nos. 2–4; 177–186.

Sharma, B.D. 1995 *Globalisation: The Tribal Encounter*, New Delhi: Har-Anand Publications.

Singh, K.S. 1972 *The Tribal Situation in India*, Simla: Indian Institute of Advanced Studies.

Sinha, Surajit and B.D. Sharma 1977 *Primitive Tribes: The First Step*, New Delhi: Government of India.

Srivatsava, V.K. 2003 "A Note on the Tribal Situation in India", *The Eastern Anthropologist*, Vol. 56, Nos. 2–4; 163–176.

3

Applied anthropology, development and cultural diversity

P.R.G. Mathur

I feel highly honoured for being selected by the Anthropological Association, Mysore for receiving the first Ananthakrishna Memorial Award. I have pleasure in accepting the award not only as a field anthropologist of 50 years' standing, but also as the Founder Member and Secretary of AICAS (Ananthakrishna Iyer International Centre for Anthropological Studies) which has done considerable work in Kerala. Prof. Ananthakrishna Iyer was not only the first Indian anthropologist to get international recognition for his fieldwork in anthropology, but he was also the Father of Anthropology in India, being the first Head of the Department of Anthropology in the University of Caluctta (from 1921 to 1937). Hailing from Lakshminaryanapuram in the suburbs of Palakkad town, Prof. Iyer was commissioned by Sir Asutosh Mukhopadhyaya to head the department of Anthropology in the University of Calcutta. Iyer used to visit the tribal areas of Mysore since 1921 or so for undertaking fieldwork. Thus the Anthropological Association of Mysore has not only honoured the pioneering work of Prof. Iyer, but also deserves congratulations for continuing his work. In selecting this humble fieldworker in anthropology hailing from a village not far from Iyer's birthplace, the Anthropological Association of Mysore has achieved the twin distinction of honouring the Father of Anthropology in India and his follower.

It is my privilege and pleasure to join in paying this tribute to the memory of the late L.K. Ananthakrishna Iyer, the father of Indian Anthropology on the occasion of this national seminar at Mysore. Nothing has been done to perpetuate his memory by Indian anthropologists, planners and administrators nor by the Central and State Governments, when anthropological researches were being challenged in Kerala in the seventies.

I conveyed a meeting of the peasants of Palakkad and narrated the life story of Professor Iyer and his contributions to the field of Urgent Anthropology in general, and particularly to the study of Scheduled Castes and Scheduled Tribes and other weaker sections of society. It was with the support of the peasant communities and the encouragement given by reputed anthropologists all over the world that the Ananthakrishna Iyer International Centre for Anthropological Studies (AICAS) was established in 1979. Iyer's three volumes of the *Cochin Tribes and Castes* (1908 and 1912), the *Anthropology of Syrian Christians* (1912), the work undertaken for his lectures on Ethnography and his four volumes (1925, 1929, 1932, 1940) on Mysore Castes and Tribes are the most outstanding among his works. Anthropologists in our country owe much to Iyer, who has not only been a great social scientist but who has left a tradition of high scholarships and scientific integrity. His works even today hold good for planners, administrators, jurists and applied anthropologists. He was indeed an indefatigable and learned field anthropologist. Iyer made several efforts to present his ethnographic data in a common theoretical framework of that time. He stressed the fundamental importance of ethnography and cultural history, which have shaped modern cultural and social anthropologists. As an ethnographer, his interests had been varied and sometimes unorthodox.

Iyer in his long and productive career had extensive contacts with Indian, British and German anthropologists and when he expired in 1937 high tributes were paid by leading anthropologists the world over. The purpose of this paper is to highlight how his ethnographic studies are still valid, not only for ethnographers, planners and administrators but also for applied anthropologists.

Anthropology without fieldwork is not worth calling a scientific discipline. Iyer had no academic degree in Anthropology like Dr. Verrier Elwin and Sarat Chandra Roy, but his lifelong interest in the way people organised their lives and his fieldwork among them earned him a unique place in the field of anthropology.

Before, I share my experience as a social anthropologist with you, it is but appropriate for me to pay my respects to my Gurus. Prof. Surajit Sinha's name should be mentioned first. I studied under Surajit Sinha for five years between 1967 and 1972, during which period, apart from other research workers he guided me to successfully complete my Ph.D. work on 'the Mappila Fisherfolk of Kerala'. I would also like to pay my tribute to Professor Nirmal Kumar Bose for his guidance, advice and encouragement to continue my anthropological researches.

As a fieldworker in social science in the 1970s on Kerala society which was at the crossroad of survival or extinction, I knew that my life was closely bound up with Malayali society and culture. I also realised that a person like me must first have a good understanding of the Kerala society and culture in which I lived, if I wished to do something meaningful and do it with a clean conscience in the era of an unprecedented upheaval. Hence, the desire and decision to probe for a scientific way of examining and studying Kerala society. Applied anthropology, as I understand it, is a science concerned with the transformation of the human society through acquiring knowledge about human beings systematically. Science should serve mankind and it is needed by man to help him develop properly. "My tutor's proposition of studying human society in the midst of man's throbbing social life was well known. It had such great appeal that I travelled all the way to him for his wise counsel. In his 1926 article, 'Myth in Primitive Psychology', written in memory of his teacher Sir James Fraser, Malinowski issued the call and I quote, 'I shall invite my readers to step up outside the closed study of the themes into the open air of the anthropological field' (Fei, 2003: 92)

Theoretical framework in historical context

The new term 'applied anthropology' was used only from 1941. The knowledge of anthropology was first put into immediate practical use in the Golden Stool incident, in 1896 when Britain was involved in costly wars with the Ashanti people of west coast of Africa. In 1921, a similar outbreak was narrowly averted when an anthropologist pointed out the tremendous symbolic significance to the Ashanti of what to the British appeared to be nearly a king's seat—the Golden Stool.

During the Second World War, many British anthropologists held important posts in the foreign office, the admiralty, British information service, wartime social survey and in the field. One of them was political adviser to the whole Middle East and another carried the main administrative burden for Egypt and Sudan. A woman anthropologist, Ursula Graham Bower, became popularly known as the T.E. Lawrence of World War II.

Just as governments have looked to geology, entomology, and the other physical and biological sciences in handling the resource of the territories concern, and to tropical medicine in meeting health problems, so they (government) have drawn on Anthropology to throw light on the exceedingly difficult problems of human relations especially the adjustment of the indigenous peoples in modern civilisation.

Forde (1953: 841–65) observed: "in any strict sense of the phrase applied anthropology in Government must refer to the actual application of anthropological knowledge by those administratively responsible in the formulation and execution of Government policy". The term 'applied anthropology' has a definite meaning for Philip Gulliver (1979) and he goes to explain that "the work may be practical use to government and international agencies" and it seems to him to imply—doing—policy making, planning, implementation and to involve responsibility. Applied anthropology is, then, research specially oriented to administrative and development problems, together with some degree of responsible participation in the process of utilising the results of such research.

Evans-Pritchard (1964: 109–15) in his lecture asked the question what is the use of knowledge about primitive societies? He answered the question by observing that "it is intended to administer a people according to their own laws and customs one has first to discover what these are. It is evident also that if it is intended to change a people's economy, for example to alter their system of land tenure, to encourage them to grown export crops, or to institute markets and a money economy, it is of some advantage to be able to estimate, at any rate roughly, what social effects these changes are likely to bring about. If, example, the system of land tenure is changed there may be repercussions on the people's family and kinship life and on their religious beliefs and cults may be closely bound up with their traditional system of tenure".

Many anthropologists and ethnologists of the 19th century and majority of social anthropologists of 20th century have, implicitly and explicitly held that social anthropology as a natural science which aims at the establishment of laws of social life, and once theoretical generalisations can be established an applied science becomes feasible. Thus, they have taken the natural sciences for their model and assumed that the purpose of Anthropology is for prediction and planning to control social change. This assumption was summed up in the phrase social engineering. Evans-Pritchard (1964: 117) did not believe that anthropological knowledge could be applied to any extent in the arts of administration and education among primitive societies in any other than in this very general cultural sense. However, he reiterated that "this does not mean that social anthropology cannot be, in a narrow and technical sense applied in anyway. It only means that it cannot be an applied science like medicine and engineering".

There is a need for the development of a more explicit and generally accepted professional code. In this connection, John Embree has observed: "Just as the medical doctor has a basic doctrine that he should prevent disease and save life, so the applied anthropologist tends to operate on a basic doctrine that he should prevent friction and violence in human relations, preserve the rights and dignity of administered groups, and that he should save lives...aid in establishing peaceful and self-respecting relations between peoples and cultures" (quoted by Kluckhohn, 1965: 168–69).

Mead (1977) also reiterated in this context that if we have the knowledge and the skill which makes us capable of applying anthropology then we cannot divest ourselves of the responsibility that goes with that knowledge. Mead asked a question, what was to be overriding value within which applied anthropologist would act as the physician was faithful to life and judge to the law. Mead concentrated on the specific ethic of applied anthropologist in the roles and interventionist and as practitioners whose work could be expedited to have identifiable consequences in the lives of human societies. As an interventionist, the applied anthropologist needed professional ethics just as the medical, or legal professions need professional ethics.

Role of applied anthropologists in planning and evaluation

Writing on the role of applied anthropologists in planning, Clyde Kluckhohn observes: "Anthropologists are being more and more drawn into the planning and administering of various types of programmes. Sometimes their role is merely that of advising or of doing background research, but an increasing number are themselves becoming administrators. Whatever the precise field of activity, there are certain general characteristics of practical anthropology. Emphasis is always placed on the importance of symbolic as well as utilitarian considerations in human relations. Communication from the administrator to his superiors and subordinates as well as to the administered group must take account of both the rational and non-rational aspects of communications. Applied anthropology has now moved beyond the phase where the primary task was that of inculcating respect for an understanding of native customs. The problem is now seen as two-sided. The content and structure of the culture of the administered group must still be analysed. The practical anthropologist must also have a systematic understanding of the special subcultures of the policy makers, the supervisory administrators, and the field operators" (1965: 160–61).

As regards the role of an applied anthropologist on the planning and implementation of projects exclusively meant for the Scheduled Tribes the following aspects have to be taken into consideration:

(i) Planning for the development of Scheduled Tribe community has to be reviewed regularly and updated throughout the programme. It must be noted that the cycle of planning and evaluation ideally operates in a continuous feedback pattern that modifies plans as a programme rolls towards its goals. Thus, planning should be constantly reviewed and updated by evaluation throughout a project, since it is an integral part of the process of planning.

(ii) Evaluation has to begin during the planning and formulation of the development programmes. Evaluation data provide valuable feedback information which can be utilised for ensuring the success of the programmes. Such information is also used to correct procedures and revise objectives.

(iii) First-hand knowledge of tribal communities gained through participant observation and the methods employed by anthropologists provide baseline data for the formulation of the programmes. It is often alleged that planners have succumbed to bureaucrats who want social reforms not to be implemented and scuttle every progressive measure. Planners are often viewed as members of the ruling elite. Charges of elitism can only be reduced in planning if the concept of cultural relativism, concept of pluralism, community study method, inductive approach and participant observation, etc., are used and the target population like the tribal community, is kept in constant contact.

(iv) Anthropologists working on development programmes have produced theories and research methodologies dealing with the process of change that are vitally important to planners and administrators in charge of the welfare of the weaker sections of the society. These theories and research tools are potentially useful in helping planners in guiding changes to understand better how a community is prone to resist change in the face of ecological, social and technological innovations.

(v) Planning for the tribal society is recommended to be decentralised. The decentralised process of planning from the bottom up will allow the tribal people to make their own priorities, while the planners will be free to concentrate on their technical side. Although this is difficult to achieve because of the larger number of members involved, plans and programmes will be more readily accepted by the target population if they feel that they are on their own. Such an interaction of the community involved with the development plans will make them more responsive to changes and bring forward their own problems, needs and priorities.

(vi) Formulation of programmes for the welfare of the Scheduled Tribes should convince planners that there is an imperative need for knowing the problems and conditions of the tribal communities involved and these are obtained by anthropologists by participant observation.

Essential features of a planned approach for the development of Scheduled Tribes may be summarised as follows:

(a) Socio-economic complexities of tribal life demand an integrated approach to development in which economic handicaps and social disabilities have to be attacked simultaneously.

(b) Primary focus should be on the betterment of the economic status of the tribal communities and social development programmes.

(c) Choice of production programmes should be such that they should fit in with the skill, attainment and managerial capabilities with regard to use of productive resources.

(d) A strong institutional support has to be built up which should be responsible for the implementation of economic programmes (production and marketing) and welfare programmes.

(e) The personnel entrusted with the task of the social and economic emancipation of the tribal communities will have to be of high calibre and appropriately motivated to it.

Another important function of an applied anthropologist is to conduct evaluation studies of the development programmes implemented for the welfare of Scheduled Tribes.

A case study of Attappady

We shall give an example of the impact of an evaluation study recently conducted in regard to one of the Integrated Tribal Development Projects in Kerala. Out of the 180 Integrated Tribal Development Projects in India in the year 1978, Kerala had only five such projects. Attappady (in the district of Palakkad) is the only tribal area where the Integrated Tribal Development Programmes had been implemented since 1975. The evaluation study conducted here revealed that the benefits have not percolated into the target population. When the anthropological study report was challenged by the administrators, planners and implementing authorities, the Government appointed a High Power Committee under the chairmanship of the Vice-Chancellor of the Kerala Agricultural University. Some of the salient observations of our study are summarised below.

While summarising the result of a decade or more development activities carried out during the TD block stage one can conclude that the tribal hamlets did not get reasonable facilities in respect of communication, water supply, education, electricity, medical aid and other amenities and the block had coordinated actions only with departments like Agriculture, Animal Husbandry, Cooperation and Panchayats. All other departments were working as watertight compartments. This was one of the reasons for the ineffective implementation of development programmes.

It was observed that over 75 per cent of the tribal families in Attappady were deprived of their lands due to various forms of exploitation. Studies based on tribal indebtedness and consequent land alienation revealed the dangerous magnitude of the problem existing in the Attappady valley. Credit and marketing were the weakest links in tribal economy and the greatest source of exploitation of the tribal communities was by non-tribals.

There was no proper coordination between the Western Ghat development projects and those of the ITDP programmes. The concept of Integrated Area Development was ignored. As an overall assessment of the benefit flow from the ITDP schemes to tribals, it can be said with confidence that the schemes failed thoroughly in some spheres and in others there were only marginal benefits to the tribesmen.

Recommendation of the evaluation study

The main emphasis given in the strategy for development is the strengthening of the tribal economic base. The programmes for economic and social development demanded the creation of a number of institutions to channelise supplies and services including legal and administrative support. Concurrently appropriate infrastructure development has to be taken up. The project must integrate with the resource endowments of the area and the level of development of the tribal communities inhabiting the valley must mainly determine the formula for the strategy which include the following: (a) utilisation of forest resources, (b) restoration of alienated tribal land, (c) rehabilitation of landless tribal families, (d) special attention and care to Kurumbas, (e) animal husbandry as a source of supplementary income, (f) credit and marketing facilities through co-operatives and co-operativisation of the entire community, (g) small tribal farmers should be assisted by SFDA projects, (h) development of road communication, (i) providing maximum impetus to education, (j) imparting training to tribal labour for acquiring new skills, (k) provision of health and medical care and health education to all people concerned, (l) provision for adequate drinking water supply to all hamlets, (m) housing schemes, (n) administration of the schemes with a forward looking, innovative and highly sympathetic administrative apparatus, (o) continuous follow-up to programmes implemented, and (p) ITD project should also develop a proper manpower resource with necessary incentive package.

The High Power Committee was appointed by the State Government to examine whether the anthropological report submitted by me was on the basis of actual field situation. The State Government appointed the committee in response to the contentions made by the implementing authorities in general and bureaucrats and planners in particular that my report was frivolous. The members of the committee toured this area and came to the conclusion that all the points I had made in my study were factual. This created a furore among the implementing authorities and officials of the concerned Integrated Tribal Development Programme. Persons in charge of development programmes, particularly for the Scheduled Tribes in India should be committed and dedicated. But, in practice, the situation is different. The use of anthropological perspective and techniques for evaluation studies have been profound, especially so during the last few decades.

The Reddiars Claim Konda Reddis' status

The Reddiars of Kerala claim their origin from Ganjam, Gundur and Nellore districts of Andhra Pradesh and Nanguneri taluk of the Tirunelveli district in Tamil Nadu. There is no doubt that the Reddiars had migrated to Kerala and had their original settlement at Samugapuram. Their migration to Kerala dates from 1886 when one Subba Tennetu Reddiar established the Vidharthi Press in Quilon. The Reddiars are generally known as Reddis in Andhra Pradesh. Each Reddiar village in Tamil Nadu has a population ranging from 500 to 1500.

Among the Reddiars of Tamil Nadu there are three different subcastes (*jatis*), viz., Kotta Reddiar, the Olavu Reddiars and the Ganjam Reddis. Intermarriage and interdining among these sub-castes is strictly prohibited. The Kotta Reddiar and Olavu Reddiars are mainly found in the Nanguneri taluk of Tirunelveli district whereas the Ganjam Reddis are found in the Bilathikulam and Kolpetti taluks of the same district. They are also found in the black soil area of Sathur and Aruppokottai taluks of Ramanad districts and Thirumangalam taluk of Madhura district in recent years. The Kotta Reddiars have even been included among the backward castes in Madhura district in recent years but Ganjam Reddiars and Olavu

Reddiars are not recognised as such. The Kotta Reddiars enjoy a superior status as they follow vegetarianism. They are found mainly in government services and are landowners. On the other hand, the Olavu Reddiars are mainly cultivators. Since this social group subsists on cultivation they are popularly known as the Olavu Reddiars in the rural areas. They do not like to be called Olavu Reddis and style themselves as Reddis solely for the purposes of enjoying benefits earmarked for the Scheduled Tribes. Ganjam Reddis are reported to be more backward in comparison to the other two sub-castes. The non-Reddiars community as well as the other subsections of the Reddiars refer or address the Kotta Reddiars as Pannayur. The Kotta Reddiars are caste Hindus. The Olava Reddiars are also caste Hindus occupying a higher social status in the regional social structure. Saiva Pillai, Konar (Yadava), Thevar (Maravar), Vaniyas, Velaar, Sambavar (Adi Dravida) and other neighbouring castes even today render traditional services to the Reddiars and Olavu Reddiars. The Reddiars worship their local deities like Pillayar, Amma and Perumal but do not worship those propitiated by the Konda Reddis. During village festivals even today all other castes maintain their ritual relations with the Reddiars. For instance, Konnar supplies the goat for sacrifices and the Maravar has the right to chop off its head. This evidence is sufficient to show that the Reddiars are caste Hindus and do not belong to a Scheduled Tribe.

The Reddiars who migrated from Tamil Nadu to Kerala mainly belonged to the Kotta Reddiar and Olavu Reddiar sub-castes. The Olavu Reddiars migrated mainly from the villages of Samugrarangapuram, Nakkaneri, Silathikulam and Parithipat whereas the Kotta Reddiars came from the village of Moolakaraipatti and Koliyankulam in the Nanguneri taluk of Tirunelveli district. The Kotta Reddiars in Kerala are mainly engaged in running hotels whereas the Olavu Reddiars have a monopoly in the textile business, especially in the erstwhile Travancore–Cochin State. For instance, some of the important hotels like the Arul Jyothi and Arya Bhavan are owned by the Kotta Reddis in Trivandrum whereas the well-known textiles shops such as Seemati, Parthas and Veera Lakshmana are owned by the Olavu Reddis. The owners of these three textile shops are related through marriage. The criteria to be adopted in deciding the status of a migrant person has been clarified by the Government of India thus: "when a person migrates from one state to another he can claim to belong to a Scheduled Caste or Scheduled Tribe only in relation to the state to which he originally belonged and not in respect of the state to which he has migrated". Generally, the clan (*gotram*) to which a person belongs in the matrix in deciding his/her caste. The clan does not change by migration. Identification of the clan is the crux of the problem in deciding the status of a community or caste.

Since the implementation of the 1976 classification Amendment Order (Act 108 of 1976), the Reddiars, especially the Olavu Reddiars, have made vigorous attempts to get themselves classified as Konda Reddis. This practice was resorted to for the purpose of getting their children admitted into professional colleges and higher studies and for appointments in government services against the quota set apart for the Scheduled Tribes. This is done by producing community certificates form revenue authorities or other competent officers who are authorised to issue such certificates. Four students belonging to the Reddiar community succeeded in getting the certificates showing their caste as Konda Reddis. On the basis of this certificate they got provisional eligibility for admission to the 1st year MBBS course in the medical colleges in the state. However, the Principal of the Medical College, Trivandrum, who made their provisional selection, withheld their admissions for further verification of their status to claim seats reserved for Scheduled Tribes. These four candidates then filed writ petitions before the Hon'ble High Court of Kerala seeking admission against the seats reserved for Scheduled Tribes. But, the High Court disposed of the above representations with the direction that the government may take decision as to whether those four petitioners actually belonged to Scheduled Tribe. The State Government directed KIRTADS to conduct an anthropological study and submit a report in this connection. Our study showed that all these four candidates seeking admissions to the medical college did not belong to the Konda Reddis, but the Olavu Reddiar (one of the sub-caste of Reddiars) community which is not recognised as Scheduled Tribe.

Migration and constitutional provisions

Since the question of migration is a salient fact, the following are the major issues involved with regard to the status of migrants from one state to another.

1. Whether a Scheduled Caste/Scheduled Tribe person on migration from the state of origin to another state will lose his status, of belonging to a reserved category.
2. Whether Scheduled Caste/Scheduled Tribe persons on migration from the original state to another will be entitled to the concessions/benefits admissible to them from the state to which they have migrated.
3. Whether Scheduled Caste/Scheduled Tribe migrants who have settled permanently in migrated state before the first notification of the Presidential Order 1950 are eligible to get concessions/benefits earmarked for them if they are not scheduled in the area to which they have migrated.
4. Whether Scheduled Caste/Scheduled Tribe persons migrated to Kerala after the promulgation of the relevant Presidential Order 1950 (where they are scheduled) are eligible to get Scheduled Caste/Scheduled Tribe benefits/concessions from the state to which they have migrated temporarily.
5. Whether the relevant order means only the Presidential Order 1950 or it includes in subsequent modification Order 1956 and Scheduled Caste/Scheduled Tribe (Amendment) Order 1976.

The Government of India in their letter No. 10014/1/12-SC and BCD-I of 6 January 1984 has clarified that "Scheduled Caste/Scheduled Tribe person on migration from the state of his origin to another state will not lose his status as Scheduled Caste/Scheduled Tribe but he will be entitled to the concessions/benefits admissible to the Scheduled Caste/Scheduled Tribe from the state of his origin and not from the state where he has migrated". In another letter No. 12017/2/85/SC and BCD dated 7.6.1985 from the Director, Government of India, Ministry of Home Affairs, it has been stated that "a person who is temporary away from permanent place of abode at the time of notification of the Presidential Order 1950 applicable in his case, to earn a living or seek education, etc., can be regarded as a Scheduled Caste or a Scheduled Tribe as the case may be, if his caste/tribe has been specified in that Order in relation to this State, but he cannot be treated as such in relation to the place of his temporary residence notwithstanding the fact that the name of his caste/tribe has been scheduled in respect of that area in any Presidential Order. He will be deemed to be treated as a migrant in relation to the latter state to which he has migrated". In the same letter, the Government of India has clarified, "if a man leaves his originating state and moves to some other state before issue of the Presidential Order 1950 applicable in his case and settles there permanently by acquiring property whether moveable or immovable that state will be regarded his/her children's ordinary place of residence (i.e., permanent abode) for the purpose of issue of the certificates to him. Her/his children will be entitled to obtain a certificate from the competent authority of the latter state provided the community to which he belonged his originating state has been recognised and scheduled in the Presidential Order applicable in his case in migrated state. He will not be eligible to obtain a certificate from his originating state to this effect. It has been stated further, "a person who has migrated temporarily for the sake of employment, etc., after the issue of the Presidential Order as already clarified in the proceeding paragraph, he will be required to obtain a certificate from the competent authority of the migrated state on the basis of the genuine certificate from his originating state to the other state, he and his children will be entitled to enjoy benefits admissible to the Scheduled Castes and Scheduled Tribes, from the state of origin and not from the state to which he migrated ".

As stated earlier, the Reddiars of Kerala are a Telugu speaking community mainly found in the erstwhile Travancore area. They are caste Hindus. They claim that they originally migrated from the districts of Ganjam, Guntur and Nellore of Andhra Pradesh and settled at Samugarangapuram, Nanguneri taluk of Tirunelveli district, Tamil Nadu. The earliest migration of the Reddiar community dates back to the 1886 when S.T. Reddiar, an immigrant from Samugarangapuram, established Vidharthi Press in Quilon, one of the oldest printing presses in Kerala. This printing press is today known as S.T. Reddiar & Sons. Towards the end of the 19th century, there were only five Reddiar families in Alleppey engaged in textile business. According to the late Veeraiyya Reddiar the founder of Seemati, his sister Seemati's husband Krishnaswamy Reddiar was one of the five earliest migrants settled in Alleppey from the Reddiar community. When Veeraiyya Reddiar's parents died, he left Samugarangapuram along with his sister Seemati in 1910 and settled in Alleppey. Seemati was a barren woman so Krishnaswamy Reddiar married again. When Veeraiyya Reddiar started his textile mill in 1915 it was named Seemati in honour of his deceased sister Seemati. Today, it has branches in Trivandrum, Quilon, Kottayam, Changanassery, Tiruvalla and Ernakulam. The Reddiars occupy a very high social position in the caste hierarchy of Samugarangapuram. They are mainly found in the cities of Trivandrum and Ernakulam and the major towns of Quilon, Alleppey, Kottarakkara, Changanassery and Kottayam. A number of Reddiars own textile, jewellery and provision shops. The Reddiars have a monopoly in textile trade in Trivandrum–Cochin.

Some of the original Reddiar migrants were printers and publishers in the 19th century. The Radha Printers in Quilon is also owned by the Reddiars. Even today they bring out some of the best sellers in Kerala like *Kunkumam, Nana, Keralasabdam,* etc. It will be evident from the above that the Reddiars are economically, educationally and socially a forward community. But, the Reddiars have infiltrated, into the fold of Scheduled Tribe Konda Reddi by producing community certificates from Nanguneri taluk in Tamil Nadu and obtained fresh community certificates to the effect that they belong to Konda Reddis from revenue officials of Kerala.

The Reddiars have been classified in former Travancore–Cochin as OBC. They are also OBC in Tamil Nadu. This position continues to be same even after the merger of Travancore–Cochin in integrated state of Kerala.

Konda Reddis of Andhra Pradesh

The Konda Reddis, one of the primitive tribes of Andhra Pradesh, mainly inhabit the districts of East Godavari, West Godavari and Kammam. The Konda Reddi habitat is characterised by the hills of the Eastern Ghats and the mighty Godavari river and its tributaries, Sabari and Pamuleru. These rivers and the deciduous forest-clad hills exercise a profound influence on the life and economy of the Konda Reddis.

None of the clans found among the Reddiars of Kerala find place among the clans of the Konda Reddis of Andhra Pradesh. This evidence is sufficient to establish the fact that the Reddiars and the Konda Reddis are not one and the same community. Moreover, the Reddiars are generally caste Hindus in Tamil Nadu whereas the Konda Reddis belong to a primitive tribe in Andhra Pradesh.

Until the Scheduled Castes and Scheduled Tribes (Amendment) Order 1976, Konda Reddis were not scheduled in the erstwhile Travancore area. But in the O.P. 293 of 1976 Dr. V. Venugopala Reddiar vs the State of Kerala, the petitioner, s/o Sankaranarayana Reddy, proprietor of Good Morning Stores, Trivandrum, Samugarangapuram residing now in Palayam, Trivandrum produced a certificate dated 1.9.1973 to the effect from the Tahsildar, Nanguneri taluk of Tirunelveli District, Tamil Nadu to the effect that he belongs to the Konda Reddi community which is classified as a Scheduled Tribe. The Tahsildar of Trivandrum also issued a certificate on 27.12.1975 stating that Dr. Venugopala Reddiar belonged to Konda Reddi community permanently residing at 13-474, Ananda Bhavan, Nanthancode, Palayam, Trivandrum since 1979. The Government of India direction makes it clear that "a person who has migrated temporarily for the sake of employment, etc., after the issue of the Presidential Order...will be required to obtain a certificate from the competent authority of the migrated state on the basis of the genuine certificates issued to his father. Further, the person who has migrated from his originating state to the other state, he and his children will be entitled to enjoy benefits admissible to the Scheduled Castes and Scheduled Tribes from the state of origin and not from the state to which he migrated". Venugopala Reddiar succeeded in getting a certificate both from Tamil Nadu and Kerala despite the fact that his father Sankaranarayana Reddiar and himself migrated temporarily for the sake of business and subsequently obtained a caste certificate from Trivandrum. But he is unaware of the fact that he will be entitled to enjoy benefits from the state of origin, i.e., Tamil Nadu. But in his school certificate (SSLC book) it is clearly stated that he belongs to Reddiar OBC community. Now, the question is whether he would be considered as a member of Scheduled Tribe in view of the fact that the Konda Reddis was not scheduled in Travancore while the same community was scheduled in Malabar. It is also listed as Scheduled Tribe in Tamil Nadu. The court held that "if a person belongs to Scheduled Tribe as classified in a particular place he will not cease to be a member of Scheduled Tribe mainly because he shifts his domicile. He continues to be a member of the Konda Reddi community which is a Scheduled Tribe. Now probably that community is not known as a Scheduled Tribe in the Travancore–Cochin area because they are not original residents of that area. There is probably no such community in that part of the state. In this connection the notification preferred to by the petitioner published by the Harijan Welfare Department would have some importance. The High Court held, "What is stated there is a Scheduled Caste and Scheduled Tribe who migrated from one state or one region to another region of the same State will be deemed to be Scheduled Castes/Scheduled Tribes provided they produce community and migration or nativity certificates". This notification was issued by the Harijan Welfare

Department and appeared in Part III of the Kerala Government Gazette dated 29.7.1975. Subsequently, the health department, as per G.O. (Rt) No. 3357/76/HD dated 14.9.1976, has issued an order that Konda Reddi may be treated as Scheduled Tribe throughout the State for the admission in the medical colleges. The court again observed: "This is a very wholesome principle which could be applied in all cases mainly because when a person migrates from one place to another he does not cease to be a member of Scheduled Tribe only on account of the fact that the said tribe is not notified as Scheduled Tribe of that area. The reason for absence of notification as a Scheduled Tribe might well be due to there is no such tribe there". But the court ignored the important constitutional provision for designating a Scheduled Tribe (Article 342 (1) that the phrase "shall be deemed to be Scheduled Tribe in relation to that State". The Government of India also clarified that the Scheduled Caste and Scheduled Tribe on migration from the state of origin to another state will not lose his status as Scheduled Caste and Scheduled Tribe. But they will be entitled to the concessions/benefits admissible to Scheduled Caste/Scheduled Tribe from the state of his origin and not from the State where he has migrated. In the case of Dr. Venugopala Reddiar it is seen that although he does not belong to Konda Reddi community, a Scheduled Tribe of Kerala, he has used the notification issued by the Harijan Welfare Department (dated 22.7.1975) and managed to get a certificate from both from Tamil Nadu and Kerala to the effect that he belonged to Konda Reddis, a recognised Scheduled Tribe of Kerala. It may be mentioned even if he is a Konda Reddi migrated from Tamil Nadu he is not entitled to the concessions and benefits admissible to Scheduled Castes and Scheduled Tribes from the migrated state, as per the Government of India direction but he is entitled to such concessions only from in his State of origin, i.e., Tamil Nadu. The very fact that he has produced a certificate from Tamil Nadu is a conclusive proof that he is a migrant and settled temporarily in Kerala. On the basis of this court verdict, Rajeswari R, a student of 1st year MBBS; Raghunathan S, 1st year BDS; Dr. Harikumar, DCH; Balaveni, MBBS; Venkittasubba Reddi, DLO and several other students produced certificates from Nanguneri taluk of Tirunelveli district and on the basis of that document fresh community certificates have been issued to them to the effect that they belong to Konda Reddi, by the Tahsildar, Trivandrum which enabled them to get admitted in Trivandrum Medical College.

Although I had submitted a detailed report on the basis of studies conducted in Tamil Nadu, Andhra Pradesh and Kerala and clarified that Konda Reddi and Reddiars are not one and the same community and those students should be sent out of medical college, it is reported that the petitioners have all completed their courses in medical college. Although some of the Reddiars who have styled themselves as Konda Reddis have succeeded in getting community certificates from the State of origin as if they are ignorant of the directions from Government of India because some of the Reddiars have migrated to Kerala about hundred years ago, long before the notification of the Presidential Order, 1950. But the major issue in this case was whether Reddiars are the same as Konda Reddis. The anthropological study had proved that Reddiars do not belong to Konda Reddis. In the case of migration, each case has to be investigated separately and the date of migration is to be ascertained in order to find out whether they have migrated temporarily to the migrated state or have their permanent abode in the migrated State.

Although Dr. Venugopala Reddiar and others have produced certificates from Tamil Nadu to the effect that they belong to Konda Reddi, a Scheduled Tribe which is classified as Scheduled Tribe in that state, they cannot claim the concessions/benefits from the migrated State or area, since Konda Reddis were not scheduled in Travancore until 1977. This is evident from the case of Appa Rao vs Post and Telegraph (AIR 1969). The facts of this case are as follows: "A postal clerk residing and working in Orissa was a member of the Konda Kapus, a group listed as Scheduled Tribe in neighbouring Andhra Pradesh but not in Orissa. After being appointed to a higher post against a reservation from Scheduled Tribe, he was reverted on the ground that Konda Kapus was not a Scheduled Tribe in Orissa where he was a permanent resident. He argued that he should be accounted a Scheduled Tribe anywhere for purposes of central government employment, since central legislation clearly outlaws state residence requirements for central government jobs". The High Court turning to the constitutional provisions for designating Scheduled Tribes (Art 342 (1)) decreed that the phrase "shall be deemed to be Scheduled Tribes in relation to that State", meant that in order to get the benefits of being a member of a Scheduled Caste or Scheduled Tribe in the matter of public employment the person claiming it should be a member of such caste or tribe in relation to the particular area or State where he is residing and where he seeks employment. Thus, the court took a restrictive reading of residence rules to be a constitutional requirement. On numerous occasions, officials and political leaders have taken the view that only a constitutional amendment could alleviate these restrictions.

In the case of A. Varadarajan vs State of Tamil Nadu, the appellant had contested and won the legislative assembly election in a reserved constituency in Tamil Nadu as ADMK candidate. But, the Supreme Court cancelled his election in 1982, although the Madras High Court had accepted his claim as Konda Reddi. Varadarajan actually belongs to Reddiar community which is recognized as OBC. Thus, he fortified his MLA status.

There are several instances of infiltration of ineligible communities into the fold of Scheduled Tribes of Kerala. For instance, the Jacobite Christians of Kottayam, Idukki and Pathanamthitta have styled themselves as Malaarayan Christians to claim the benefits of Scheduled Tribes. The Arayan, a fishing community of southern Kerala, have usurped the benefits of Hindu Malaarayan, a Scheduled Tribe of the state. Paniakkals, ritual priest of Mukkuvan, have become Paniyan, a Scheduled Tribe of Kerala. The Odda Naickans have claimed the benefits of Kattunaickan, a primitive tribe of Wayanad. The Pandaram, the garland makers, have styled themselves as Malapandaram to enjoy the benefits of that Scheduled Tribe. The anthropological studies conducted on these communities have shown that they do not belong to Scheduled Tribes but they belong to backward classes. The classification of communities was first introduced in Kerala, a separate verification cell was established in KIRTADS and in the Secretariat since 1979. This helped to prevent the infiltration of forward communities into fold of Scheduled Caste and Scheduled Tribe communities and also restore the benefits to the actual Scheduled Caste and Scheduled Tribe communities and thus protect and preserve their constitutional safeguards. Today, in Kerala, if anybody wants to change his/her social status in public records it is possible only after conducting anthropological studies.

Mahadeo Kolis and Kolis

In Madhura Patil case (Civil Appeal No. 5854 of 1994), the Supreme Court held that the appellants (Madhuri Laxman Patil and her sister Sujithra Laxman Patil) do not belong to the 'Mahadeo Koli', a Scheduled Tribe of Maharashtra, but they actually belonged to Hindu Koli, an OBC community.

The Apex Court directed the State and Central Governments to streamline the procedure for the issuance of community certificate, by their Secretaries on the basis of certain criteria:

1. All the State Governments shall constitute a scrutiny committee of three officers, viz., (i) Additional or Joint Secretary or any higher in rank of the Director of the Department, (ii) Director, Social Welfare/ Tribal Welfare/Backward Class Welfare as the case may be, (iii) in the case of Scheduled Caste another officer who has intimate knowledge in the verification and issuance of social status certificate. In the case of Scheduled Tribes the Research Officer who has intimate knowledge in identifying the tribes, tribal communities, parts of or groups of tribes or tribal communities; each directorate should constitute a Vigilance Cell headed by a Superintendent of Police.
2. Application for verification of community certificate by the scrutiny committee shall be filed atleast six months in advance before seeking admission into education institutions or appointment to a post.
3. The order passed by the scrutiny committee shall be final and conclusive and subject only to appeal under the procedure of Article 226 of the Constitution.
4. The High Court would dispose of these cases as expeditiously as possible within a period of three months. In case, as per its procedure the writ petition/miscellaneous petition/matter is disposed of by a single judge, no further appeal would lie against that order to the Division Bench, but subject to special leave under Article 136 before the Supreme Court.
5. In case the certificate obtained or social status claimed is found to be false, the parent/guardian/the candidate should be prosecuted for making false claim.

Madhuri Patil sought admission for BDS and her sister Sujithra Patil, for MBBS. They were able to procure bogus community certificates to the effect that they belonged to Mahadeo Koli, a Scheduled Tribe of Maharashtra, although they actually belonged to Koli, an OBC community.

The Supreme Court upheld the cancellation and certification of their social status as Mahadeo Koli as ordered by the scrutiny committee and affirmed by the order of the appellate authority and High Court in that behalf subject to the above modification the appeal was dismissed without cost.

Mahadeo Kolis are forest dwellers living by agriculture, collection of minor forest produce and forest labour. On the other hand, Koli, a fishing community, inhabit the coastal areas of Maharashtra and is recognised as a backward class. They belong to the Hindu Koli caste. On the other hand, Mahadeo Koli is a Scheduled Tribe as per SC and ST Order of 1950, 1956 and also SC and ST Amendment Act of 1976.

In consequence of Madhuri Patil case the Government of Kerala enacted a law popularly known as Act 11 of 1996 (Restriction on Issue of Community Certificates) for constituting the scrutiny committee consisting of the Secretary, SC and ST Department, Director of SC and ST Department and Director of Tribal Development Department and Director of KIRTADS. Under the Act of 1996, a Vigilance Cell was also established in KIRTADS. The Act also stipulated that those who have succeeded in getting false certificates as SC and ST and also those who have issued a false community certificates and also the office in charge of Vigilance Cell can be prosecuted if they are responsible for issuing false community certificates.

Conclusion

Applied anthropology in India in general, and in Kerala in particular, cannot be ignored if the scientific identification and classification of communities is desired. Competition is high, especially in securing admission to professional courses and government jobs as a result people try to manipulate provisions of the constitution in such a way that they get a certificate of community belonging to reserved category. With the majority among the weaker sections remaining still ignorant about their rights it becomes easier for the members of the majority community to exploit the situation in their favour. The formulators of our Constitution have stipulated a definite time limit for the extension of benefits of reservation but after nearly six decades of independence, we are yet to reach anywhere near the original target. Why, one may ask? The above mentioned situations clearly indicate the state of our administration has landed itself into.

The preparation of ethnographic notes on different communities, particularly the primitive and backward ones, is fast gaining importance, which are useful for planning development programmes. Monographic studies focusing attention of one or more (educational, economic, etc.) areas of a community are of great help. Applied anthropologists as researcher-cum-trainers must develop skills and tools for transmitting knowledge to implementing and development personnel in order to equip them to evaluate and analyse programmes for making suitable changes, arrangements and suggestions, as the situation demands. The success of any development programme can be ensured only by the involvement of such trained personnel. Applied anthropologists can serve as a bridge between the government and the community, and action anthropologists could work with the community to solve its problems. While applied anthropologists are primarily analysts and communicators, action anthropologists are, besides these, also interventionists. They should intervene in the community, the government and other seats of power and decision-making. The objective of their action should neither be the immediate gain of the community nor that of the power elite in isolation but the broader vision of humanity.

Acknowledgement

I am extremely grateful to Prof. P.K. Misra for his criticism and comments on the Ananthakrishna Memorial Lecture titled 'Applied Anthropology: Development and Cultural Diversity'.

■ References

Eddy, E.M. and William L. Patridge 1978 *Applied Anthropology in America*, New York: Columbia University Press.

Evans-Pritchard, E.E. 1964 *Social Anthropology*, London: Cohen and West Ltd.

Fei, Xiaotong 2003 *Towards a People's Anthropology*; 90–101, Collection of Anthropology and Ethnology in China No. 4 of the Application Materials China Applicant Committee for the 16th Congress (2008) of IOAES May, (2003), Beijing: New World Press.

Forde, E.D. 1953 "Applied Anthropology in Government: British Africa", In *Anthropology Today*, A.L. Kroeber (ed.), Chicago: University of Chicago Press.

Gulliver, P.H. 1979 *Disputes and Negotiations: A cross-cultural perspective*, New York: Academic Press.

Iyer, L.K.A. 1908 *Tribes and Castes of Cochin*, Vol. 1 (1908) and Vol. 2 (1912), New Delhi: Cosmo Publications.

Kluckhohn, Clyde 1965 *Mirror for Man,* New York: McGraw Hill Book Co.

Mathur, P.R.G. 1977 *Tribal Situation in Kerala,* Trivandrum: Kerala Historical Society.

——. 1980 "The Cholanaickans: Caveman of Kerala", Paper presented at the ICAES, New Delhi 1978, Ministry of Home Affairs.

——. 1989 "Applied Anthropology, Planning and Development Administration—Law and Practice", in *Human Science.* Special Number: 112–132.

Mead, M. 1977 "Applied Anthropology: The State of the Art". In *Perspectives on Anthropology,* A.F.C. Wallace (ed.), Washingdon D.C.: American Anthropological Association.

4

The concept of tribe in the Indian context

T.B. Subba

The Shillong Times of October 3, 2007 had a headline title "Purno opposes ST status to others", which carried a statement given by NCP General Secretary and former Lok Sabha Speaker Purno A. Sangma, at the annual conference of Akhil Bharatiya Adivasi Vikas Parishad held in Jaipur, Rajasthan. Among other things he reportedly said: (1) "We (tribals) are classless and casteless people and not going to let anyone to dilute our tribal character", and (2) "A tribal status is given to one who is primitive, has distinct culture, geographical isolation and has shyness of contact".

The above attempt to define a tribe by a tribal leader assumes a lot of significance not only because of the stature of the person but also because this heralds a new era of self-definition. The innumerable attempts to define a tribe have otherwise been made almost exclusively by anthropologists belonging to Anglo-Saxon origin. They used words like primitive, savage, segmentary, egalitarian, animistic, totemic, kinship-based, linguistically and culturally homogenous, occupying definite territories, geographically isolated or living in forests, hills and distant places, and so on to define the tribes they studied but were acutely aware of the fact that there were other tribes who did not strictly fit into the definitions they had proposed. Hence, most of them chose to propose only a working definition that would be relevant only to the tribes they had studied. The problem continues today even if we seek to confine our definition of tribe to a single country like India, which is the focus of the present seminar.

Over the years, we have come to such a pass that we have begun to talk about what a tribe is not, rather than what it is. This is understandable in view of the immense variation the tribes in India show in terms of size and distribution of population, level of literacy and technology, linguistic diversity, religious and occupational affiliations, and the degree of their integration with other communities. This diversity owes its origin partly to the diverse, arbitrary and politically expedient ways of scheduling a community as a tribe in the Constitution of India for the past five decades or so. This diversity creates a huge challenge for anthropologists to define a tribe in the acceptable label. The criterion "dispossessed and deprived people" (see Xaxa, 1999) might make sense in the plains of India but certainly is not equally relevant to north-east India. Thus, in the context of India, the label itself is a major problem because tribes of north-east India do not wish to be labelled "*adivasi*", as the tribes in India's plains do. The English word "tribe" is well accepted by the former and arguably gives them a sense of "self-esteem and pride" (ibid: 3589).

But, as Beteille has rightly pointed out, finding an acceptable definition of tribe is not only an academic requirement but in many countries like India, also a legal and constitutional one (1998: 187). It is certainly not enough to say that tribes in India refer to those communities which are listed in the Constitution. The Constitution simply designates a certain community as a Scheduled Tribe without defining what a tribe, according to it, is and if we continue to get daunted by the great diversity among tribes within India (see Sinha, 2006) or continue to blame the colonial administration for creating this mess about concepts like caste and tribe it does not speak well of the intellectual ability of the postcolonial Indians, who I suspect have not made any serious effort to define a tribe. While till 1990s there were several efforts to contrast caste with tribe, despite dissenting voices (see Misra, 1977), the efforts after 1990s have been more or less limited to showing the conceptual similarities and differences between tribes and indigenous people (Roy Burman, 1992; Beteille, 1998; Xaxa, 1999).

Politics of definition

Before I attempt to define a tribe, here, I would like to dwell briefly on the politics of defining a community as a tribe. Definition of a people as a tribe becomes important from administrative point of view so that the state can decide whether or not to extend a certain constitutional privilege to a particular community. National resources being limited in a country like India the state must prioritise the beneficiaries on the basis of certain criteria. But more importantly perhaps defining a community as a tribe means bringing the people being so defined under some kind of conceptual control and bringing certain degree of certainty, and hence predictability about them and their behaviour. And once a tribe is so controlled other people even begin to see such people bearing certain characteristics that might not have been noticed prior to being so labelled. Labelling is based on certain characteristics but the act of labelling generates new characteristics—for those who label as well as those who are so labelled—that in turn help to identify a community so labelled differently (see Scheff, 1966; Rosenhan, 1973; Thoits, 1985 on labelling and identity).

I would further argue that defining a community as a tribe also amounts to stereotyping it, highlighting some of its characteristics and ignoring others, thereby *fossilizing its personality*. That it is a tribe becomes the foremost and often the only identity of the community and rest of its qualities or shortcomings simply fall in place according to its dominant identity.

Defining a tribe is, from this point of view, an act of homogenising not only from outside but also from within. The expected gains from a tribal identity gradually mould them to project a homogenous and externally expected image of them and all contradictory features are dismissed as aberrations. It is a process in which the community itself participates actively in the hope of a better future, a more secured landholding, regaining traditional rights over now "reserved forests", priority in employment, etc. I clearly recall how in 2005 the leaders of various communities in the process of being labelled as tribes in Sikkim welcomed the members of the group of "experts" which included me, who visited Sikkim to prepare ethnographic reports on them, which were expected to be completed soon and be the "passports" to the "heavenly" world of tribes where there is only happiness and prosperity. Once they become tribes, they think that, that would be the end of their suffering, misery, stagnation and poverty. That is why they provided us with every possible document—photographs of exotic rituals and practices. They also presented to us self-prepared ethnographic reports in hard copy as well as in CDs. Above all their eyes showed how keen they were to attain the tribal identity. The success of their neighbouring Limbus and Tamangs, who were in no way different from themselves, in being scheduled as tribes in January 2003 had filled them with the necessary hopes and aspirations.

Defining a community as a tribe is perhaps the greatest challenge anthropologists face today because it calls upon them to find that common thread that connects the now 700 odd tribes spread over the length and breadth of India and belonging to different races, languages, religions, literacy levels, modes of livelihood, and so on. In the remaining part of my presentation I have tried to do that exactly, although I had the choice to simply bring out the difficulties of defining a tribe in the Indian context. Doing so would be easy, but a bad caricature of what Andre Beteille (1974) has so well done. I decided to go for the more challenging of the two options I had while preparing this article. The basic premise on which I would like to rest my effort to define a tribe is that it should be based on a common and positive attribute shared by most of the tribes in India rather than a host of negative attributes assigned to them over the last couple of centuries. The task is daunting and the acceptability of what I propose may be limited, but the effort is worth making.

Sangma's definition of tribe

Let me begin defining a tribe by referring to what Purno A. Sangma, one of the best known tribal leaders of India, is quoted to have said at Jaipur in 2007, reference to which is made in the very beginning of my article. There are three important words he has used in his address, viz., primitive, casteless and classless. I would like to argue that none of these three concepts, individually or together, define a tribe. There are of course some tribes who may be labelled as "primitive, casteless and classless," but all the three concepts indicate the absence of something—culture, caste and class, respectively. In that sense, the concepts used by Sangma to define a tribe are negative concepts. If I were to choose a negative concept to define a tribe today I would choose "backwardness" to do so not only because tribes are thought to be backward by their neighbours but they themselves think that they are backward vis-à-vis the people they come in contact with. If tribes were not considered "backward" why would advanced societies seek withdrawal of such privileges from those who they now reckon as "forward" tribes, who in other words may have become peasants, castes and the like.

But I choose not to define a tribe on the basis of backwardness because this is not only a relative but also a negative concept and I think a community ought not to be defined negatively.

To go back to Sangma's definition it must be remembered that a tribe shares several characteristics with a caste. A tribe is also a localised and endogamous group like a caste, and is often stratified if not hierarchical in the ritual sense of the term. There is also a shared consciousness about membership and a sense of belonging to a tribe, which is also seen in case of a caste today. The only difference I can see between the two concepts is not religious, as many would expect, but linguistic: each tribe has a language of its own, but castes are part of a larger, regional linguistic communities. About castes being organic and tribes segmentary suffice to say here that there are segmentary castes—especially in the middle rung—as well as organic tribes or those who have been brought to the fold of Hinduism. Sangma also claims that tribes have distinct cultures, geographical isolation and shyness. The distinctiveness of culture is a debatable concept. Every tribe, like every caste, has something distinctive about its culture, notably a language, but it also shares very many material and non-material traits with neighbouring communities who may be tribes or castes. Geographical isolation is similarly problematic. The tribes themselves were not geographically isolated from each other; they were relatively isolated from perhaps the plains Hindus or Muslims, as the case may be, who were equally isolated (or not) from the hill tribes. So why look at the tribes from the perspective of the plainsmen even if we accept for the moment that there was no interaction between the hill tribes and plains castes, who, in fact, had regular contact through market centres. But the most difficult issue to agree on is perhaps the "shyness of culture". If the hill tribes largely remained in the hills in the past it was more perhaps due to climatic reasons and/or the lack of linguistic confidence to mix with the plains people than their shyness. The hill people were also scared of contacting malaria or their pockets being picked while in the plains. But why are the plains people not considered to have "shyness of culture"? Was it because they wanted to infiltrate the hills and exploit the hill people, as suspected by Elwin (1966), but the administrative policies like Inner Line Permit and Restricted Area Permit stopped them from doing so.

I have consciously dwelt on the definition of tribe given by Sangma in some details here because in doing so I saw an excellent opportunity to illustrate how the self-definition of a tribe can in no way be different from the definition given by the dominant Other. While there is nothing new about etic-emic debate in anthropology (Headland, Pike and Harris, 1990), adoption of the categories of the dominant Other by Sangma may be read as a strategy to gain more economic and political mileage out of the dominant discourse on tribes in India. This is likely because Sangma is aware that there is growing resentment in many parts of India against the rich tribes enjoying all the privileges without paying income tax or giving anything back to the nation. His arrogant statement that the existing tribes would not allow any new communities to join the category of tribes further indicates his sensitivity to the above.

Search for a definition of tribe

Coming back to my effort to define a tribe in the Indian context, what is that common thread that passes through all the tribes that are already scheduled and are yet to be scheduled? What is that single most common denominator of all tribes in India? As I was contemplating to prepare this article I threw this question open to some of my tribal colleagues and students. If I am to summarise their responses in one word it is "backwardness", which was incidentally a common criterion mentioned in the reports of all the 14 State Governments who were asked to suggest criteria for identification of Scheduled Tribes in 1950 (Sinha, 2006). "We are backward in comparison to the plains people", "We are kind of laid back people", "We are not concerned about our future", "We do not think of the consequences of our actions", "We are not clever like the plainsmen", "We are of course backward, why else would the government give us those constitutional facilities?" Such were the instances of what they responded. Something that comes out consistently in all these responses is a sense of something lacking in them. This is what Verrier Elwin referred to by his famous expression "loss of nerve" (Elwin, 1966). Why did they not come up with a single statement that indicated something positive? I was and am still perturbed, albeit I am fully conscious of the fact that these were not responses based on a properly designed scientific research.

The fact that my tribal colleagues and students, who represent almost the whole of north-east India, did not volunteer a single positive attribute of tribe to define it is something I would like to dwell on briefly before moving further. One should remember that the hill tribes of the region, who represented my universe for eliciting the above responses, do not otherwise always have a positive view of the plains people. The plains people are seen as source of all the vices like theft, cunningness, untrustworthiness, not respecting one's own word, and so on. Even baldness of head and darkness of skin are considered as characteristics received from the plains people.

In the course of my conversations with my subjects I prodded further on what they thought were the positive attributes of the tribes. Some of the oft-repeated expressions were as follows: "We are simple", "We are honest", and "We are straightforward". Can these positive attributes be summarized to define a tribe? I am tempted to do that for I am aware that even those who are not tribes themselves tend to agree with the above attributes of tribes. But I am also aware of the serious hazards of stereotyping national characters (Subba, 2006a), which is what the above can lead to. Is it not possible that at least a few among the tribes are not simple, not honest, not straightforward, and so on? Even if there are very few such persons among the tribes—say less than 10 percent—a definition based on such attributes will still exclude such people from the category of tribes.

Let me briefly argue here that an act of defining necessarily involves exclusion. Defining a group of people is a positivistic exercise in highlighting the regularities, the patterns, and the commonalities in the group, which would automatically mean exclusion of those attributes that do not fall in the pattern, are atypical, and are aberrant.

Seen from this perspective, any definition of tribe includes something and excludes something else that belongs to the universe of tribes. Unless we accept this premise one can make no further progress in this regard because an all-inclusive definition of tribe is theoretically or empirically impossible. Reservations expressed by many anthropologists about earlier definitions of a tribe mainly revolve around the issues of exclusion of attributes of certain tribes. While the usage of the word "tribe" is quite universal, our encounters with tribes have resulted in a bewildering variety of experiences that cannot be easily subsumed under any concept. Our concepts and theories must be regularly exposed to various empirical situations, but the latter being what they are will not make sense until they are brought under some kind of conceptual framework knowing fully well that such an act will be a violation of many an empirical reality.

Tribes and evolution

It will not be too gross a statement to say that we do not yet have a definition of a tribe that is inclusive of the diversity in tribal situation in India. Hence, I must caution that perception of the tribal situation in India will of course vary depending on the conceptual framework of the researcher.

Theoretically speaking, the perception of tribal situation in India, or elsewhere, has largely been in the evolutionary perspective—as people occupying an earlier stage in the evolution of mankind compared to the stage of those who are not considered as tribes. This is the most dominant perception in administrative circles as well as among the lay. This is why non-tribal people ask why certain tribes who have made perceptible progress during the past 50 years or so should continue to receive the constitutional privileges meant for less developed tribes (Sinha, 2006). Such questions are necessarily based on evolutionary perspective.

So, how do I define a tribe in the Indian context? Or rather, would I still like to try and define a tribe? I think yes, because it is time now to see whether the word "tribe" has any relevance or see if it is time to replace it with something more inclusive, less pejorative, and less loaded word. Some effort has already been made towards replacing the word "tribe" with other words like "native", "indigenous people", "backward Hindus" (Ghurye, 1943), "aboriginals" (Elwin, 1943), and the Indic words "*janajati*" and "*adivasi*". However, the fact remains that no one has been able to replace the word "tribe", which means, it carries a certain meaning, or meanings, that other words have failed to carry. What is it in the word "tribe" that other words do not seem to carry? It is certainly the wide currency of the word to refer to a group of people who are, in the eyes of the neighbouring communities as well as the administration, "different" from others in terms of food habits, sexual relations, marriage customs, religious beliefs, and so on. The word, therefore, carries a sense of people who have been living on the edge of human civilisation, eking their livelihood from Mother Nature, and maintaining some kind of symbiosis with nature. Such romanticisation of the tribes has received critical attention of several anthropologists, but continue to lurk on the horizon of tribal anthropology in India.

If there is no better word than "tribe" to represent the tribal world, is it reasonable to try and define the word once again? My answer to this question is again yes, but such a definition must go beyond the existing definitions in which "homogeneity" is an accepted norm—they are seen as people who speak the same language, share the same culture and religious beliefs and practices, etc. By contrast, those who are not tribes are "heterogeneous" in terms of language, culture, customs, beliefs, practices, and so on. I have no clear answer to how this contrast might have developed about the tribal and non-tribal communities, but I strongly suspect that the evolutionary perspective of anthropologists must have contributed to such a dichotomisation between tribes and non-tribes. Organisms, as we all know, evolve from simple to complex and homogeneous to heterogeneous structures. The people called tribes being lower in the evolutionary scheme of things must be homogenous. How else would the anthropologists, who belonged to the "higher" level of evolution, distinguish themselves from their objects and justify their studying the tribes?

If the tribes are both diverse and heterogeneous, as indicated above, is there any possibility of an inclusive definition that takes care of the variation in tribal situations in India? This is one last question I would like to ask before the patience of my audience wears out to listen to how I would like to define a tribe. Honestly, what I am trying so long is not to delay the job I have assigned myself to, but to analyse every possible question that is likely to engage any attempt to define a tribe. My answer to the above question is yes, because I see some kind of psychological bridge across all tribes in India, started by those who have moved out of their villages for higher education and other opportunities. They share a certain common sentiment, a kind of bonding, mutual trust and support among themselves. This solidarity is based on shared ecology, common legends, origin myths and stories, and the like. I have been a beneficiary of this sentiment and been deprived of it at the same time, depending on how they have identified me— as a Nepali or a tribal, as if a Nepali cannot be a tribal, or a tribal Nepali (Subba, 2011).

Conclusion: Tribe as reciprocal people

I would like to define a tribe in India as a "reciprocal people". Their economic pursuits—be they shifting cultivation, foraging, gathering, animal husbandry, trade or settled agriculture—would not be possible without reciprocity in the absence of or nebulous form of monetised economy. They received the impact of monotised economy relatively later than the non-tribes due to their habitation in less accessible geographical locations with poorly developed market networks and had lesser impact due to their lesser dependence on market, which in turn was due to the fact that reciprocity was a dominant value in tribal societies across the globe. Any textbook on Economic Anthropology would amply illustrate this point.

Reciprocity is still an important value in tribal societies. An instance of this can be seen in the Khasi folktale about the origin of *kwai* or areca nut and betel leaf with a dash of lime, which is offered to visiting guests as a symbol of hospitality in Khasi society. In this folktale, a poor man and a rich trader are known to be bosom friends. After being much obliged to his rich friend the poor man invites him to his house one evening but realises that he has nothing to offer his friend in return. Having nothing to cook for the rich friend, the wife of the poor man kills herself leaving a kettle boiling in the hearth. When her husband goes in to check out if some food was ready he finds his wife dead. Realising the reason for her death he too kills himself with a sword. When the rich trader goes in to find out why his friend did not return for so long he finds both his friend and his wife dead by the hearth and the kettle still boiling. Out of remorse for driving his friend to kill himself, he too kills himself with the same sword.

In brief, this story shows the value of reciprocity and how a man and his wife kill themselves for not being able to reciprocate the gesture of the rich friend. There may be many such folktales among other tribes as well. But I have been particularly impressed by the high level of participation of community members in all events of crisis, which I presume is driven by the need to oblige in order that the one who is obliged reciprocates in times of need.

Agricultural operations, marriage and death rituals, construction and repair of houses, and other such events in tribal societies bring a large number of families to work together, to pool their meagre resources to accomplish what would otherwise be impossible for a family. Such a family keeps mental or written record of who had helped and in what form and the same is recalled when it is time for the family to reciprocate. It is also seen that the amount or value given in reciprocation is not less than the amount or value originally received. If this is ignored the defaulter may be gossiped about and even criticised if such a family is rich enough to reciprocate an equal or greater amount. A sense of guilt is inevitable if a family is unable to reciprocate, which is a lot more powerful mechanism for perpetuating reciprocity than a punishment for having failed to do so.

Even the blood revenges that were so common among many tribal communities until recently could be seen as negative reciprocities. Although blood revenges have been virtually non-existent today, the principle of an eye for an eye, and a tooth for a tooth still seems to appeal the tribal people. Without strong and democratically constituted traditional policies one would certainly see more of negative reciprocities that we see them today.

Reciprocity may be seen as a survival strategy adopted by the tribes in the wake of rapid erosion of their resources after the coming of the British. They experienced land alienation, displacement, and other forms of exploitation like no other communities did, not even the Scheduled Castes, who mainly suffered from social disabilities but did not have to be displaced nor did they have land to be alienated. In a situation where they felt threatened of their survival not only in the hands of resource hungry states but also the ruthless administrators and greedy traders they seem to have used reciprocity as the key to their survival. It not only ensured mutual survival but also survival of their language, songs, dances, art and rituals to a large extent.

Finally, I would dwell briefly on how one is to identify a reciprocal community for the purpose of protective discrimination. An answer to this question must be provided because the policy of protective discrimination is more likely than not to continue in India, for good as well as bad reasons. Hence, ethnographic report to consider whether or not a community is to be brought under protective discrimination may first of all ascertain whether or not such a community has a language of its own, either extinct, eroded or extant, but not owned by other tribes as well. Once this is confirmed, the report may consider the extent of monetisation of the economy because it is directly linked with reciprocity. My theoretical premise here is this—greater is the monetisation of economy less reciprocal and communal the community becomes. The monetisation of economy may be studied, for the purpose of such ethnographic reports, on the basis of cash income vis-à-vis kind income. If the cash income of a community exceeds its kind income it may be disqualified for the purpose of affirmative action because such a community is not only likely to be less reciprocal but also less backward. I am hopeful that the above proposal provides an alternative approach to the vexed issue of reservation in India even if it is not accepted for implementation.

References

Beteille, Andre 1974 *Six Essays in Comparative Sociology,* New Delhi: Oxford University Press.

——. 1998 "The Idea of Indigenous People", *Current Anthropology*, 39 (2): 187–91.

Elwin, Verrier 1943 *The Aboriginals,* Oxford Pamphlets on Indian Affairs, No. 14, London: Oxford University Press.

——. 1966 *Loss of Nerve,* Bombay: Oxford University Press.

Ghurye, G.S. 1943 *The Scheduled Tribes,* Bombay: Popular Prakashan.

Headland, T.N., K.L. Pike and M. Harris (eds) 1990 *Emics and Etics: The Insider/Outsider Debate,* Newbury Park: Sage.

Misra, P.K. 1977 "Caste-Tribe: A Non-Issue", *Journal of the Indian Anthropological Society,* 12(2): 137–50.

Rosenhan, D.L. 1973 "On Being Sane in Insane Places", *Science,* 179: 250–58.

Roy Burman, B.K. 1992 "Indigenous and Tribal Peoples, Global Hegemonics and Government of India", *Mainstream,* September 5, 31–35.

Scheff, T. 1966 *Being Mentally Ill: A Sociological Theory,* New York: Aldine.

Sinha, A.C. 2006 "Culture Change Among the Tribes of North-east India: Some Conceptual and Methodological Issues". Paper presented at the national seminar on "Christianity and Cultural Change Among the Tribes of North-east India", held on October 26–28, 2006 and organised jointly by the Department of Anthropology, NEHU, Don Bosco Centre for Indigenous Cultures and Sacred Heart Theological College, Shillong.

Subba, T.B. 2006a "Culture and Personality", An electronic reading material hosted by National Science Digital Library in collaboration with CSIR, Government of India.

——. 2011 "From Caste to Tribe: An Autobiographical Essay", in P.K. Misra, H.K. Bhat and Dipali G. Danda (eds) *Tribe, State and Empowerment: The Indian Experience.* Jhargram: Indian National Confederation and Academy of Anthropologist. Mysore: Anthropological Association.

Thoits, P.A. 1985 "Self-labelling Processes in Mental Illness: The Role of Emotional Deviance", *American Journal of Sociology,* 91: 221–49.

Xaxa, Virginius 1999 "Tribes as Indigenous People of India", *Economic and Political Weekly,* December 18, 3589–95.

5

Tribal development and security of land

P. Ishwara Bhat

To be secure is to be free from dangers, troubles and attacks. Security gives a feeling of self-confidence, protects against uncertainties and enables development. In the context of tribal development, security connotes protection of land and other natural resources for their reasonable use, protection from exploitation by moneylenders, land grabbers and contractors, protection of environment, especially forest and safeguarding of their customs, traditional knowledge and culture. It is a concept supported by the ideals and practices of self-government and social justice. The constitutional and legal principles in providing security to tribes through protection of their land will be analysed in this paper.

For a primarily agro-based community like tribes, land is an invaluable resource. Earth is provider of food, medicine, shelter and clothing; it is the seat of spirituality, the foundation of culture and language; it is the keeper of history and memory of forefathers.[1]

The ILO Convention Concerning Indigenous and Tribal Peoples in Independent Countries, 1989 has recognised the rights of the tribal people to land by reiterating the principles declared in earlier international instruments. Article 15 states, "The rights of the peoples concerned to the natural resources pertaining to their land shall be specifically safeguarded. These rights include the right of these peoples to participate in the use, management and conservation of these resources". In cases where the state retains ownership over sub-surface minerals and other resources, exploration and exploitation of them could be done after consultation with the concerned peoples and after following the procedures in order to protect their interests. According to Article 16, the peoples concerned shall not be removed from the lands which they occupy only in exceptional circumstance, except after obtaining their free and informed consent and by following procedure for their appropriate rehabilitation. The relocation shall be subject to their right to return to the land in case the ground for relocation ceases to exist. The alternative land provided in rehabilitation shall, in quality, use, dimension and title, be at least equal to the land previously occupied. Agenda 21 of the Rio Declaration, 1992 recognises that the land of indigenous people should be protected from activities that are environmentally unsound or that the indigenous people consider to be socially and culturally inappropriate (26.3 1). Article 26 of the UN Declaration on the Rights of Indigenous Peoples, 1994 recognises their right to own, develop, control and use the lands and territories, including the total environment. The right to restitution of lost lands, the right to restoration of the total environment and right to just and fair compensation in the form of equal land in case of relocation are included in the constitution (Articles 27, 28). The Indian Constitution also recognises right to compensation at market value when land under personal cultivation and within ceiling limit is taken away by the State (Article 31A Proviso).

Historically tribal areas remained distinct from the general land management system due to their inaccessibility. Inadequacies in land records coupled with poverty and illiteracy gave scope for their exploitation by zamindars, contractors and middlemen. The protective measures introduced by the British to deal with the situation included recognition of community ownership in some area and prohibition of transfer of land from tribals to non-tribals.[2] Considering the past experience and the exploitation of the tribals' simplicity and truthfulness by the non-tribals, it became imperative by statutory safeguards to preserve the land which is their natural endowment and mainstay for their economic empowerment. As Simon Commission report said, in view of the fact that the tribals were primitive people, simple, unsophisticated and frequently improvident, "there was a risk of their agricultural land passing to the more civilised section of the population, and the occupation of the tribals was for the most part agricultural; and, secondly, they were likely to get into the wiles of the money lenders". Accordingly, in the Government of India Act, 1935 appropriate provisions for protection of land of the tribals were made.

Para 5(2) of the Fifth Schedule to the Constitution provides that the Governor may make regulations for the peace and good government of any area in a state which is for the time being a Scheduled Area. Without prejudice to the above general power, special power has been conferred under clause (a) to prohibit or to restrict the transfer of land by or among members of the Scheduled Tribes in such area and under clause (b) to regulate the allotment of land to members of the Scheduled Tribes in such area; clause (c) regulates money-lending to the tribals in the Scheduled Area. According to the Supreme Court, "The predominant object of Para 5(2) of the Fifth Schedule of the Constitution and the Regulation is to impose total prohibition of transfer of immovable property to any person other than a tribal for peace and proven good management of tribal area; to protect possession, right, title and interest of the members of the Scheduled Tribes held in the land at one time by the tribals. The non-tribals, at no point of time, have any legal or valid title to immovable property in Agency tracts unless required with prior sanction of the Government and saved by any law made consistent with the Fifth Schedule".[3]

Para 3 (1) (a) of the Sixth Schedule to the Constitution reads as under:
"3. Powers of the District Councils and Regional Councils to make laws:

(1) The Regional Council for an autonomous region in respect of all areas within such region and the District Council for an autonomous district in respect of all areas within the district except those which are under the authority of Regional Councils, if any, within the district shall have power to make laws with respect to

(a) the allotment, occupation or use or the setting apart of land other than any land which is a reserved forest, for the purposes of agriculture or grazing or for residential or other non-agricultural purposes or for any other purposes likely to promote the interests of the inhabitants of any village or town:

Provided that nothing in such laws shall prevent the compulsory acquisition of any land, whether occupied or unoccupied, for public purposes by the Government of Assam in accordance with the law for the time being in force authorising such acquisition;

(b) the management of forest not being reserved forest;

(c) the use of canal or water course for the purpose of agriculture;

(d) the regulation of the practice of jhum cultivation".

The words 'allotment, occupation or use or the setting apart of land' have been interpreted restrictively so as not to include transfer in *Miss Sitimon*[4] case and hence a statute imposing restriction upon transfer of land from tribal to non-tribal was considered as ultra vires of the District Council's power, and violative of right to equality under Article 14. The argument based on legislative history of the provision to the effect that the Sub-Committee and Advisory Committees had intended to allay the fears of hill tribes about exploitation by the more advanced people from the plains, and the purpose was to control immigration of non-tribals into the tribal areas, was not accepted. It is submitted, from the angle of land security to tribals and effective protection of their social and economic interests under the canopy of social justice, a restrictive and literal interpretation of the provision is not justified. It is to be remembered that the Fifth and Sixth Schedules form an integral scheme of the Constitution with direction, philosophy and anxiety is to protect the tribals from exploitation and to preserve valuable endowment of their land for their economic empowerment to elongate social and economic democracy with liberty, equality, fraternity and dignity of their person.

In exercise of the powers under the above clauses, States and Regional Councils have enacted laws. There are also pre-constitution laws like the Chota Nagpur Tenancy Act, 1908 providing for protection of tribal people's interests in land. The Santhal Pargana Tenancy (Supplementary Provisions) Act, 1959 and the Bihar Scheduled Areas Regulations, 1969 prohibit the alienation of land to the tribals or when converted for urban use, to given them equivalent lands. As early as in 1901, in Gujarat, some measures of protection were provided (when it formed part of the Bombay Province) by amendment of Sections 73-A and 79-A in the Bombay Land Revenue Code, 1879, and imposed ban on transfer of land of tribes in those scheduled villages in which survey and settlement had not been introduced without previous permission of the Collector. Section 4 of the Agency Tracts and Land Transfer Act, 1917, a Madras Province legislation, provided that any transfer of immovable property situated within the Agency Tracts by a member of a hill tribe shall be absolutely null and void unless made in favour of another member of a hill tribe, or with the previous consent in writing of the Agent or of any other prescribed officer. In case of contravention, the Agent or any other prescribed officer may on application by any one interested, decree ejectment against any person in possession of the property claiming under the transfer and may restore it to the transferor or his heirs. The Tribal Areas Dastur-Ul-Amal 1947 also had protective policy. The Scheduled Areas Land Transfer Regulation 1959 reiterated the above policy but became ineffective because of failure to enact detailed rules. In the background of Srikakulam rebellions, in 1970 total prohibition was imposed upon transfer of land from tribals to non-tribals.

The Maharashtra Land Revenue Code and Tenancy Laws (Amendment) Act, 1974 and Maharashtra (Restoration of Lands to Scheduled Tribes) Act, 1974 also prohibit alienation and ensure restoration of alienated lands to the tribes. The Kerala Land Reforms Act, 1963 contains similar provision. The Kerala Scheduled Tribes (Restriction of Transfer of Land and Regulation of Alienation of Lands) Act, 1975 was enacted for the same object. According to section 3 (1) of the Andhra Pradesh Agency Regulation, 1970 notwithstanding anything in any enactment, rule or law in force in the Agency tracts any transfer of immovable property situated in the Agency tracts by a person, whether or not such person is a member of a Scheduled Tribe, shall be absolutely null and void, unless such transfer is made in favour of person, who is a member of a Scheduled Tribe or a society formed under the Andhra Pradesh Cooperative Societies Act, 1964 (Act 7 of 1964) which is composed solely of members of the Scheduled Tribes. When the constitutionality of section 3 of the Regulation was impugned as violative of Articles 19(1) (f) and 14 of the Constitution, the Supreme Court, in *P. Rami Reddy vs. State of Andhra Pradesh*[5] upheld its validity holding that the Regulation aims to restore the lands to the tribals which originally belonged to them but passed into the hands of non-tribals. It would be unjust, unfair and highly unreasonable merely to freeze the situation, instead of reversing the injustice and restoring the status quo ante. The non-tribal economic exploiters would get no immunity and not be accorded a privileged treatment by permitting them to transfer the lands and structure, if any, raised on such lands to non-tribals and to make profits at the cost of the tribals.[6]

How a devious method of land grabbing could be dealt can be seen by looking to a case from Madhya Pradesh. In *State of Madhya Pradesh vs. Babu Lal*[7], a non-tribal had filed a suit for declaration against a ST for declaration that his name be recorded in the revenue record as Bhumiswami. The defendant did not contest the suit and the parties filed a compromise conceding to the claim of the plaintiff. The MP Land Revenue Code, 1959 had imposed restrictions on the transfer of land by members of a Scheduled Tribe. The State Government intervened and filed a petition in the High Court seeking a writ of certiorari for quashing the judgment of the Civil Court based on compromise. The High Court dismissed the petition, holding that the state could pursue the alternative remedy of filing a suit for declaration that the decree was null and void. In appeal by special leave, the Supreme Court set aside the judgment of the High Court and issued a writ of certiorari to quash the judgment and decree passed.

In *Manchegowda vs. State of Karnataka*[8] the Supreme Court upheld the Karnataka Scheduled Castes and Scheduled Tribes (Prohibition of Transfer of Certain Lands) Act (2 of 1979), which provided for resumption or restitution of the granted land to SC/ST grantees in case they had alienated to any person in violation of land grant rules. The court held that the Act did not violate right to property, and was justified as a special provision for SCs/STs under Article 15(4), 19(5) and Article 46. The court looked to the rationale underlying the non-alienation clause contained in the existing Land Grant Rules and the statutory scheme needed for restoration of land to the original grantees in view of the fact that ignorance and poverty of the Scheduled Castes and Scheduled Tribes grantees was exploited by persons belonging to the affluent and powerful sections to obtain sales or mortgages either for a nominal consideration or for no consideration at all and they have become victims of circumstances. In *Lingappa Pochanna Appelwar vs. State of Maharashtra*[9] the court upheld the constitutionality of similar provisions of Maharasthra Restoration of Lands to Scheduled Tribes Act, 1974.

The Supreme Court in *Amerndra Pratap Singh vs. Tej Bahadur Prajapati*[10] took another pro-tribe approach by holding that loss of land belonging to the tribal because of adverse possession by a non-tribal amounted to 'transfer', which was prohibited under the Orissa Scheduled Areas Transfer of Immovable Property (by Scheduled Tribes) Regulations (2 of 1956). According to the court, this would ensure that a member of an aboriginal tribe indefeatably continues to own the property and that non-tribals do not succeed in making inroads amongst the tribals by acquiring property and developing roots in the habitat of tribals. The court observed: "The tribals need to be settled, need to be taken care of by the protective arm of the law, and be saved from falling prey to unscrupulous device so that they may prosper and by an evolutionary process join the mainstream of the society."

In spite of legal measures, land grabbing has been practised through forcible eviction, benami transactions, collusive decrees, mortgage, share cropping, marriage with a tribal woman, adoption of a non-tribal by a tribal, and entry of land records in the name of a tribal farm servant. Acquisition of tribal land by the government for various developmental projects has also resulted in loss of substantial land. Some of the deficiencies in the present legal regime include: confinement of restriction on land transfer only to notified area; lack of clear policy about adverse possession; absence of suo motu actions by governmental bodies; infirmities in land records; lack of stringent penal provisions; disposition of tribal land on account of non-payment of bank loan; and absence of adequate provisions for restoration of land to tribals irrespective of the issue whether it is granted one or not. Because of these factors, as reported on the basis of empirical research, the extent of land holding by the STs in some of the villages in Andhra Pradesh has drastically reduced.[11]

Security of forest dwellers' right to land

The symbiotic relationship between the tribals and forests is well established over the years both in temporal and spiritual sense. The National Policy on Forests, 1894 introduced state control over forests and curtailed the rights and privileges of the tribals over forest resources. The new forest policy of 1952 contemplated withdrawal of facility of free grazing in forests and efforts to wean the tribals from the traditional practice of shifting cultivation. In order to increase the forest cover, treeless lands were also taken for forest development, and settlers in those areas were declared as encroachers liable for eviction. The Forest Act of 1980 prohibits deletion of reserved forest or the diversion of forest land for any 'non-forest' purpose and prevents cutting of trees in a forest without prior approval by the Central Government. The forest policy of 1988 prohibited plantation of horticultural crops in forests and banned assignment or lease of forestland to people or institutions not wholly governed by government.

It is common knowledge that the adivasis and other backward people living within the jungle used the forest area as their habitat. They had raised several villages for generations and had been using the jungles around for collecting the requirements for their livelihood, fruits, vegetables, fodder, flowers, timber, animals by way of sports and fuelwood. When a part of the jungle became reserved forest and in regard to other proceedings under the Act were taken, the forest officers started interfering with their operations in those areas. Criminal cases for encroachments and also other forest offences were registered and systematic attempt was made to obstruct them from free movement. When approached for remedy through a Public Interest Litigation in *Banawasi Seva Ashram* the Supreme Court on 22 August1983 asked the parties to work out a formula under which claims of adivasis or tribals in Dudhi and Robertsganj tehsils, to be in possession of land and to have regularisation of such possession might be investigated by a High Powered Committee with a view to reach at a final decision in regard to such claims. Meanwhile, no further encroachments shall be made on forest land nor will any of the adivasis or tribals be permitted under cover of this order or any previous order to cut any trees and if any such attempt is made it will be open to the state authorities to prevent such cutting of trees and to take proper action in that behalf but not so as to take away possession of the land from the adivasis or tribals. The establishing, functioning and outcome of High Powered Committee was monitored by the Supreme Court through subsequent orders.

The problem of encroachment of forest land resulting in destruction of the forest in Andaman Islands in which Onge tribes were dwelling came up before the Supreme Court in Godavarman case (1999) on behalf of the tribe some NGOs filed interlocutory application.[12] The Supreme Court discussed in 2002 the proposal of Amicus Curiae for removal of all encroachers who did not meet the deadline of 1980 for regularised encroachments, and called for responses of states within six weeks. The proposal was confirmed, and the MoEF issued a directive to all states that they summarily evict all illegal encroachers on forest land and regularise only eligible encroachments before 1980. The directive had detrimental effect upon the tribal community. Destruction of huts and homes of the tribals by using elephants in Assam, lack of opportunity to dispute the eviction notice and eviction without reaping the standing crops in Maharashtra received pro-tribe public sympathy. Failure of tribals to maintain proper documents owing to their illiteracy, inability to prove their residency before 1980 and inaccurate departmental surveys identifying non-forest area as forest had resulted in unjustified eviction.[13] In 2002–03 about 1.68 lakh families were evicted. With the change of government after election in 2004 the issue of effective protection of forest dwellers' right gained political attention. On 13th December, 2005, the Minister for Tribal Affairs introduced the Scheduled Tribes (Recognition of Forest Rights) Bill, 2005 into parliament, "to recognise and vest the forest rights and occupation in forest land in forest dwelling Scheduled Tribes who have been residing in such forests for generations but whose rights could not be recorded and to provide for a framework for recording the forest rights so vested and the nature of evidence required for such recognition and vesting in respect of forestland". The bill was then referred to the Joint Parliamentary Committee. The committee suggested for inclusion of 'other traditional dwellers' as beneficiaries; for recognising Gram Sabha's power to identify the beneficiaries and for prohibiting diversion of the forest for other use.

The Scheduled Tribes and Other Traditional Forest Dwellers (Recognition of Forest Rights) Act, 2006 came into being on 29th December, 2006. The main aim of the Act is to recognise and vest upon forest dwelling Scheduled Tribes (FDSTs) and other traditional forest dwellers (OTFDs), who have been residing in forest from generations but whose rights could not be recorded, their forest land rights and occupation in forest land. It imposes responsibilities upon, and confers authority to them for sustainable use, conservation of biological diversity and maintenance of ecological balance and thereby strengthening the conservation regime of the forest while ensuring livelihood and food security of the FDSTs and OTFDs who are integral to the very survival and sustainability of forest ecosystem. It has tried to address the long standing insecurity of tenurial and access rights of FDSTs and OTFDs including those who were forced to relocate their dwelling due to state development interventions.

FDSTs the members or community of the Scheduled Tribes who primarily reside in and who depend on the forests or forest lands for bonafide livelihood needs and includes the Scheduled Tribe pastoralist communist. OTFDs include any member or community who has for at least three generations (25 years each) prior to the 13th December, 2005 primarily resided in and who depend on the forest or forest land for bonafide livelihood needs.

The forest rights of the FDSTs and OTFDs mean (Section 3 Clause 1) the following rights, which secure individual or community tenure or both, on all forest lands, namely:

(a) right to hold and live in the forest land under the individual or common occupation for habitation or for self-cultivation for livelihood by a member(s) of an FDST or OTFD;

(b) community rights such as nistar, by whatever name called, including those used in erstwhile princely states, zamindari or such intermediary regimes;

(c) right of ownership, access to collect, use and dispose of minor forest produce[14] which has been traditionally collected within or outside village boundaries;

(d) other community rights of uses or entitlements such as fish and other products of water bodies, grazing (both settled or trans-human) and traditional seasonal resource access of nomadic or pastoralist communist;

(e) rights including community tenures of habitat and habitation for primitive tribal groups and pre-agricultural communities;

(f) rights in or over disputed lands under any nomenclature in any state where claims are disputed;

(g) rights for conversion of *pattas* or leases or grants issued by any local authority or any State Government on forest lands to titles;

(h) rights of settlement and conversion of all forest villages, old habitation, unsurveyed villages and other villages in forests, whether recorded, notified or not into revenue villages;

(i) right to protect, regenerate or conserve or manage any community forest resource which they have been traditionally protecting and conserving for sustainable use;

(j) rights which are recognised under any state law(s) of any Autonomous District Council or Autonomous Regional Council or which are accepted as rights of tribals under any traditional or customary law of the concerned tribes of any state;

(k) right of access to biodiversity and community right to intellectual property and traditional knowledge related to biodiversity and cultural diversity;

(l) any other traditional right customarily enjoyed by the FDSTs or OTFDs, as the case may be, which are not mentioned in clauses (a) to (k) but excluding the traditional right of hunting or trapping or extracting a part of the body of any species of wild animal; and

(m) right to in situ rehabilitation including alternative land in cases where the Scheduled Tribes and OTFDs have been illegally evicted or displaced from forest land of any description without receiving their legal entitlement to rehabilitation prior to the 13th December 2005.

Under Section 4, the Central Government recognises and vests the above forest rights in the FDSTs and OTFDs. This is subject to the condition that such Scheduled Tribes or tribal communities or OTFDs had occupied forest land before the 13th December 2005. The right shall be heritable but not alienable or transferable and shall be registered jointly in the name of both the spouses in case of married persons and in the name of the single head in the case of a household headed by a single person and in the absence of a direct heir, the heritable right shall pass on to the next of kin (Section 4 c 4). Such land shall be under the occupation of an individual or family or community on the date of commencement of the Act and shall be restricted to the area under actual occupation and shall in no case exceed an area of four hectares (Section 4 c 6). The vesting of land is without any encumbrance (Section 4 c 7). The right is also available to the FDSTs and OTFDs who can establish that they were displaced from their dwelling and cultivation without land compensation due to state development interventions, and where the land has not been used for the purpose for which it was acquired within five years of the said acquisition (Section 4 c 8). While Section 3 (1) (m) gives right to alternative land for evictions done prior to 13th December 2005, this clause is prospective in operation, and gives protection against displacement without rehabilitation. In the light of *Narmada Bachao Andolan* judgment that insisted on forest dwellers' right to rehabilitation the statutory recognition of this right has a potentiality for avoiding eviction without meaningful rehabilitation. No FDST and OTFD shall be evicted or removed from forest land under his occupation till the recognition and verification procedure is complete (Section 4 c 5).

However, the Central Government shall provide for diversion of forest land whose width is less than one hectare with the permission of Gram Sabha for the following facilities managed by the government which involve felling of trees not exceeding 75 trees per hectare, namely, schools, dispensary or hospital; anganwadis; fair price shops; electric and telecommunication lines; tanks and other minor water bodies; drinking water supply and water pipelines; water or rain water harvesting structures; minor irrigation canals; non-conventional source of energy; skill upgradation or vocational training centres; roads; and community centres (Section 3 c 2).

The Act has tried to strike a fair balance between protection of wild life and forest rights of FDST and OTFD. It defines critical wildlife habitat as "such areas of national parks and sanctuaries where it has been specifically and clearly established, case by case, on the basis of scientific and objective criteria, that such areas are required to be kept as inviolate for the purpose of wildlife conservation as may be determined and notified by the Central Government in the Ministry of Environment and Forests after open process of consultation by an Expert Committee". Quite importantly, the Act provides that (Section 4 c 2) the forest rights recognised under the Act in critical wildlife habitats of national parks and sanctuaries may subsequently be modified or resettled, provided that no forest rights holders shall be resettled or have their rights in any manner affected for the purposes of creating inviolate areas for wildlife conservation except in case all the following conditions are satisfied, namely:

(a) the process of recognition and vesting of rights as specified in section 6 is complete in all the areas under consideration;
(b) it has been established by the concerned agencies of the State Government, in exercise of their powers under the Wild Life (Protection) Act, 1972 that the activities or impact of the presence of holders of rights upon wild animals is sufficient to cause irreversible damage and threaten the existence of said species and their habitat;
(c) the State Government has concluded that other reasonable options, such as, coexistence are not available;
(d) a resettlement or alternatives package has been prepared and communicated that provides a secure livelihood for the affected individuals and communities and fulfils the requirements of such affected individuals and communities given in the relevant laws and the policy of the Central Government;
(e) the free informed consent of the Gram Sabhas in the areas concerned to the proposed resettlement and to the package has been obtained in writing; and
(f) no resettlement shall take place until facilities and land allocation at the resettlement location are complete as per the promised package.

Provided that the critical wildlife habitats from which right holders are thus relocated for purposes of wildlife conservation shall not be subsequently diverted by the State Government or the Central Government or any other entity for other uses.

The concern for ecological balance is also reflected in the duties imposed upon the FDSTs and OTFDs, Gram Sabha and village level institutions. They are empowered (Section 5) to (a) protect the wildlife, forest and biodiversity; (b) ensure that adjoining catchments area, water sources and other ecological sensitive areas are adequately protected; (c) ensure that the habitat of FDSTs and OTFDs is preserved from any form of destructive practices affecting their cultural and natural heritage; and (d) ensure that the decisions taken in the Gram Sabha to regulate access to community forest resources and stop any activity which adversely affects the wild animals, forest and the biodiversity are complied with.

Grass roots democracy is relied upon in decision-making process regarding identification of the genuine occupants. The Gram Sabha shall be the authority for determining the extent of individual or community forest rights or both given to FDSTs and OTFDs without the local limits of its jurisdiction. It will be responsible for claims consolidating and verifying of them and preparing a map delineating the area of each recommended claim. Gram Sabha shall pass resolution to the forward copy to sub-divisional level committee.[15] Any aggrieved party of Gram Sabha may prefer petition to the sub-divisional committee within 60 days from the date of passing resolution by Gram Sabha with reasonable opportunity given to him to present his case.[16]

The sub-divisional level committee shall examine resolution and prepare a record of the forest rights and forward it through the sub-divisional office to district level committee for a final decision.[17] If any person is aggrieved by the decision of sub-divisional level committee, he can prefer an appeal to the district level committee within 60 days which shall consider the petition but it cannot be made directly against Gram Sabha.[18] The State Government shall constitute district level committee to approve record of forest rights prepared by sub-divisional level committee and the decision becomes final.[19] Further, the state government shall constitute a state level monitoring committee to monitor the process of recognition and vesting of forest rights and to submit to the nodal agency the reports.[20] It is significant that self-determination has been invoked as a mechanism for settling the claims of forest dwellers.

There is a wide appreciation about the Act of 2006. CPM stalwart Brinda Karat has termed the law as a significant victory for the forest dwelling communities and a big step forward in their struggle for rights and in mitigating the historic injustices in many respects. According to Jayati Ghosh, it is one of the most important and progressive new laws, and is extremely important not only for providing justice to forest dwellers, but also for conserving the forest themselves.[21] There are two critically important aspects of this Bill: it recognises communities' rights and it also democratises the system of forest conservation. Both are vital to the health of forests and forest communities. It also requires forest rights holders to refrain from any activity that would adversely affect the forest and the biodiversity in the local area, and also enjoins the local community to stop any activity which adversely affects wildlife forests and biodiversity, whoever might be responsible for that activity, rather than officialdom.

Security from deforestation and environmental pollution

"Ninety percent of the Scheduled Tribes predominantly live in forest areas and intractable terrains; 95 percent of them are below poverty line and totally depend upon agriculture or agriculture-based activities; and some of them turn out as migrant construction labour due to their displacement from hearth and home for the so-called exploitation of minerals and construction of projects" observed Justice K. Ramaswamy in *Samata.*[22] Legal measures for protection of forest have responded to this factual situation. Para 5 (2) of the Fifth Schedule empowers the Governor to restrict or prohibit the transfer of land by or among the members of ST or to regulate the allotment of land to STs has been understood in broader sense to include the power to restrain the use of land for non-forest purposes. In *Samata*, protection of forest against its depletion through mining was the issue. The Supreme Court relied on the provision under Forest Conservation Act 1988 which provided that no State Government or other authority shall make, except with prior approval of the Central Government (i) any order directing that any reserved forest or any portion thereof shall cease to be a reserved forest; (ii) that any forest land or portion thereof may be used for any non-forest purpose; (iii) that any forest land or any portion thereof may be assigned, by way of lease or otherwise, to any private person or to any authority or corporation, agency or any other organisation, not owned, managed or controlled by the government; and (iv) that any forest land or any portion thereof may be cleared or trees which have grown natural in the land or portion for the purpose of using it for reforestation. Since transfer of land in V Schedule area for mining purpose amounted to violation of the FC Act, the Court disallowed future use of mining leases, except the state sponsored one, that too, subject to strict compliance with the FCA.

Under para 3 (1) of the VI Schedule, the Regional Council has the power to manage any forest other than reserved forest and to regulate the practice of jhum or other forms of shifting cultivation. Regarding reserved forest identified under Assam Forest Regulation, the Council has no power of intervention.

The efforts to exclude human intervention in national parks and sanctuaries have necessitated balancing between interests of the forest dwelling tribals to collect minor forest produce and to exercise other traditional rights on the one hand, and conservation of forest and wildlife on the other. In *Animal and Environment Legal Defence Fund*[23] the Supreme Court accommodated both the claims by subjecting the licensed fishing activity in Pench National Park to extensive monitoring and regulation in order to ensure that fishing does not disturb the wildlife situation. Issuing of photo identity card to tribal fishermen, limits on seasons and timings for fishing, restraints on entry and exit points and prevention of use of fire are some of the measures directed by the court. In *Pradeep Krishen*,[24] where constitutionality of Madhya Pradesh government's order permitting collection of tendu leaves from sanctuaries and national parks by villagers was in issue, the Supreme Court directed the state government to complete the procedure for final declaration on sanctuaries and national parks within six months. In *Niyamavedi*[25] the Kerala High Court declines to interfere with the ouster of adivasis from six ancient settlements in the context of establishing a biological park in an evergreen forest on the ground that the park would promote conservation of flora and fauna of the Western Ghats. This can be contrasted to the Guwahati High Court judgment[26] that quashed the governmental order that ordered for shifting of villages, which fell within the sanctuary. It is important to note that the security of both forest and tribals is a balancing task in the socio-economic reform.

Conclusion

In view of immense importance of land for the security and development of the tribal people, the legal system has positively responded to their problems. Quite consistent with international and constitutional values, the statutes and judicial decisions have tried to protect their genuine claims. It is significant that human rights values have primarily reflected the goals of social justice in the context of indigenous people. Security of land is one of its components and means. Protection of forest and of right to dwell in forest or collect minor forest produce have been looked from the angle of right to livelihood, especially in the background of varieties of exploitations and continued denials. The Act of 2006 is a triumph of tribal people and a promise of happy and harmonious life.

■ Notes

1. The World Council of Indigenous Peoples: according to K. Ramaswamy: "Land is their most important natural and valuable asset and imperishable endowment from which the tribals derive their sustenance, social status, economic and social equality, permanent place of the abode and work and living. It is a security and source for economic empowerment. Therefore, the tribes too have great emotional attachment to their lands. The land on which they live and till, assures them equality of status and dignity of person and means to economic and social justice and potent weapon of economic empowerment in social democracy". Samata vs. State of Andhra Pradesh (Year (1997) 8 SCC 191).
2. The Scheduled Districts Act, 1874 and the Agency Tracts and Land Transfer Act of 1917 contain such provision. Section 4 of the Act of 1917 reads: "(1) Notwithstanding any rule of law or enactment to the contrary, any transfer of immovable property situated within the Agency Tracts by a member of a hill tribe shall be absolutely null and void unless made in favour of another member of a hill tribe, or with the previous consent in writing of the Agent or of any other prescribed officer".
(2) Where a transfer of property is made in contravention of sub-section (1), "the Agent or any other Prescribed Officer may on application by any one interested, decree ejectment against any person in possession of the property claiming under the transfer and may restore it to the transferor or his heirs".
3. Samata vs. State of Andhra Pradesh (1997) 8 SCC 191 para 49.
4. District Council of U.K. and J. Hills, Shillong vs. Sitimon Sawian AIR 1972 SC 787.

5. (1988) 3 SCC 433: (AIR 1988 SC 1626).
6. The Court observed: "These tribal communities were in occupation of lands and lived by shifting cultivation and gathering whatever produce that was available... The non-tribals who arrived in these areas late in the 19th century in certain areas and the early 20th century in certain other areas found the tribals who were in occupation of these lands an easy prey for the schemes of exploitation. The non-tribals were lending money to the tribal communities and taking the land belonging to them as security though nothing was taken in writing from a tribal. The rates of interest charged ranged between 25 to 50 per cent and in certain cases even 100 per cent ... It is absolutely necessary to create conditions for peace and maintain peace and prevent the new non-tribals from settling down in the scheduled area. If the alienations are permitted to the non-tribals there is a danger of large scale exploitation by the new non-tribals again with the result peace will be disturbed in that area ... Unless new entrants into the scheduled areas are prevented from settling down in the scheduled areas by purchasing properties either from tribals or non-tribals, it is not possible to prevent the exploitation of the unsophisticated tribals".
7. 1977 (2) SCC 435.
8. (1984) 3 SCC 301: (AIR 1984 SC 1151).
9. (1985) 1 SCC 479: (AIR 1985 SC 389).
10. AIR 2004 SC 3782.
11. According to T. Prabhakar Reddy, in Narnour village it declined from 90 per cent in 1978 to 21 per cent in 1988 and in Boagutta village from 86 per cent to 23 per cent. (Tribal Land Alienation in Andhra Pradesh, *Economic and Political Weekly*, July 15, 1989), also see S.N. Dubey and Ratna Murdia (eds.), *Land Alienation and Restoration in Tribal Communities in India* (Himalaya Publishing House, Bombay), also see Prof. Haimendrof, *Tribes of India: The Struggle for Survival* (University of California Press, Berkeley). On the other hand, excessive land possession by some tribal individuals has not been effectively dealt by application of law. See for discussion, Dr. P.V. Ramesh, "Land Reforms, Land Transfer in Scheduled Area", in "Scheduled Tribal and Social Justice", pp. 178 and 202.
12. Meanwhile the Calcutta High Court had issued interim order in 1999 prohibiting felling of naturally grown trees on the islands.
13. In Banawasi Seva Ashram vs. State of Uttar Pradesh (1992) 2 SCC 202; AIR 1992 SC 920 the Supreme Court had directed the empowered committee to conduct an inquiry, receive testimonies of inhabitants and related documents filed by local government in cases where the claims were not supported by documents.

14. "Minor forest produce" includes all non-timber forest produce of plant origin including bamboo, brush, wood, stumps, cane, tussar, cocoons, honey, wax, lac, tendu or kendu leaves, medicinal plants and herbs, roots, tubers and the like (Section 2).
15. Section 6(1) of the Act 2006.
16. Section 6(2) of the Act 2006.
17. Section 6(3) of the Act 2006.
18. Section 6(4) of the Act 2006.
19. Section 6(5) and (6) of the Act 2006.
20. Section 6(7) of the Act 2006.
21. *Frontline*, June 18 to July 1, 2005.
22. Para 11.
23. Animal and Environmental Legal Defence Fund vs. Union of India, AIR 1997 SC 1071.
24. Pradeep Krishen vs. Union of India, AIR 1996 SC 2040.
25. Niyamavedi vs. State of Kerala, AIR 1997 Ker 262.
26. AIR 1983 Gau 18.

6

Tribal development in north-east India vis-à-vis national integration: An overview

R.K. Kar

I

The term 'tribe' in the Indian context refers to the indigenous *janas* (people). They are commonly designated as *adivasi* (original settlers), *adimjati* (primitive people), *girijan* (hill dwellers), *janajati* (tribals), *vanyajati* (forest dwellers), and by their respective ethnic and cultural appellations too.

From time immemorial the tribal communities constitute an important segment of the Indian society. They constitute around 8 per cent of the country's total population; and are distributed in 426 tribes and 165 subtribes (Das Gupta, 1997: 99). Indian Constitution designates certain indigenous communities as Scheduled Tribes (STs) as per Article 342, as they are socially and educationally backward classes. They belong to the weaker section of Indian population along with the Scheduled Castes (SCs), and are thus entitled to protection against social injustice and all forms of exploitation as per Article 46 of the Constitution of India.

Anthropologists have always considered tribe as a social type; and have clubbed them into particular socio-economic categories. A *tribe* may be defined as a homogeneous social group with undifferentiated social structure and a territorial affiliation. It has a common dialect or language, and its economy is pre-industrial and non-market oriented. It is governed by its hereditary political functionaries by means of customary laws, norms and values; and it maintains its socio-cultural identity by recognising social distance from other tribal and caste groups. The world view of a tribe is generally archaic; and by and large, the members are animists. These criteria, though account for the ideal type of a tribal community, in reality, however, the situation today is very often different. Nowadays, the tribal communities are undergoing such a sea of change that it would indeed be difficult to identity a number of tribal communities as such on the basis of the criteria discussed above.

Development of the tribes has always been a matter of concern in independent India. Quite a good number of innovative initiatives have been undertaken with regard to the strategies of tribal development since independence. Provisions were made in the Indian Constitution under the V and VI schedules to protect the tribal interests to save them from outside exploitation. The First Five-Year Plan was introduced in 1951 with a comprehensive programme of community development. It was however, only during the Fifth Five-Year Plan that the concept of Tribal Sub-Plan was adopted. But, in any case, while making an objective evaluation of all these endeavours, during the last ten Five-Year Plans, what do we really observe? Even though there has been some significant development, the fact remains that the tribal people, by and large, continue to show a dismal scenario almost in all spheres. The results as a whole, in terms of improvement in the quality of life of the people do not seem to be commensurate with the inputs. It is relatively more conspicuous in case of the tribes of north-east India.

"The idea of *development*, as a matter of fact, has been guiding the policies of the vast majority of the countries of the world since more than last six decades. As the major ideology of our times, development has shaped the purpose and efforts of states; and of great public as well as modest private organisation" (Sutton, 1989: 137). More critically, development has been characterised as a secular theory of salvation (Nandy, 1987); and as a modernising myth (Celso Furtado, quoted in Wolfe, 1981).

The origins of the concept of *development* may be traced to the nineteenth century ideas of *progress*. These, in turn, draw on the work of the philosophers of the 18th century, who held that *stationary races* could catch up with the *advanced races*—primarily through the application of science and enlightened governmental intervention (Sutton, 1989; Adas, 1989). However, the concept really came into its own with the emergence of new nations following World War II (Guha, 1994). Thus, in his inaugural address on 20th January 1949, the American President, Harry S. Truman defined as *under-*

developed, the emerging nations of Asia, Africa and Latin America (quoted in Sachs, 1990). In acknowledgement of this definition, decolonisation inevitably involved the constitution of states wedded to the idea of rapid economic development. While formulating the policies and programmes, the new nations drew their inspiration from models that posited a linear continuum having themselves at one end of the spectrum; and the already industrialised western nations at the other. The idea of development thus succinctly captured the evolutionary and linear perspective; and was considered to be a smooth process that would be free of any conflict. But, in reality, the development experience quickly revealed a sharply skewed distribution of benefits among the prospective beneficiaries. In the 1950s and 1960s though a large number of the Third World countries (including India) achieved their growth targets (as measured by the rates of increase in the Gross National Product and the per capita income), the levels of living and quality of life of the masses (tribal, peasant and the urban poor) for the most part remained unchanged (Todaro, 1985: 84). Some particular social groups appeared to be gaining a disproportionate share of the gains from development. The problem of *equity* and *social justice* thus emerged as a basic dilemma of the development experience. It is a dilemma that is as yet largely unresolved, and around which much of the anthropological exercises continue to focus.

In the late 1960s, therefore, *development* was redefined in terms of alleviation or elimination of poverty, inequality, unemployment, disease and illiteracy (Seers, 1969: 3), thus the concept is now being "conceived of as a multidimensional process involving major changes in social structures, popular attitudes and national institutions as well as the acceleration of economic growth, the reduction of inequality and eradication of absolute poverty" (Todaro, 1985: 85). In the specific context of tribal communities, development has always to strike a balance between economic and social domains, and has to be culture specific (Behura, 1999: 10). In other words, the development efforts, particularly in the context of tribal communities, should have a holistic perspective. As a matter of fact, "the main issues in tribal development in India today are not philosophical" (Sharma, 1978: 11). It is a question of better appreciation of their tradition as well as the nature of socio-politico-economic forces, either in operation or are likely to operate as these areas get opened up. The need for a harmony between long term economic development and socio-political tradition is no longer a debatable issue. An understanding of the framework of social structure and social organisation of any group is essential before contemplating some action plan in order to bring planned development in the community.

In the socio-cultural life of the Indian tribes, though there are certain common characteristics that cut across the geographical regions, there do exist some strong local variations that deserve due consideration. Besides, antecedents, social and cultural tradition, the nature of the terrain is also an important factor that forms the matrix of social life. All societies depend on it for their basic needs. All these factors interact in a kind of functional relationship that is again relativistic in nature. Each community, as a matter of fact, has certain distinctive characteristics rooted in the remote past which bear the impress of that culture. Sometimes, an arbitrary or a generic term is used to denote a group of tribes living in a certain territory. All the tribes occupying the same geographic region are called by the outsiders by the same common term. The different tribes of the groups, however, might have their own linguistic and socio-political traditions. This type of an apparent expansive identity is a recurrent feature in the north-eastern region. Thus, for example, the formal label *Naga* refers to the people of Nagaland. But, it includes the tribes like the *Angami, Ao, Chakesang, Chung, Khienmungan, Konyak, Lotha, Phom, Rengma, Sangtam, Sema, Yunehung* and *Zeliang* (c.f. Kar, 1990: 72). Similarly, the *Kukis* of Manipur (c.f. Das, 1945; Steward, 1985), the *Adis* of Arunachal Pradesh (c.f. Vidyarthi and Rai, 1977), the *Paharis* of Rajmahal hills (c.f. Vidyarthi, 1963), the *Gadabas* of Orissa and the *Gonds* of Central India (c.f. Haimendrof, 1948) are not homogenous populations in respect of ethnicity, language, social history and tradition. A good deal of insight in social and other dimensions is, therefore, necessary for formulating the right strategy of development for any tribal community.

II

North-east India, popularly known as Sat Bhoni (Seven Sisters), comprises the states of Assam, Arunachal Pradesh, Manipur, Meghalaya, Mizoram, Nagaland and Tripura. According to 2001 census, the total population of the region is around 38.5 million, distributed over an area of 2.6 lakh sq km. For administrative purpose, of late, Sikkim has also been included in north-east India (population—540,493 according to 2001 census).

The region is considered as a cultural corridor between India and south-east Asia and has a tremendous strategical importance, not only because of its geography but also because of its history, demography and culture. The region provides shelter to numerous people of various ethnic affiliations having different social structures, cultural heritages and cultural linkages across the international borders. International borders, as a matter of fact, accounts for around 98 per cent of the north-east's total border area (Bhushan, 2004). There is a rich assembly of tribal cultures and communities in this rugged expanse of the eastern Himalayas. There are more than 140 major tribal groups in north-east India, having a quite good number of sub-tribes. In other words, around one-third of the total number of the listed tribes for the whole of India, are to be found in this region. The tribal population in different stages range from 11 (Assam) to 94 (Mizoram) per cent to the total population of the state. The average percentage of tribal population in the region is 22 (Kar, 2001).

Connected with the main body of the country by a 22 km wide corridor; having a 5,000 km international boundary with Bangladesh, Bhutan, China, Myanmar and Nepal (Narayanan, 2004); and having cultural linkages with trans-Himalayan societies, north-east India has shot into limelight in the recent decades owing to a series of ethnic-cultural movements, mostly reflecting sub-national sentiments. At times, the spirit and content of some of the movements apparently become threatening even to our national integration.

Politically, many parts of the north-east have become integral administrative parts of India only with independence; and culturally, most of the region has always been outside the mainstream of Indian culture and civilisation. Educational, political, economic and other advantages as per the provision of the Indian constitution have no doubt contributed significantly to widen the social universe of the once isolated or nearly isolated communities in the region. But, progressively increasing contact and interaction with other hill and plains peoples and cultures seem to have highlighted the cultural differences and have enhanced the awareness of collective self-identities among the different communities of the region.

The sudden extension of civil administration into the entire region against the British policy of treating it as "partially and totally excluded areas", the drawing of international boundaries in this part of India with greater rigidity, the existence of a large number of culturally as well as ethnically different communities, and the keen interest, shown by our unfriendly neighbours in creating tensions in the border regions in India, have all significantly and negatively influenced the process of nation building. It is important for us not only to know intimately the aspirations and problems of the people of the region, but to find ways to reduce, if not remove, the causes of their disaffection and to help them achieve their aspirations within the framework of social justice and broadly defined national interests. In the context of north-east India, it thus appears that though political integration through effective administrative control has largely been achieved, emotional integration (i.e., integration in terms of acceptance by the people of a common set of values, understandings and norms) to the required extent has yet to be achieved. The lack of proper physical, cultural and emotional links between the people of mainland India and the north-east has bred a deep sense of alienation that very often seems to manifest itself as a violent struggle for liberation and independence. It is believed that the inadequate and inefficient development efforts as well as the inequitable distribution of the benefits of the development exercises are the major factors that have contributed towards the present state of affairs in the region.

III

V.N. Narayanan (2004) observes: "north-east and its unique geopolitical location and economic isolation after partition has not been properly understood and assimilated into national perspectives even now". The perception and treatment of the north-east as a national security zone divided into different states with different degrees of insurgency and the mass media's portrayal of the region almost wholly in terms of insurgency and turbulence have so perverted the scenario that the opportunity of treating the region as one socio-economic zone with tremendous potential for generation of wealth and prosperity has been frittered away. The north-east thus seems to be a victim of perceptions of the government as well as the media.

The developmental efforts for the region have very often been made use by military forces and the sporadic offerings of economic packages without any well thought-out plan for development. "New Delhi's attempts at resolving the north-east's problems have been either to throw money at it or to send in additional security forces. The greater portion of the development funds sent from New Delhi is divided among the ruling elite as a matter of right. The extortion demands of the militant groups are merely "their shares" of the loot. The security forces sent to curb militancy do not always behave towards civilians in a manner befitting a democracy" (Bhushan, 2004).

The social scientists in general, and the anthropologists in particular, working in this region, I believe have a special role to play to make the government aware of its proper role that would have set the region on the road to social cohesion, lasting peace and rapid economic development.

Being considered as one economic zone, the region is endowed with an extremely rich biodiversity and natural beauty; and it has great potentialities for oil and mineral resources, generation of hydroelectric power (estimated at 35,000 MW) and ecology-based tourism, to name a few.

The huge biodiversity of the north-east region, besides acting as a resource base, provides numerous ecosystem services, free of cost (Das, 1995). These include moderation of local climate, binding of top soil on steep, erosion-prone slopes in the hills, conservation of water and nutrients, mitigation of floods, droughts and landslides, providing recreation and so on and so forth. The forests have also supported over the ages the subsistence economy of the tribals and other ecosystem people of this region along with the evolution of strong forest–culture interactions as evident from the folklores and traditional customs. The indigenous people of the region realised the importance of forest and initiated traditional conservation measures in the form of sacred groves and community forest reserves (Syngai, 1999). However, the transition from subsistence economy to consumerism is fast eroding these traditional value systems while the alternative secular conservation measures are yet to evolve and strike roots in the tribal mindset. Similarly, sustainable hunting for food has been replaced by large-scale killing and poaching of valuable wild life in the forest. Such a void in value systems typical of a society in transition has been fully exploited by the wild life trade mafia, timber tycoons and the other interested ones who have lured the rural tribals and other ecosystem people in destroying their own life support system. The practice of *jhuming*, the pillage and plundering by the MNCs, foresters and trafficker are also considered as contributing factors for the steady decrease of biodiversity and forest cover (both in terms of quantity and quality) in north-east India.

In order to devise ways and means for conservation of forest resources, a realistic assessment of the pressure on forests due to *jhuming*, timber- logging, fuel wood extraction and others need to be made on priority basis. Although *jhuming* has often been held primarily responsible for the loss and degradation of forests in the north-east, the fact remains that the annual area under shifting axe cultivation is about 2.3 per cent of the forest area, while the total area affected by *jhum* amounts to nearly 8.9 per cent (Gupta, 2000). Besides, in view of the fact that a substantial area of forest remains under the control of district councils/clans/communities, the age-old safety measures in the form of sacred groves and community forest reserves need to be revitalised through involvement and empowerment of the village councils and other local bodies and the NGOs. Formulation of proper policy/ies and a prudent management of the area would undoubtedly open wide vistas and economic prosperity for the people of the region as well as for the country as a whole.

North-east India has a tremendous *eco-tourism* potential. A fascinating range of scenic viewing and wild life can draw a huge range of national and international tourists. Concerted efforts need to be made to organise the entire chain of transport and communication links (both internal and external), packaged or chartered tours, hotels, guides, festivals and entertainments, river cruises, wild life safaris, angling, tea garden tours, trekking, mountaineering, handicrafts emporia and the likes. Growth of eco-tourism can, not only provide employment opportunities but also attract funds from abroad for research and development projects.

With regard to hydro-electric power potential also north-east India has a tremendous prospect. At present, the total hydel power generation is only around 500 MW whereas, as noted earlier, the region has the potential of around 35,000 MW (ibid.). Likewise, there are huge potentialities of oil and mineral resources as well as industrial (e.g., agro-based, forest-based and mineral-based industries in addition to the small-scale ones) development in the region that need to be explored systematically and in sustainable means and ways, so that the benefits are equitably shared by all sections of people.

■ References

Adas Michael 1989 *Machines as the Measure of Man: Science, Technology and Ideologies of Western Dominance.* New Delhi: Oxford University Press.

Behura, N.K. 1990. "Tribes, Their Development and Quality of Life", *Man and Life,* 25(1 & 2) 5–40.

Bhushan, Bharat 2004 "Engaging North-east Militants", *The Telegraph,* 11 October.

Das, G. 1995 "Some Issues in Understanding the Underdevelopment of North-eastern Region: A Note on Historical Perspective", in *Regional Development in North-east India,* in B.J. Deb (ed.), New Delhi: Reliance Publishing, pp. 42–49.

Das, T.C. 1945 *The Purums,* Kolkata: University of Calcutta.

Das Gupta, Biplab 1997 "India's Tribal Population: An Overview", *Jr. of the Anthropological Society,* 32(2): 99–138.

Guha, Ramachandra 1994 *Sociology and the Dilemmas of Development,* New Delhi: Indian Council of Social Science Research.

Gupta, Abhik 2000, "Environment and Development in North-east India: A Holistic Appraisal". An unpublished paper presented in the seminar on *The Development of Scheduled Tribes and Scheduled Castes in North-east India in the New Millennium*, held in the Department of Sociology, Assam University, Silchar on 8–9 December, 2000.

Haimendorf, C.F. 1948 *The Rajgonds of Adilabad*, London: Macmillan and Co.

Kar, R.K. 1990 "Socio-Political Organisation and the Process of Development: An Appraisal of the Himalayan Societies", in S*trategy of Development in the Himalayas*, in S.K. Biswas (ed.), Kolkata: Institute & Social Research and Applied Anthropology, pp. 70–116.

Kar, R.K. 2001 Anthropo-historical Appraisal of a Migrant Population in Assam, North-East India, *Man and life*, 27 (3 & 4): 139–62.

Malinowski, B. 1922 *Argonauts of Western Pacific*, New York: Duttan.

Nandy, A. 1987 *Traditions, Tyrannies and Utopias*, New Delhi: Oxford University Press.

Narayanan, V.N. 2004 "North-East: Gateway to South East Asia", *The Assam Tribune* (A Daily published from Guwahati), 7th October.

Sachs, Worlfand 1990 "On the Archaeology of the Development Idea", *Lokayan Bulletin*, 8(1): 7–37.

Seers, D. 1969 "The Meaning of Development", Unpublished paper presented in the Eleventh World Conference of the Society for the International Development, New Delhi.

Sharma, B.D. 1978 *Tribal Development: The Concept and the Frame*, New Delhi: Prachi Prakashan.

Steward, Lieut R. 1985 "Notes on Northern Cachar", *Journal of the Asiatic Society of Bengal*, 24: 9–16.

Sutton, F.F. 1989 "Development Ideology: Its Emergence and Decline", *Daedalus*, 118(1): 10–16.

Syngai, D. 1999 "Sacred Groves of Meghalaya", in B. Kharbuli, D. Syiem and H. Kayang (eds), *Biodiversity: North-East India Perspectives*, Shillong: North Eastern Biodiversity Research Cell, NEHU, 70–76.

Todaro, M.P. 1985 *Economic Development in the Third World*, New Delhi: Orient Longman Ltd.

Vidyarthi, L.P. 1963 *The Male*, Calcutta: Bookland.

Vidyarthi, L.P. and B.K. Rai 1977 *The Tribal Culture of India*, Delhi: Concept Publishing Company.

Wolfe, Marshall 1981 *Elusive Development*, Geneva: United Nations Research Institute for Social Development.

7

Genetic architecture of Indian people

V.R. Rao and A. Chandrasekar

India with rich genetic, social, cultural, ecological diversities with central geographical location and an extended period of human occupation necessitate Anthropological Survey of India to take up a project, "DNA Polymorphism in Contemporary Indian Populations" to trace out ancient successive human migrations, peopling of India and to understand variation in Indian gene pool.

The International Human Genome Project and the ongoing International Hap Map Project help us understanding human biological variation at molecular level. In human genome, 99.99 per cent is similar to all humans. Only 0.01 per cent explains individual and population variation. This variation in human population is the magnificent legacy of our evolutionary past, diseases and health. The genetic variation explains more than 40 per cent of the variation of most common diseases and more than 70 per cent for diseases like schizophrenia in a population. Human genome has about 10 million Single Nucleotide Polymorphisms (SNPs). Some of these polymorphisms predispose us to the common diseases in combination with other variants and with the environment. Polymorphism in human genome is often not independent of one another. A new mutation is associated with particular polymorphism present on the same chromosome. Knowing these polymorphisms offer tremendous advantage in the study of human disease and variable response to treatment.

The human body consists of about 60 thousand billion cells of which nearly every single cell contains our entire genetic information, the DNA. Each cell consists of two kinds of DNA—nuclear DNA is found inside the nucleus (chromosomal DNA, consisting of autosomal DNA, X chromosomal DNA and Y chromosomal DNA) and mitochondrial DNA that is present outside the nucleus in the mitochondria.

DNA polymorphisms reveal a population's genetic structure, migration and admixture in the past, susceptibility to illness and genetic causes of diseases. Human Genome, DNA sequencing offer an evidentiary alternative fossil based prehistoric reconstructions about origin and evolution of human beings. The uniparental inherited non-recombining haploid mtDNA and Y chromosome became an extremely powerful tool in phylogenetic studies.

Mitochondrial DNA and its role in human evolution

During the process of fertilisation, mitochondria that is present in the sperm cannot enter into the egg and die away, and the embryo is only left with maternal mitochondria. As such, we share the same mtDNA as our brothers and sisters, but not our father's.

MtDNA is also passed down nearly unchanged from generation to generation. So we share the same mtDNA-type as our mother, our maternal grandmother, our maternal great grandmother and so on. In fact the same mtDNA code will track our direct genetic line back until the point at which a natural mutation in the mtDNA code.

Each cell contains around 10,000 mitochondria. Mitochondrial DNA is a circular double-strand DNA molecule about 16.5 kb in length. The origin of mitochondria, in eukaryotic cells can be best explained by endosymbiosis theory. This theory posits that mitochondria are the direct descendants of a bacterial endosymbiont that became established at an early stage in a nucleus-containing (but amitochondriate) host cell. Gene sequence data strongly support a monophyletic origin of the mitochondrion from a eubacterial ancestor shared with a subgroup of the α-Proteobacteria. However, recent studies of unicellular eukaryotes (protists), some of them little known, have provided insights that challenge the traditional serial endosymbiosis based view of how the eukaryotic cell and its mitochondrion came to be. These data indicate that the mitochondrion arose in a common ancestor of all extant eukaryotes and raise the possibility that this organelle originated at essentially the same time as the nuclear component of the eukaryotic cell rather than in a separate, subsequent event.

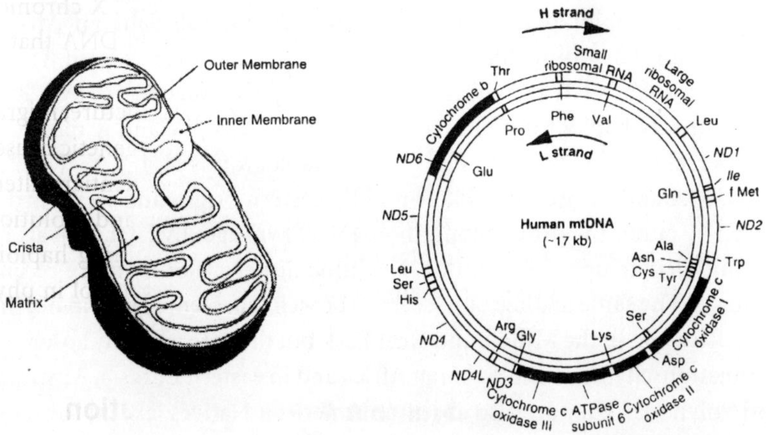

Human mitochondria

Due to the lower efficiency of DNA repair as well as to a higher frequency of DNA replication errors, mitochondrial DNA and in particular the non-coding region is highly polymorphic. The generation of mtDNA variability can only occur through new mutations. In vertebrates the mutation rate of mitochondrial genes is ten-fold higher compared to nuclear genes. Consequently, mtDNA rapidly accumulates sequence changes along radiating female lineages, thus providing a detailed record of ancient migration patterns.

Human origin and migration

Studies on mtDNA, Y chromosome and many autosomal regions support that modern humans originated in Africa between 166,000 and 249,000 years ago, then expanded throughout Africa and into rest of the world with little or no interbreeding between modern humans and archaic populations lived elsewhere in the old world, including the Neanderthals in Europe and Homoerectus in Asia.

mtDNA haplogroups in the world

In the absence of selection, genetic drift and founder effects have played a major role in shaping haplotype frequencies, giving rise to haplogroups and sub-haplogroups that are often restricted to specific geographic areas and/or population groups. The most ancient mtDNA haplotypes are L1, L2 and L3. Haplotypes L1 and L2 are specific for sub-Saharan Africa. Haplogroup L3 with its lineages, M and N arose in north-eastern Africa and subsequently left to colonise Asia and Europe between 50–70 kyrs ago. In Europe, N haplogroup lineages, H, I, J, B, T, U, V, W and X make up >80 percent of the mtDNA. The mtDNA haplogroups H, I, J, K, T, U2e, U3, U4, X and W are most likely middle-eastern origin and were introduced by either the protocolonisation 45–50 kyrs ago, by later arrivals in the middle/late upper Paleolithic, Neolithic dispersals or by more recent contacts. The same haplogroups seem to be well represented also in northern Africa and in the Middle and Near East, but they are virtually absent in populations, living in sub-Saharan Africa and in eastern Eurasia, Australia and Polynesia. They are also absent in American Natives, except for haplogroup X, which has found its way to some northern American Amerind populations. Native Americans belong to A, B, C, D and X lineages of M and N haplogroups. In Asia, macrohaplogroups N and M contributed equally to mtDNA radiation, with a plethora of derivative mtDNA lineages being generated within south-eastern and central Asia. However, in Siberia, northward from the Altai Mountains and the Amur River, only six mtDNA haplogroups (A, C, D, G, Z, and Y) make up 75 per cent of the mtDNAs. In contrast, south of Tibet and Korea, haplogroups A, C, D, and G represent only 14 per cent of the mtDNAs, and haplogroups Y and Z are rare. Thus, there is a five-fold enrichment of A, C, D, and G mtDNAs between central Asia and Siberia (Torroni et al., 1993). In Native American populations, only five Old World mtDNA haplogroups (A, B, C, D, and X) encompass 100 per cent of the mtDNA variation (Wallace et al., 1999). Haplogroups A, C, and D, which represent 58 per cent of Siberian mtDNAs, came to the Americas from northern Siberia across the Bering land bridge. Haplogroup B may have arrived later, because it is virtually absent in Siberia and rare in northern North America, and its sequence diversity in Native Americans is less than that of A, C, or D. In Asia, B is found primarily along the Asian coast and out into the Pacific. Hence, it might have come to the Americas via a coastal route, thus bypassing the extreme north. Finally, native American haplogroup X is concentrated in north-central North America and is distantly related to European X. Hence, it probably also arrived in the Americas via a northern route.

Indian scenario

The initial dispersal of modern humans from east Africa en-route north and east Africa has now been documented, following the African mtDNA haplogroups into Saudi Arabia and then west India. Indian subcontinent, due to its geographical location and ecological conditions played a pivotal role in the initial dispersal of modern humans.

The earliest imprints of human activities in India dates back to the Paleolithic ages roughly between 400,000 and 200,000 BC. Stone implements and cave paintings from that period have been discovered in many parts of South Asia. In Indian subcontinent, Dryopithecus, remains of Ramapithecus, Sivapihtecus and Gigantopithecus and species like Indicus, Punjabicus and Bilaspurensis of Miocene and Pliocene times were found. Indian Lower Paleolithic cultures (Sohan, Kolhan, Madrasian) show an existence of one or more subspecies of Homoerectus. On the banks of Narmada and its tributaries an assemblage of mammalian fossils and stone tools made by Lower Paleolithic man, a right portion of skull cap and a right clavicle of early stone age man were discovered. Its age was estimated to about 0.5 million years BC. Narmada man was identified as an archaic homosapien. Thus, earliest periods of Indian civilisation is known through the reconstruction based on archaeological evidence. Historically, India experienced many waves of migrations. Several groups entered India as merchants, invaders and migrants during the last millennium.

There are at least four major components to the genetic structure of India. The first one is the early Paleolithic component. The second is the migration of farmers, possibly speaking Proto-Dravidian languages, from the western Iran during Neolithic period. Third component corresponds to the arrival of Indo-European speakers roughly 3,500 years ago, who mostly introduced caste system. The fourth component is associated with Austro-Asiatic and Tibeto-Burman speakers, who affiliate others with east Asia.

Topology of Indian mtDNA

Indian specific mtDNA branches, M and N encompass all the populations in India irrespective of their social rank, caste or tribe. The demographic history of India inferred by mtDNA tree revealed, that there is no clear separation into genetically distinct groups along caste, tribe or language lines (Mountain et al., 1995; Kivisild et al., 1999a; Bamshad et al., 2001), although a low number of shared haplotypes indicate limited gene flow across linguistic, caste and tribe borders (Bamshad et al., 1998; Bhattacharyya et al., 1999; Roychoudhury et al., 2001). In India, the frequency of haplogroup M ranges from 54 to 97 per cent. This haplogroup is most common in the tribal population (for example, 96.7% amongst the Kotas of the South) and decreases as we go up in caste (reaching 18.5% amongst the Brahmins of Uttar Pradesh). Based on high frequency and diversity haplogroup M in India and elsewhere in Asia, some authors have suggested its origin in south-west Asia (Roychoudhury et al., 2000, 2001; Richards et al., 2003) against Ethiopia, where M, has been found in fair frequency (Quintana-Murci et al., 1999). The presence of M1 without accompanying L lineages in the Caucasoid (Tambets et al., 2000) leaves the question about the origin of haplogroup M still open (Metspalu et al., 2004).

The topology of M in India has remained largely undefined except a few. India specific M sub-haplogroups are M2, M3, M4, M5, M6, M18, M25, M30, M31, M32, M33, M34, M35, M36, M37, M38, M39, M40, M41, M42, M43, M45, M48, M49, M50, M51–M64 (Chandrasekar et al., 2009). M2 is the most frequent and oldest clade in India with coalescence time of 70,600±21,000 years. Due to the increased frequency towards the southern part of India, M2 is significantly more frequent among the Dravidian speakers (9–13%) where as it ranges from 0.7 to 8 per cent among Austro-Asiatic groups and 3–5 per cent among Indo-European speakers who are spread in central and northern region of India. It is more geography rather than linguistics or caste/tribe behind this pattern (Metspalu et al., 2004; Kumar et al., 2008). Most numerous subgroups of macrohaplogroup N in India are Indian specific variants of the phylogenetic node R including haplogroups R5, R6, U2 (a,b,c) (Kivisild et al., 1999a, 1999b; Quintana-Murci et al., 2004) and R7, R8, T30, R31 and N5 (Palanychamy et al., 2004). Haplogroup U is found frequently after M haplogroup in India. Presence of haplogroup M and U in India are best explained by separate late Pleistocene migrations of modern humans to India. One of them, possibly arriving by the southern route, brought to India an African carrying haplogroup M and was spread further eastward. The second migration brought the ancestors of haplogroup U. Haplogroup U is not present among Mongolians. Haplogroup U entered India after eastward migration of M, explaing the absence of haplogroup U lineages among Mongoloid. Haplogroup U is also present in Ethiopia. Haplogroup U thus neither originated in Europe nor in India, it might have originated in Ethiopia (Kivisild et al., 1999a). R5 is the second most frequent sub-clades of R in India after haplogroup U. The coalescence age estimate for R5 was similar to that of M2. Though R5 is absent in Austro-Asiatic tribe, it is spread across the other language boundaries. In contrast to M2, R5 is more frequent among castes than among tribal populations. Together with Indian specific sub-clades of haplogroup U2, haplotypes M2 and R5 can be discriminated as a package of Indian specific mtDNA clades harbouring extremely deep coalescence times around 50,000–70,000 YBP (ibid.). An extensive deep late Pleistocene genetic link between contemporary Europeans and Indians, is provided by the mtDNA haplogroup U, which encompasses roughly a fifth of mtDNA lineages of both populations. The U haplogroup is most common among the north Indian Muslim community (more than 30%), present at 15–20 per cent in the various castes, and less than 10 per cent among the tribals. The relative frequency of U2i sub-haplogroup compared to the haplogroup U in general is highest amongst the tribals. Conversely, the tribals almost entirely lack the west Eurasian sub-haplogroup U2e which is more common among the upper castes and shows a caste linked gradation. The other subgroups significantly represented in Indian population are U1 and U7. The estimated time for the split between the Indian and western Eurasian U2 lineages was 53,000+4,000 yrs BP, which is close to the suggested time for the peopling of Asia and the first expansion of anatomically modern humans in Europe. Only a small fraction of the Caucasoid-specific mtDNA lineages found in Indian population can be ascribed to a relatively recent admixture, which can be equated with Indo-Aryan invasion to India some 4,000 years ago (ibid.). Genetic distances indicate that Tibeto-Burman speaking tribal populations (from eastern India) were more closely related to Asian than to other Indians

(Cordaux et al., 2003). However, Indian caste populations were more closely related to Europeans than to eastern Asians.

The demographic history of India inferred by mtDNA, Y chromosome and autosomal genes revealed some clustering according to caste, tribe affiliation, there was no clear separation into genetically distinct groups along caste or tribe lines. There is no correlation of mtDNA and Y chromosome with matrilocal and patrilocal communities. In the caste–tribe hierarchy, we can find upward female gene flow and two way gene flow of male genes. We can observe differential pattern of mtDNA and Y chromosome in case of Parsis. Historical records say Parsis migrated from Iran and settled in northwestern Indian province of Gujarat around 900 AD and eventually moved to Mumbai in India and Karachi in Pakistan. DNA data also reveals the same. Among Parsis of Karachi, in mtDNA and Y chromosome composition 60 per cent of mtDNA belongs to Indian M haplogroup and 100 per cent of Iran Y chromosome admixture (Qamar et al., 2002). Both results suggests male-mediated migration of the ancestors of the present day Parsi population, from Iran to India, where they married local females, or local directional mating in Gujarat between Iranian males and local women, through time leading to loss of mtDNAs of Iranian origin.

It would be highly speculative to infer the earliest inhabitants of India from the extant mtDNA pools of Indo-European, Dravidian and Austro-Asiatic linguistic groups, because language families present today in India are all much younger than the majority of indigenous mtDNA lineages found among their present day speakers at high frequencies (Metspalu et al., 2004). Recent linguistic and archaeological evidence place the spread of Austro-Asiatic languages in the Neolithic, in conjunction with the dispersal of rice cultivation from the Ynagtze river basin (Higham, 2003). If this were the case, it would imply that the arrival of this linguistic phylum in India was not associated with female gene flow (Metspalu et al., 2004).

The Negrito people of Andaman Islands comprises of the Great Andamanese, the Onge (Thangaraj et al., 2005) and the Jarawa (Barik et al., 2008) possess sub-lineages of haplogroup M, M31 and M32. They show close affinity with south-east Asians than Africans. Andaman-specific mtDNA clades M31a1 and M32a provide evidences for very recent settlement of Andaman islands (ibid.).

Population located west of Indus Valley possess mainly Eurasian Lineages, with a very limited contribution from south Asia and western

Eurasia. South-Asian Lineages M* & U are absent in this region. The Caucasoid lineages, U9, R*, R2, R5, R6, N1d, HV2 make up >50 per cent of the haplogroup profile in the adjacent Indus Valley. U7 is the most wide-spread deep-rooting local lineage (~38000 YBP), and the other lineages (HV2, R2, R5, U2) in the Indus Valley and India show signals of *in situ* differentiation. The Brahui population of Indus Valley speaks Dravidian language which is now mainly restricted to south India and Sri Lanka. The Brahui population is characterised by high prevalence of west Eurasian mtDNAs (55%) accompanied by high frequency of the Y chromosome haplogroup J (McElreavey and Quintana-Murci, 2005).

Genetic links with west Eurasians

Indians have genetic link with west Eurasians through mtDNA haplogroup U, which roots deep into late Pleistocene. West Eurasian mtDNA haplogroups represent 6–7 per cent of north and central tribes, which are located in the area where Indo-European languages are spoken.

Genetic links with east Eurasians

East Eurasian specific mtDNA haplogroups M7, 8, 9, 10, M–D, M–G, N9, R9 are less common in India. Indian caste populations harbour only about 4 per cent of such mtDNA's compared to 17 per cent of west Eurasian ones. Tibeto-Burman speaking tribal populations of eastern and northern India exhibit the highest frequencies of east Eurasian specific mtDNA haplogroups.

Genetic links with Australians

Genetic link between Indian and Australian was consistent with mtDNA. It has been hypothesised that the peopling of Sohul (PNG and Australia) may have been the result of an early migration from east Africa through the Indian subcontinent following the southern route (Lahr and Foley, 1994). A shared mtDNA lineage between Indians (Munda, Madia and Pauri Bhuiya) and Australian aborigines provides direct genetic evidence of an early colonisation of Australia through south Asia, following the "southern route" (Kumar et al., 2008).

Y chromosome and haplogroup nomenclature

The Y chromosome contains the largest non-recombining block in the human genome. By virtue of its many polymorphisms it is now the most informative haplotyping system, with applications in evolutionary studies, forensics, medical genetics, and genealogical reconstruction. There has been a keen interest in using polymorphisms on the NRY to examine questions about paternal genetic relationships among human populations. These polymorphisms are particularly useful because of their low rate of parallel and back mutation, which makes them suitable for identifying stable paternal lineages that can be traced back in time over thousands of years. As the number of known binary polymorphisms increased, resulting emergence of several unrelated and non-systematic nomenclatures for Y-chromosomal binary haplogroups have become an increasing source of confusion. To resolve this issue, Y Chromosome Consortium constructed a comprehensive haplogroup tree for the human NRY. A single most parsimonious phylogeny was constructed for the 153 binary haplogroups observed. A simple set of rules was developed to unambiguously label the different clades nested within this tree. In order to devise a nomenclature system at a reasonable scale, YCC assigned a capital letter to several of the major clades, beginning with the letter A and continuing through the alphabet to the letter R. The letter Y was assigned to the most inclusive haplogroup comprising haplogroups A–R. Deciding which clades are to receive the highest labelling level can only be, to some extent, arbitrary. Here, those clades which labelled with single capital letters seem to represent the major divisions of human NRY diversity. This hierarchical nomenclature system supersedes and unifies past nomenclatures and allows the inclusion of additional mutations and haplogroups yet to be discovered.

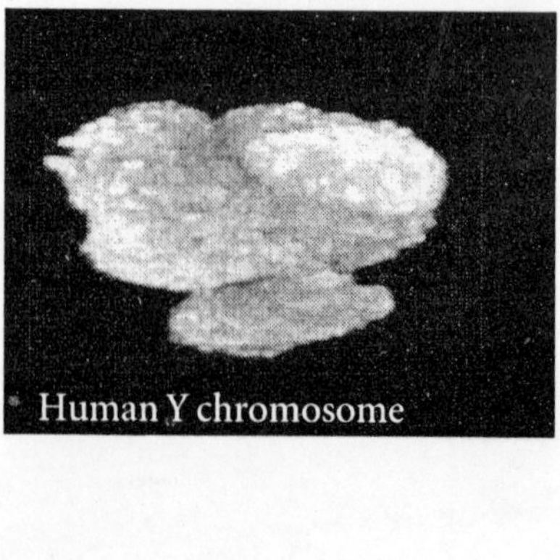

Human Y chromosome

Y chromosome lineages

Y chromosome studies reveal an extreme geographic structure in global populations in which the oldest clade represents Africans and the younger ones some non-African populations. One Y chromosome polymorphism (C to T mutation) at the M168 locus is shared by all non-African populations and was originally derived from Africa on the basis of a study of 1062 globally representative male individuals (Underhill et al., 2001). The age of M168 was estimated at 44,000 yrs (35,000–89,000) marking the recent out-of-Africa migrations. Under the M168 T lineage there are three major derieved sublineages—lineages D and E, defined by polymorphisms at loci YAP (Alu insertion), lineages F–R defined by the marker M89 (C to T mutation), and lineage C defined by the marker M130 (C toT mutation, also called RPS4Y). Therefore, these three markers can be used to test the completeness of the orgin and migration of modern human.

Topology of Indian Y chromosome

Indian Y chromosome lineages show affinity with the south/southeast Asia cluster K* (xO,P), though north India has a large fraction of R1a (M17). The Central Asian P* is significantly rarer among the tribals. The European ancestral lineage BR* is more common among the tribals, especially the Dravidian tribals, than the caste populations.The Tibeto-Burmese and to a smaller extent Austro-asiatic, tribals have higher frequencies of K*. It has been suggested that clines towards haplogroup J shows diffusion of agriculture from the middle-east: Indian data does not show any clear evidence of this. The 'Indoeuropean' R1a and the L haplogroup are also found in significant numbers. The major European haplotype (M173 or R1b) is pretty rare, but some European haplotypes are found amongst the upper castes, and in Punjab and Pakistan. The early formation of a non-African sub-cluster C is present among Australians, Newguinean, south-east Asians, Japanese and Central Asian. It is present in low frequencies in India. No Yap + chromosomes (clade D and E) were detected in either the caste or tribal populations (Kivisild et al., 2003). Haplogroup D was found among Andaman Islanders (Thangaraj et al., 2003, Chandrasekar et al., 2007) In comparison with castes, tribal populations showed higher frequency of haplogroup H1. South Indians

Y chromosomes exhibit high frequency of haplogroup H followed by R, L, J, F and O lineages. These H, J, L, R lineages penetrated into Bali (12%) and took a major role in peopling Bali.

Among Indian tribes, predominant Y chromosome haplogroups are H (45%) and O (40%). The Dravidian linguistic groups have very high frequency (94%) of haplogroup H. Haplogroup H is nearly completely restricted to India, Srilanka and Pakistan. Among Austro-Asiatic groups, south-east Asian haplogroup O is predominant (68–88%) followed by haplogroup H (8–11%). Haplogroup R is absent among them. The Indo-European linguistic groups have 50 per cent of O haplogroups and haplogroup H follows next. The Kolarian groups exhibits less or nil frequency of O haplogroups. These two linguistic groups have R allele. The Indo-European linguistic groups seem to be a newsynthesis of Dravidian, Austro-Asiatic and Indo-European gene pools. R1 allele is believed to be originated in Eurasian steppes, north of Black Caspian Sea. This lineage might have originated in a population of the Kurgan culture, known for the domestication of the horse (approximately 300 BCE). These people were also believed to be first speakers of the Indo-European language group. This lineage is currently found in central and western Asia, India and in Slavic populations of eastern Europe. Haplogroup J2 ranges from 0–17 per cent in India. It originated in the northern portion of the Fertile Crescent where it later spread throughout central Asia, the mediterranean and south into India. It is associated with Neolithic demic diffusion. Y chromosome genetic distance estimates showed that the chromosomes of Indian caste populations were more closely related to Europeans than to eastern Asians (Bamshad et al., 2001).

Thus, the combination of molecular age and geographical structure makes mtDNA and the NRY a sensitive genetic index capable of tracing the micro-evolutionary patterns of novel modern human diversity. Mitochondrial DNA and Y chromosome studies in Indian populations reveals affiliation with Europeans, east Asians, Austro-Melanesians and *in situ* development of deep-rooted whose relative clustering and coalescence ages suggests shaping of Indian gene pool during late Pleistocene.

Additional efforts are required to identify new coding region breakers of mtDNA and Y chromosome groups, to further improve the classification of Indian mtDNA's and Y haplogroups. Present ongoing works may contribute towards dispelling the hanging clouds.

References

Bamshad, M.J., Kivisild, T., et al. 2001 "Genetic Evidence on the Origins of Indian Caste Populations", *Genome Res*, 11: 994–1004.

Bamshad, M.J., Watkins, W.S., et al. 1998 "Female Gene Flow Stratifies Hindu Castes", *Nature*, 395: 651–52.

Barik, S.S., Sahani, R., et al. 2008 "Detailed mtDNA Genotype Permit a Reassessment of the Settlement and Population Structure of the Andaman Islands", *Am J Phy Anth*, 136: 19–27.

Bhattacharyya, N.P., Basu, P., et al. 1999 "Negligible Male Gene Flow Across Ethnic Boundaries in India, Revealed by Analysis of Y-chromosomal DNA Polymorphisms", *Genome Res*, 9: 711–19.

Cordaux, R., Saha, N., et al. 2003 "Mitochondrial DNA Analysis Reveals Diverse Histories of tribal Populations from India", *Eur J Hum Genet*, 3: 253–64.

Chandrasekar, A., Saheb, S.Y., et al. 2007 "YAP Insertion Signature in South Asia", *Annals of Human Biology*, 34(5): 582–86.

Chandrasekar, A., Kumar, S., et al. 2009 "Updating Phylogeny of Mitochondrial DNA Macrohaplogroup M in India: Dispersal of Modern Human in South Asian Corridor", *PLoS ONE*, 4(10): e7447, doi:10.1371/journal.pone.0007447

Higham, C. 2003 "Languages and Farming Dispersals: Austroasiatic Languages and Rice Cultivation", in P. Bellwood and C. Renfrew (eds), *Examining the Farming/Language Dispersal Hypothesis*, Cambridge: The McDonald Institute for Archaeological Research.

Kivisild, T., Rootsi, S., et al. 2003 "The Genetic Heritage of the Earliest Settlers Persists both in Indian Tribal and Caste Populations", *Am J Hum Genet*, 72: 313–32.

Kivisild, T., Bamshad, M.J., et al. 1999a "Deep Common Ancestry of Indian and Western-Eurasian Mitochondrial DNA Lineages", *Curr. Biol.* 9: 1331–34.

Kivisild, T., Kaldma, K., et al. 1999b "The Place of the Indian Mitochondrial DNA Variants in the Global Network of Maternal Lineages and the Peopling of the Old World", in S.S. Papiha, R. Deka and R. Chakraborty (eds), *Genomic Diversity*, New York: Kluwer Academic/Plenum Publishers, 135–52.

Kumar, S., Padmanabham, P.B.S.V., et al. 2008 "The Earliest Settlers' Antiquity and Evolutionary History of Indian Populations: Evidence from M2 mtDNA Lineage", *BMC Evol Biol*, 8: 230.

Kumar, S., Ravuri, R.R., et al. 2009 "Reconstructing Indian-Australian Phylogenetic Link", *BMC Evol Biol*, 9: 173. doi: 10.1186/1471-2148-9-173.

Lahr, M.M. and Foley, R.A. 1994 "Multiple Dispersals and Modern Origins", *Evol Anth*, 3: 48–0.

McElreavey, K. and Quintana-Murci, L. 2005 "A Population Genetics Perspective of the Indus Valley through Uniparentally-Inherited Markers", *Ann. of Hum. Bio*, 32: 154–62.

Metspalu, M. et al. 2004 "Most of the extant mtDNA boundries in south and south-west Asia were likeky shaped during the initial settlement of Eurasia by anatomically modern humans", *BMC Genet*, 5: 26.

Mountain, J.L., Hebert, J.M., et al. 1995 "Demographic History of India and mtDNA-Sequence Siversity", *Am J Hum Genet*, 56: 979–92.

Palanichanay, M.G. et al. 2004 "Phylogeny of mitochondrial DNA macrohaplogroup N in India, based on complete sequencing: Implication for the peopleing of South Asia, *American Journal of Human Genetics*, 75: 966–978.

Qamar, R., Ayub, Q., et al. 2002 "Y Chromosomal DNA Variation in Pakistan", *Am J Hum Genet*, 70: 1107–24.

Quintana-Murci, L., Semino, O., et al. 1999 "Genetic Evidence of An Early Exit of Homo Sapiens from Africa through Eastern Africa", *Nat Genet*, 23(4): 437–41.

Quintana-Murci, L., Chaix, R., et al. 2004 "Where West Meets East: The Complex mtDNA Landscape of the Southwest and Central Asian Corridor", *Am J Hum Genet*, 74: 827–45.

Richards, M., Rengo, C., et al. 2003 "Extensive Female-mediated Gene Flow from Sub-Saharan Africa into Near Eastern Arab Populations", *Am J Hum Genet*, 72(4): 1058–64.

Roychoudhury, S., Roy, S., et al. 2000 "Fundamental Genomic Unity of Ethnic India is Revealed by Analysis of Mitochondrial DNA", *Current Science*, 79(9): 1182–92.

——. 2001 "Genomic Structures and Population Histories of Linguistically Distinct Tribal Groups of India", *Hum Genet*, 109(3): 339–50.

Tambets, K., Kivisild, T., et al. 2000 "The Topology of the Maternal Lineages of the Anatolian and Trans-Caucasus Populations and the Peopling of the Europe: Some Preliminary Considerations", in C. Renfrew and K. Boyle (eds), *Archaeogenetics: DNA and the population prehistory of Europe*, Cambridge: Cambridge University Press, 219–35.

Thangaraj, K., Singh, L., et al. 2003 "Affinities of the Andaman Islanders: A Vanishing Human Population", *Current Biology*, 13: 86–93.

Thangaraj, K., Chaubay, G., et al. 2005 "Reconstructing the Origin of Andaman Islanders", *Science*, 309: 996.

Torroni, A., Sukernik, R.I., et al. 1993 "mtDNA Variation of Aboriginal Siberians Reveals Distinct Genetic Affinities with Native Americans", *Am. J. Hum. Genet*, 53: 591–608.

Underhill, P.A., Passarino, G., et al. 2001 "The Phylogeography of Y Chromosome binary Haplotypes and the Origins of Modern Human Populations", *Ann Hum Genet*, 65: 43–62.

Wallace, D.C., Brown, M.D. and Lott, M.T. 1999 "Mitochondrial DNA Variation in Human Evolution and Disease", *Gene*, 238: 211–30.

8

Bio-cultural aspect of sickle-cell trait in tribal populations of India

R.S. Negi

Human bio-cultural evolution has been the outcome of complex and largely uncontrolled interactions between human biological endowment and the environmental factors and culture. The life ways of different human societies are largely the manifestations of these interactions.

Health, nutrition and sanitary practices taken together are generally seen as indicators of life conditions. Health status of any population is determined by both biology, that is, genetic make up and its interaction with environmental factors including nutritional adaptation, as well as cultural factors which may enforce the hygienic and sanitary practices. Here, we will take into consideration the delimiting influences exhorted by one of the hereditary conditions, that is, sickle-cell trait on human populations.

Sickle-cell is caused by an abnormal haemoglobin S. It was first discovered in a person of African origin and was believed to have spread from Africa through physical migrations, as it was found to be harboured by populations in east, west and north Africa and around mediteranean basin. But recent advances in recombinant DNA technology provide evidence to show that sickle-cell mutation arose independently in different parts of the world. In homozygous condition, that is double doze, the sickle-cell gene causes severe anaemia known as sickle-cell anaemia or disease. The condition is lethal and usually causes early death. However, in heterozygous condition, that is in single doze known as sickle-cell trait, it has a selective advantage as the condition is known to be resistant to falciparum malaria. It is estimated that sickle-cell anaemia causes about 1,00,000 deaths worldwide per year. In USA, where the gene is to the extent of 8 per cent, mostly in people of African origin, about 40,000–50,000 individuals suffer from the disease. In India, sickle-cell trait has a rather peculiar but wide distribution.

Its occurrence is largely confined to the tribal populations of peninsular India and some Scheduled Caste population. After a large-scale survey, it was demonstrated that sickle-cell trait attains high frequencies among the tribal population inhabiting:

- Nilgiri–Wynad plateau,
- South Gujarat–Malwa plateau, and
- Middle Indian belt from Nagpur region in the west to the south-eastern Orissa and coastal Andhra Pradesh.

The population inhabiting the regions of high frequency of the trait are a number of small populations in the southern part of India and coastal Andhra Pradesh, 'Bhil' group of population in western India and 'Gond' group of population in the middle Indian region. However, no estimates are available from Indian populations of individuals suffering from sickle-cell anaemia/disease, very few as such studies have so far been made.

It has been well established that the sickle-cell gene is maintained in the different populations world over due to the adaptive response to the enormous selective pressure produced by falciparum malaria is or was till recently endemic. It has been shown experimentally that heterozygous sickle-cell trait carriers are resistant to falciparum malaria. Thus, in malarial environment, the sickle-cell trait was being perpetuated and maintained through the mechanism of natural selection.

Malaria, one of the greatest killer disease, was unknown to humankind before the advent of agriculture. In other words, till the humans were mainly subsisting through hunting and gathering, they were free from the disease. It was due to the clearing of tropical forest for shifting or slash and burn cultivation that created conditions for mosquito-breeding in the vicinity of human settlements. For agriculture, patches of land were cleared in the forest on the one hand and on the other the human beings changed their lifestyle from the hunter gatherer nomads to the food producing sedentary settlers in early villages or settlements. The mosquitoes found breeding ground in the cleared patches of land and also the human sedentary populations to feed upon. Thus, malaria struck human being for the first time and eventually produced tremendous selective pressure. Malaria depleted human population significantly and produced pressure on the human force needed for agricultural activities. Malaria was direct result of the cultural modification to the environment by human activity but it also created a biological situation in depletion of active work force. No doubt human beings were biological responses too, and the sickle-cell mutation was one such adaptive response. Population inhabiting the malarial environment responded by the greater resistance of sickle-cell trait carriers, but there is cost implication too. The greater fitness of the heterozygous trait carrier had a better reproductive performance but that also increased the probability of heterozygous matings and elimination of the homozygous offspring through sickle-cell disease. There is, therefore, a counter balance between the reproductive performance of the heterozygous carriers and elimination of homozygous anaemic.

With this background picture let us examine the implications of the occurrence of sickle-cell trait in tribal India. For the purpose of this paper we will limit our treatment to the south Indian tribal populations inhabiting the Nilgiri–Wynad region including parts of the three states of Karnataka, Tamilnadu and Kerala.

The very first study to detect sickle-cell trait in India was made in Nilgiri by Lehman and Cutbush (1952). Thereafter, a number of studies have been undertaken in this region for sickle-cell trait. Table 1 shows the incidence of sickle-cell trait in various populations inhabiting Nilgiri–Wynad region as reported by different investigators. It has been observed that there is wide range of variation in the trait frequencies among different populations. In case of some populations like Paniyan, Irula and Kurumba there is variation in trait frequencies in different sample originating from different localities.

The Nilgiri–Wynad region is mostly a forest habitat. Almost all the tribal populations claim to have come from other parts except the Paniyan who claim to be autochthones of Wynad. This could be so or they may have migrated to Wynad quite far back in time so that the fact of migration is erased from their collective memory. The habitat has malarial environment and till recently was endemic for falciparum malaria.

It is a matter of speculation whether the environmental conditions were same during the Neolithic period when ragi was being cultivated in south India especially in Andhra Pradesh, Karnataka and Tamilnadu. Most of the tribal population has the collective memory of having migrated from Karnataka and Tamilnadu. It is reasonable to presume that their ancestors had the knowledge of ragi cultivation and when they were pushed into the forest and hilly fasthood by people possessing advanced technology they cleared the patches in the forest for their settlements and shifting cultivation. It is interesting to note that all these populations do have ragi cultivations even if they are practising hunting and gathering. As a matter of fact there are no true hunter and gatherers among these populations except perhaps Cholanaickan and Pathinaickan, who are immigrant people and have not taken to shifting cultivation in their new habitat. However, this does not rule out their practising some kind of cultivation in their previous habitat.

Recession into the thick forest by these population resulted in cultural modifications of the environment of human activity. Conditions were created for the mosquito-breeding in the vicinity of human settlements and ultimately introduction of malaria.

For the past 2,000 years malaria had been one of, the most potent killer in human history. Observed parallelism between the distribution of high frequencies of sickle-cell trait and malaria substantiates the belief that malaria is the selective agent maintaining these high frequencies of the trait. It has been said that in malarial environment the heterozygous carriers not only are resistant to malaria but have also better reproductive performance so as to counter-balance the loss of homozygous offspring. Unfortunately, besides mapping out the distribution of the trait in India, further studies to examine the malaria–sickle-cell relationship or the comparative reproductive performance of the heterozygous carriers have not been carried out.

It has been proposed that there is a relationship between sickle-cell trait, malaria and agriculture. But not all agricultural systems have the same effect on development of malaria and higher frequencies of sickle-cell trait. Wisenfeld (1967) propounded that communities practising what is known Malaysian system of agriculture that is slash and burn cultivation, and roots and tree crops have higher frequencies of the trait. Such communities have higher dependence on agriculture. Communities practising advanced agricultural system with intensive irrigation and having cereal crops have lower frequencies of the trait and they have lower dependence on agriculture.

Table 1 *Showing the incidence of sickle-cell trait in tribal population of Nilgiri–Wynad region*

Sl. No.	*Population*	*Locality*	*Number tested*	*Number sickler*	*% of sickler*	*Investigator*
01	Paniyan	Nilgiri	61	21	34.43	Lehman, 1954
	Paniyan	Nilgiri & Wynad	74	22	29.73	Buchi, 1955
	Paniyan	Wynad	38	8	21.05	Negi, 1977
	Paniyan	Wynad	955	265	27.5	Das & Bose, 1959
	Paniyan	Wynad	109	47	43.12	Sastry (Unpublished)
02	Badaga	Nilgiri	191	26	13.61	Lehman, 1954
	Badaga	Nilgiri	30	2	6.67	Lehman & Sukumaran, 1956
03	Toda	Nilgiri	84	3	03.57	Lehman, 1954
	Toda	Nilgiri	50	2	2.00	Lehman & Sukumaran, 1956
	Toda	Nilgiri	60	1	03.33	Kirk et al., 1962
04	Irula	Nilgiri	124	39	31.45	Lehman, 1954
	Irula	Nilgiri	18	4	22.23	Lehman & Sukumaran, 1956
	Irula	Nilgiri	15	6	40.00	Kirk et al., 1962
	Irula	Nilgiri	254	86	33.85	Sastry (Unpublished)
	Irula	Palghat	184	30	16.30	Negi, 1977
05	Kurumba	Nilgiri	16	3	18.75	Lehman, 1954
	Kurumba	Nilgiri	112	20	17.86	Buchi, 1955
	Kurumba	Nilgiri	43	10	23.26	Kirk et al., 1962
	Kurumba	Nilgiri	26	7	26.92	Lehman & Sukumaran, 1956
	Kurumba	Wynad	56	10	17.86	Negi, 1987

06	Urali	Wynad	42	8	19.05	Negi, 1977
07	Muduga	Palghat	100	6	06.00	Negi, 1977
08	Jenu Kuruba	Coorg	107	3	02.83	Negi, 1977
		Mysore	75	29	38.67	Sastry (Unpublished)
09	Beta Kuruba	Coorg	48	4	08.33	Negi, 1977
		Mysore	67	28	41.79	Sastry, 1977
10	Yerava	Coorg	135	32	23.70	Negi, 1977 (Unpublished)
	Yerava	Mysore & Coorg	51	17	33.33	Sastry, 1977
11	Adiyan	Wynad	75	24	32.00	Negi, 1977 (Unpublished)
	Adiyan	Wynad	114	34	29.82	Sastry, 1977
12	Malasar	Coimbatore	41	3	07.32	Negi, 1977 (Unpublished)
13	Soliga	Coimbatore	115	30	26.09	Negi, 1977 (Unpublished)
	Soliga	Mysore	102	41	40.59	Sastry, 1977
14	Mullu Kuruba	Nilgiri	101	39	38.61	Sastry, 1977
15	Cholanaikan	Nilambur	28	4	14.29	Negi et al. (Unpublished)
16	Pathinaickan	Nilambur	29	6	20.69	Negi et al. (Unpublished)
17	Kattunaickan	Wynad	24	7	29.17	Negi et al. (Unpublished)
18	Kundu Vadian	Wynad	14	5	35.71	Negi et al. (Unpublished)

In view of the above observation, the sickle-cell trait–malaria–agriculture relationship could be placed in the following evolutionary sequence:

(i) Human beings were free from malaria in the hunting gathering stage.
(ii) Advent of agriculture in forest environment was in the form of clearing of patches for slash and burn agriculture.
(iii) Clearing of patches created condition for mosquito-breeding in the vicinity of human settlement and introduction of malaria into human populations.
(iv) One of the biological adaptive response to the selective pressure produced by malaria was sickle-cell mutation.
(v) Higher frequencies of sickle-cell to counter-balance the high mortality due to malaria.

By inference, therefore, the high frequencies of the trait would be in those population inhabiting malarial environment and practising shifting or slash and burn cultivation. The trait should be absent in hunter-gatherers and of low incidence in population practising intensive agriculture.

It would be worthwhile to examine the proposition in relation to the south Indian tribal populations. Table 2 shows the classification of this population according to the mode of subsistence and the percentage of sick-ling. The populations are classified as hunter-gatherers, shifting cultivators and agriculturists. It would be stated that the classification is only an approximation as there are no true hunter and gatherer, since all those population classified as such do practice some sort of agriculture specially shifting cultivation. Similarly, the shifting cultivation is supplemented by other subsistence activities. The classification is based on the information available in published ethnographic accounts and is perhaps true to conditions a few generations ago.

Cholanaickan and Pathinaickan although now pursuing hunting and gathering mode of subsistence are recent migrants and were probably offshoot of the Kattunaickan who practice shifting cultivation.

All the population is second category that is shifting cultivation with the exception of Muduga, Malasar and perhaps Soliga harbour very high frequencies of the trait. In the third category, the frequencies of the trait is expected to be lower. But here also the situation is not so simple. The Mullu Kurumba has recently taken to intensive cultivation, and probably belong

Table 2 *Mode of subsistence and sickle-cell trait in south Indian tribal population*

Hunting-gathering		*Agriculture*		*Shifting cultivation*	
Population	*% sickler*	*Population*	*% sickler*	*Population*	*% sickler*
Malapandaram	—	Muduga	6	Badaga	7–14
Upladam	—	Malasar	7	Adiyan	30–32
Kanikar	—	Soliga	7–27	Kundu Vadiyan	36
Kadar	—	Kurumba	18–27	Mullukurumba	39
Malavedam	—	Kattunaickan	29		
Cholanaickan	14	Yerava	24–33		
Pathinaickan	29	Irula	16–40		
Jenu Kurumba	3–39	Paniyan	21–43		
Betta Kurumba	8–42				

to the second category rightfully. The position of Kundu Vadian is not very clear. It is a very small population recently migrated to Wynad. They practice intensive agriculture at present.

By the foregoing it can be said, though not conclusively, that high frequencies of the sickle-cell trait are found among the population who are or were till a few generations ago practising shifting cultivation.

However, the situation is not so simple and far from clear. In 1947, the Nilgiri–Wynad region was hyper endemic for falciparum malaria. Soon after in fifties and sixties under Malaria Control Programme followed by Malaria Eradication Programme there had been extensive DOT spray to root out the mosquito-breeding grounds and thus eradicate malaria. For some time, the situation was well in control. But, natural selection operated on the mosquitoes also which gave rise to the DDT resistant varieties. For past few years, malaria has reappeared and is in upward swing. What implications these factors will have on the human populations specially those inhabiting malarial environment and harbouring sickle-cell trait should be the concern for detailed studies. Another important factor is large-scale increase in the incidence of malaria with consequent increase in the frequency of sickle-cell trait. We can only speculate until detailed studies are undertaken, may be, with a generational time gap.

Although sickle-cell trait anaemia is usually lethal, the trait in single doze is not associated with disease for all practical purposes. Matings of two trait carriers produce 25 per cent offspring with double doze who suffer from sickle-cell disease. It is, therefore, important to first study the populations known to have sickle-cell for correct estimates of the gene among them so that effective measures could be taken to improve the health conditions, which would reduce the severity of the disease. In some of the African countries and USA the severity of the disease has been blunted, the disease is not as severe because adult homozygous individuals are known to survive even under the poor health conditions, which is by and large present in the remote tribal areas (Singh et al., 1956; Brittenham et al., 1977). The mutant gene in Indian populations, is most probably different from that in African populations and that is the reason that its effects in double doze are not so severe. It is a somewhat fortunate situation and full advantage must be taken to minimise the severity of sickle-cell disease by effective medical intervention and health measures. Apart from health measures, genetic counselling is one method that could eliminate the disease but how far that will be successful among the pre-literate tribal populations, at the present juncture, is a moot question.

■ References

Brittenham, G., B. Lozoff and J.W. Harris 1977 "Sickle Cell Anaemia and Trait in a Population of Southern India", *Anthropological Journal of Hematopogy*, 2: 25–32.

Buchi, E.C. 1955 "Is Sickle a Wedded Trait?", *The Anthropologist*, 1: 25.

Kan, Yuet Wai and Andree M. Dozy 1980 "Evolution of Haemoglobin S and C Genes in World Populations", *Science*, 209: 388–91.

Kirk, R.L. et al. 1962 "The Blood and Serum Group of Selected Populations in South India and Ceylon", *AJPA*, 70: 485–97.

Lehman, H. and M. Cutbush 1952 "The Findings of the Sickle-cell Trait in Pre-Dravidians of South India", *Man*, LIII: 10.

Lehmann, H. 1954 "Distribution of the Sickle-cell Gene", *Eug. Rev.* 46, 101.

Lehman, H. and P.K. Sukumaran 1956 "Examination of 146 South Indian Aboriginals for Haemoglobin Variants", *Man*, 56: 95.

Livingstone, R.B. 1958 "Anthropological Implication of Sickle-cell Gene Distribution in West Africa", *American Anthropologist*, 60: 533.

Mathur, P.R.G. 1977 *Tribal Situation in Kerala*, Trivandrum: Kerala Historical Society.

Negi, R.S. 1968 "Sickle-cell Trait in India: A Review of Known Distribution", *Bull. Anthropol. Survey India*, XVII(4): 439–49.

—— 1977 "Population Dynamics of Sickle-cell Trait Distribution in India", unpublished Ph.D. Thesis, Calcutta University.

Saha, N. and B. Banerjee 1973 "Haemoglobinopathics in the Indian subcontinent", *Acta Genet Med Gemellol*, 22: 117–38.

Sastry, D.B. 1977 Sickle-cell Disease in Tribes of South India. Unpublished paper read in Seminar on Human Variation in India.

Singh, J., B.A. Rao and S.P. Ram Krishnan 1956 "National Malaria Programme in India", *Indian Journal of Malariology*, 195.

Wisenfeld, S.L. 1967 "Sickle-cell Trait in Human Biological and Cultural Evolution", *Science*, 157: 1134.

9

Nutritional status based on anthropometry of tribal children of Paschim Medinipur district, West Bengal

Sanjib Ganguly, Argina Khatun, Samiran Bisai, Subal Das and Kaushik Bose

Child growth is widely used to assess adequate nutrition, health and development of individual children, and to estimate overall nutritional status and health of population. Compared to other health assessment tools, measuring child growth is relatively inexpensive, easy to perform and non-invasive. Children have special nutritional needs because of their extensive growth and development. Undernutrition among children is an important health problem in India including West Bengal.

Three commonly used internationally recommended indicators are child stunting (low height-for-age), underweight (low weight-for-age) and wasting (low weight-for-height). We used stunting (ST) and underweight (UW) to assess nutritional status. While ST reflects a failure to reach linear growth potential due to sub-optimal health and/or nutritional conditions, UW reveals low body mass relative to chronological age, which is influenced by both, a child's height and weight.

In view of this, the present investigation was undertaken to determine age and sex variations in height and weight as well as to evaluate the levels of ST and UW among 8–18 years tribal school children of Paschim Medinipur district of West Bengal.

Materials and methods

The present study was undertaken at five schools in Paschim Medinipur district of West Bengal. The schools were :

1 Khasla Indumati High School, PO Bhaudi, PS Salboni; Paschim Medinipur.
2 Rangamati Kiranmoyee High School, PO Rangamati, PS Kotwali; Paschim Medinipur.
3 Rangamati Kiranmoyee Prathamik Vidyalaya, PO Rangamati, Paschim Medinipur.
4 Khola Patna Prathamik Vidyalaya, PO Khola Patna, Paschim Medinipur.
5 Gokulpur Bidhan Chandra Vidyabhaban, PO Gokulpur, Paschim Medinipur.

A total of 431 children (296 boys and 135 girls) aged 8–18 years were measured. Ethical permission was obtained from relevant authorities.

> All anthropometric indicators were determined using the internationally accepted standard techniques. Height and weight measurements were recorded to the nearest 0.1 cm and 0.5 kg respectively. ST and UW were used to evaluate the nutritional status of the subjects. The United States National Centre for Health Statistics (NCHS) age and sex specific –2 z scores were followed to define ST and UW. The following scheme was utilized:
>
> ST: < –2 HAZ
> UW: < –2 WAZ
>
> where HAZ and WAZ refer to height-for-age and weight-for-age z scores, respectively, of NCHS.

We followed the WHO [1] classification for assessing severity of malnutrition by percentage prevalence ranges of these three indicators among children. The classification is:

	Low (%)	Medium (%)	High (%)	Very High (%)
ST	<20	20–29	30–39	≥40
UW	<10	10–19	20–29	≥30

All statistical analysis was undertaken using the epi-info statistical package.

Results

The distribution of the subjects by age and sex are presented in Table 1. Boys and girls comprised 68.7 per cent and 31.3 per cent of the subjects, respectively. The bar chart of the subjects by age and sex is presented in Figure 1.

The means and standard deviations of weight by age and sex are presented in Table 2. Girls were heavier than boys until 12 years. However, boys were heavier during 13–18 years.

The means and standard deviations of weight by age and sex are presented in Table 3. Girls were taller than boys until 12 years. Thereafter, the trend was reversed.

The mean z scores for WA (WAZ) of the subjects presented in Table 4 revealed that the mean z scores of WA were less than those of NCHS guideline at 9 and 10 years age in boys and at 18 years age in girls.

Table 1 *Distribution of subjects by age and sex*

Age (years)	*Frequency*	*Percentage*	*Boys*	*Girls*
8	15	3.5	46.7	53.3
9	12	2.8	41.7	58.3
10	14	3.2	50.0	50.0
11	58	13.4	69.0	31.0
12	77	17.9	66.2	33.8
13	73	16.9	72.6	27.4
14	58	13.5	69.0	31.0
15	40	9.3	62.5	37.5
16	31	7.2	74.2	25.8
17	19	4.4	89.5	10.5
18	34	7.9	82.4	17.7
Total	431	100.0	68.7	31.3

Figure 1 Bar chart showing the distribution of population by age and sex.

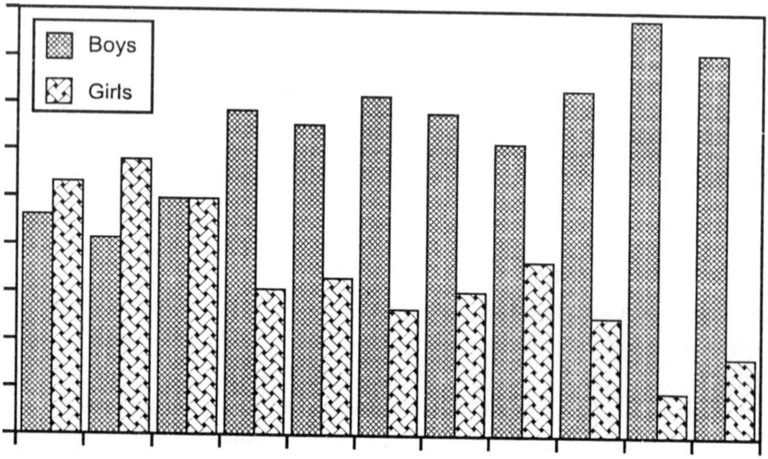

Table 2 *The means and standard deviations of weight by age and sex.*

Age (years)	*Boys*		*Girls*	
	Mean	*SD*	*Mean*	*SD*
8	20.3	2.8	24.3	9.0
9	20.5	1.9	22.6	4.0
10	22.5	2.7	24.0	3.2
11	27.3	3.9	29.5	5.2
12	31.0	6.8	33.6	6.3
13	36.8	8.5	34.5	7.2
14	39.3	7.9	38.7	6.4
15	43.4	8.6	40.5	3.9
16	47.7	7.0	47.5	10.1
17	51.1	5.1	43.5	3.5
18	52.5	5.2	41.3	2.4

The mean z scores for HA (HAZ) of the subjects presented in Table 5 revealed that the mean z scores of HA were less than those of NCHS guideline at 17 and 18 years age of girls.

The frequencies of ST and UW are presented in Table 6. The overall (age and sex combined) rates of ST and UW were 23.2 per cent and 24.6

Table 3 *The means and standard deviations of height by age and sex*

Age (years)	*Boys*		*Girls*	
	Mean	*SD*	*Mean*	*SD*
8	121.1	6.9	124.2	15.2
9	120.3	3.4	124.2	6.7
10	129.0	5.2	130.2	4.3
11	135.5	7.9	138.8	8.0
12	141.1	9.6	144.6	7.7
13	148.1	9.6	144.7	7.2
14	151.4	8.9	147.1	6.6
15	156.3	10.3	148.2	4.9
16	160.0	8.9	151.7	5.9
17	162.4	3.7	145.2	3.0
18	164.5	4.6	149.6	4.4

Table 4 *Distribution of weight for age (WAZ) z score by age and sex*

Age (years)	*Boys*		*Girls*	
	Mean WAZ	*SD*	*Mean WAZ*	*SD*
8	−1.44	1.10	−0.37	2.20
9	−2.18	0.80	−1.54	1.30
10	−2.86	0.60	−1.33	0.70
11	−1.35	0.70	−0.83	1.00
12	−1.28	0.90	−0.95	0.90
13	−1.67	1.10	−1.28	0.90
14	−1.31	0.90	−1.19	0.80
15	−1.32	1.10	−1.43	0.50
16	−1.31	0.70	−0.94	1.20
17	−1.56	0.60	−1.66	0.50
18	−1.69	0.70	−2.07	0.30
Total	−1.37	0.91	−1.14	1.02

per cent, respectively. The rate of ST was higher among girls (25.2%) compared with boys (22.3%). The rate of UW was higher among boys (24.3%) compared with girls (21.5%). Based on WHO classification of severe malnutrition, the overall (age and sex combined) prevalence of UW was high (20–29%) while those of ST (20–29%) were medium.

Table 5 *Distribution of height-for-age (HAZ) z score by age and sex*

Age (years)	*Boys*		*Girls*	
	Mean HAZ	*SD*	*Mean HAZ*	*SD*
8	−0.62	1.00	0.07	2.50
9	−1.86	0.70	−1.27	1.20
10	−1.12	0.80	−0.71	0.60
11	−1.06	0.10	−0.29	1.10
12	−1.00	1.30	−0.66	1.20
13	−0.99	1.20	−1.40	1.20
14	−1.17	1.00	−1.77	0.90
15	−1.18	1.20	−1.92	0.80
16	−1.40	1.00	−1.55	0.90
17	−1.76	0.50	−2.71	0.50
18	−1.80	0.80	−2.27	0.70
Total	−1.204	1.09	−1.73	1.32

Table 6 *Nutritional status of the subjects based on WAZ and HAZ*

Age (years)	*Boys*		*Girls*	
	UW	*ST*	*UW*	*ST*
8	28.6	14.3	12.5	12.5
9	40.0	40.0	42.9	28.6
10	42.9	0.0	28.6	0.0
11	17.5	17.5	22.2	5.6
12	23.5	17.7	15.4	11.5
13	22.6	18.9	20.0	25.0
14	25.0	25.0	11.1	38.9
15	24.0	28.0	20.0	46.7
16	13.0	17.4	25.0	25.0
17	17.7	35.3	0.0	1.0
18	42.9	35.7	66.7	66.7
Total	24.3	22.3	21.5	25.2

Discussion

Anthropometric indicators have been widely used in population-based studies directed to nutritional evaluation. Although they are proxy indicators, that is, they represent indirect measures of undernutrition that do not take into account nutrient intake or biochemical examination, their wide use is justified due to the ease of the method and its high sensitivity to nutritional alterations in a population. Cohort studies, ideal for nutritional conditioning monitoring, suffer, in Third World countries, from the logistic difficulties usually associated with population studies of large magnitude. In such cases, cross-sectional studies can provide relevant elements for understanding the connection between health status and physical conditions of life. These studies have the advantage of relatively low costs, and they can also provide fundamental information for the implementation of health surveillance systems and the definition of long-term health intervention strategies.

Undernutrition continues to be a cause of ill-health and premature mortality among children in developing countries like India [16]. The most commonly used indicators of undernutrition among children are ST (low height-for-age) and UW (low weight-for-age). ST is an indicator of chronic undernutrition, the result of prolonged food deprivation and/or disease or illness. UW reveals low body mass relative to chronological age, which is influenced by both, a child's height and weight.

These indices are compared against an international reference population developed from anthropometric data collected in the United States by the NCHS. Children whose measurements fall below –2 z scores of the reference population median are considered undernourished, i.e., to have ST or to be UW. These indices reflect distinct biological processes, and their use is necessary for determining appropriate interventions.

The results of the present study clearly indicated that, based on WHO classification of severity malnutrition, the overall (age and sex combined) prevalence of UW was high (20–29%) while those of ST (20–29%) was medium.

It has been suggested that since undernutrition is a function of both food deprivation and disease, which are in turn the consequences of poverty, anthropometric indices can serve only as proxies for evaluating the prevalence of undernutrition among children. Efforts to reduce undernutrition, morbidity and mortality depend on reducing poverty and raising people's living standards by improving the quality of homes and by increasing access to clean drinking water and adequate sanitation. Such interventions have positive impacts on health, and implementing these also goes some way towards fulfilling people's basic human rights. Since the nutritional status of the subjects of the present study is not satisfactory, immediate nutritional intervention in the form of dietary supplementation is required.

Acknowledgements

Financial assistance [Grant Number 233(Sanc.)/ST/P/S & T/9G-4/2005] of Government of West Bengal, Department of Science and Technology (WBDST) is gratefully acknowledged. The staff of these schools as well as all the subjects are also gratefully acknowledged for their help and cooperation.

■ References

Bishnol, P., K. Sehgal and A. Kwatra 2004 "Anthropometric Measurements of Preschool Children as Effected by Socioeconomic Factors", *Asia Pac J Clin Nutr*, 13(Suppl): S132.

Blossner, M., M. deOnis and R. Uauy 2006 "Estimating stunting from underweight survey data", in K. Bose (ed.), *Culture, Ecology, Nutrition, Health and Disease*, Delhi: Kamla Raj Enterprise.

Hamill, P.V. et al. 1979 "Physical Growth: National Center for Health Statistics Percentiles", *Am J Clin Nutr*, 32: 607–29.

Kumar, S. and L. Bhawani 2005 "Managing Child Nutrition in a Drought Affected District of Rajasthan: A Case Study", *Indian J Public Health*, 49: 198–206.

Lee, R.D. and D.C. Nieman, (2003). *Nutritional Assessment*, New York: McGraw Hill.

Martorel, R., J. Rivera and H. Kaplowitz 1996 "Consequences of Stunting in Early Childhood for Adult Body Size in Guatemala", *Ann Nestle*, 48: 85–92.

Mustaphi, P. and M. Dobe 2005 "Positive Deviance: The West Bengal Experience", *Indian J Public Health*, 49: 214–17.

Nandy, S. et al. 2005 "Poverty, Child Under Nutrition and Morbidity: New Evidence from India", *Bull WHO*, 83: 210–16.

Post, C.L. and C.G. Victoria 2001 "The Low Prevalence of Weight-for-Height Deficits in Brazilian Children is Related to Body Proportions", *J Nutr*, 131: 1133–34.

Rajaram, S., T.S. Sunil and L.K. Zottarelli 2003 "Analysis of Childhood Malnutrition in Kerala and Goa", *J Biosoc Sci*, 35: 335–51.

Ray, S.K. 2005 "Action for Tackling Malnutrition: Growth Monitoring or Surveillance", *Indian J Public Health*, 49: 214–17.

Satyanarayana, K. et al. 1989 "The Adolescent Growth Spurt of Height Among Rural Indian Boys in Relation to Childhood Nutrition Background: An 18

Year Longitudinal Study", *Ann Hum Biol*, 16: 289–300.

Saxena, N., D. Nayar and U. Kapil 1997 "Prevalence of Underweight, Stunting and Wasting", *Indian Pediatr*, 34: 627–31.

Waterlow, J.C. et al. 1977 "The Prevention and Use of Height and Weight Data for Comparing the Nutritional Status of Group of Children Under the Age of 10 Year", *Bull WHO*, 55: 489–98.

World Health Organization 1995 *Physical Status: The Use and Interpretation of Anthropometry*, Technical Report Series No. 854, World Health Organization, Geneva.

Yadav, R.J. and P. Singh 1999 "Nutritional Status and Dietary Intake in Tribal Children of Bihar", *Indian Pediatr*, 36: 37–42.

10

Some biological factors associated with infant mortality among the Kol of Madhya Pradesh: A multivariate analysis

Ajay Kumar Gharami

"Children health tomorrow's wealth" is a very well-known saying. In reality, birth of a child occupies a special position in people's life and children are generally loved all over the world. Unfortunately, a large number of children die every year in our country due to various kinds of illnesses. Such child death always brings sorrow to the families.

Though, human life begins with the stage of conception, there are several antecedent and sequential factors from both endogenous and exogenous sources that affect the growth and decay of infant and children at several stages of their development. The life process is affected through preconception stages, ecology culture, family and marriage subsequently through parents, conception, pregnancy, prenatal and postnatal care, infant and child rearing practices interventions and several other developments. Apart from these factors, on a concurrent basis morbidity, natural calamity and accident either directly or through the preceding list of factors affect life. Each of these critical factors and progressive stages in life has several specific variables that may affect human development. There are also factors, which are yet to come to light but may emerge in course of time. Whatever caused factors are already known may change their influence and several new factors may come to light through further advancement in knowledge. Besides, the same variable may affect mortality differently at different stages in life and in different contexts. For instance, minimum financial resources may be required for a peasant family to support a pregnant mother but meeting the cost of delivery in a modern urban-oriented clinic may be a financial burden for the same family. This is how income may influence life, differently at different stages of its growth. Similarly, certain cultural practices are healthy but others are fatal. Further, several specific variables individually or collectively, directly or through other factors, favourably or adversely, influence life process once or on several occasions at different critical periods of human development. Hence, it was decided to select a comprehensive term called life affecting variables for explaining the numerous and diverse determinants of mortality (Mahadevan, 1986b).

India has a large population of Scheduled Tribes. They account for 8.08 per cent of the total population. They are spread far and wide, but the largest concentration is found in the central India. Attention on tribal health, however, has not been adequate. This is because of three reasons, firstly, there was a general belief that living close to nature they enjoyed an environment which is conducive to good health. Secondly, the tribals have been regarded as not very amenable to western systems of medicine as they still depend very much on supernatural cures. The third reason possibly was the difficult terrain occupied by the tribals, where it is difficult to reach health services adequately. The Kol of Satna district, Madhya Pradesh, represent a more or less the same situation.

The proposed study will emphasize on the generation of critical information required for effective planning and formulation of health care strategies among the Kol of Satna district. The investigation will lay emphasis on life affecting variables and other environmental correlates. The study addresses itself to the evaluation of health profile of infants and children prevalent diseases and health seeking behaviour etc. It has been planned that local health authorities will be closely involved in the collection of data on infant mortality, life affecting variable and screening of the affected families. The result of the study will be provided to the state and district health authorities for augmentation of preventive and promotional health care. It is expected that proposed study will find out those factors, which can solve the problem of poor health of the Kol tribe and uplift the standard of life. In short, the present study will be useful in improving the health standard of the Kol tribe of Satna district, Madhya Pradesh.

Infant mortality is used as a marker of the socio-economic development of a nation (Gubhaju et al., 1991). The same is also used as a reliable indicator of health status and well being of children. Sandhya (1991) is of the opinion that there are certain socio-cultural factors which play a more important role in determining the level of infant mortality, than such factors as public health engineering, control of certain communicable diseases such as malaria, cholera, etc. She also said that one hardly finds the details on socio-cultural and demographic characteristics of the infant deaths from secondary sources.

In another study, Pandey et al. (2001) examined the association between a few social and biological factors with the infant mortality level in Kamars, a primitive tribe of Madhya Pradesh. They found that while the biological factors like age of mother and order of birth are found highly associated with the infant mortality, the factors like type of household, main occupation and household annual income have weak association.

It is well established that many a social and biological factors are associated with survival and well being of a child. The determinants of infant mortality, however, vary between the regions, between cultural groups, and also between geographical regions of different economic status. Unfortunately, a very few anthropological studies have so far been carried out on this aspect in the state of Madhya Pradesh (Basu, 1989; Talwar, 1988; Sharma, 1999). The present study is an attempt to examine the effects of biological and other variables on infant mortality among the Kol of Satna district, Madhya Pradesh.

Materials and methods

The Kol is a Scheduled Tribe of India. They are mainly found in the Satna district of Madhya Pradesh. The study area comprised total geographical area of Satna district of Madhya Pradesh. It extends between the latitudes 23°55' and 25°11'18' North and the longitudes 80°23' and 80°23' East. For the present study data was collected from the villages of Nagod, Suhawal, Majhgawan and Uchohara blocks of Satna district, Madhya Pradesh, during the period between March and May, 2001. Information on general demographic and socio-economic variable was collected by visiting the families of these blocks. In this connection, 444 Kol women were interviewed.

The Kol are divided into several endogamous groups and each of these groups contains exogamous lineage groups. Monogamy is the most common form of marriage among them though a few cases of polygamous marriages are also noticed. Their religion is of animistic character but nowadays many of them profess Hinduism. A large section of the Kol depends on agriculture and daily wage labour for their subsistence economy.

The present investigation was conducted through interview schedule. Simultaneously, group discussion and informal interview methods were also used. The observation was made through structured-schedules and semi-participant method with the following aspects:

1. A door-to-door survey was undertaken among the Kol of Satna district of Madhya Pradesh using structure schedules;
2. To find out the causes of the death, the family data and data from public health centres were taken into consideration and
3. The deaths within 0–1 year were considered as infant deaths respectively.

Score assigned

For the purpose of bivariate as well as multivariate analysis, 20 factors were assigned independent scores which are given below:

SCORE ASSIGNED

	Variables		*01*	*02*	*03*	*04*
	DEPENDENT VARIABLES	**CODE**				
1	Infant mortality	YI	Nil	01	02	03
	INDEPENDENT VARIABLES					
Biological Variables						
1	Mother's age at marriage	XI	Upto 14 years	15–17 years	17 years & above	
2	Breast feeding duration	X2	Upto 1 year	1–2 years	2 and above	
3	Birth order	X3	1–3	4–6	7–9	10+
4	Material applied to the cord	X4	Ash	Oil	Medicated power	
5	Previous LB interval	X5	<1 year	1.1–1.6 years	1.7–2.0 years	2.1 years
6	Mother's age	X6	<20 years	21–30 years	31–40 years	41+
Other Variables						
1	Medical check-up of mother before delivery	X1	Yes	No		
2	Delivery attendant	X2	Medical person	Indigenous Dai		
3	Immunization of child	X3	Yes	No		
4	Place of delivery	X4	Home	PHC	Hospital	
5	ANM check-up	X5	No	Yes		
6	Family planning	X6	No	TT	Condom	Others

Results and discussion

1. **Infant Mortality:** The infant mortality among the studied population is shown in Table 1. Percentage of infant mortality is found to be 13.77 among the Kol, which indicates strikingly high percentage of

infant deaths. When this has been calculated in neo-natal and post-neo-natal stages, deaths in post neo-natal period (7.76 per cent) is found to be considerably higher than that of neo-natal period.

Sex differences: When infant mortality is compared between two sexes, it is found that in neo-natal period, infant deaths is considerably higher among the males (6.47) than that of the females (5.51). In post neo-natal period, a dissimilar trend is noticed in which females (8.37) are found to be major contributors than that of the males (7.19). In case of total infant deaths the females (13.88) are found with slightly higher percentage than that of the males (13.67). It reveals from the binomial test of equality of proportion that difference between the sexes is insignificant in this respect.

2. **Age at marriage**: Table 2 exhibits that infant mortality is comparatively higher among the mothers who married at an early age than that of the mothers who married at a later age. In case 18 years and above at marriage this mortality is, however, found in lowest frequency (12.36 per cent). When λ^2 test is performed it is found that there exists no significant association between age at marriage and infant mortality.
3. **Duration of breast feeding of the first child:** Table 3 shows that infant mortality is lowest (12.32 per cent) in case of 2 to 2.6 years breast feeding duration and highest (17.61 per cent) in case of 2.6–4 years birth interval. When λ^2 test is performed it is found that there exists no significant association between breast feeding duration and infant mortality.
4. **Infant mortality by birth order:** Table 4 shows that in respect of birth order and infant mortality no definite trend is noticed, which is found to be highest (23.53 per cent) in 10 and above order and lowest (10.19 per cent) in 4–6 birth order. The result of λ^2 analysis shows that there exists significant association between birth order and infant mortality. The result of λ^2 analysis shows that there exists no significant association between birth order and infant mortality.
5. **Material applied to the umbilical cord**: Table 5 shows that infant mortality is found to be lower, in case of medicated powder applied to the cord than that of the ash and oil. The number of mothers in this category, is however found to be very low. The result of λ^2 analysis shows that there exists no significant association between material applied to the umbilical cord and infant mortality.

6. **Birth interval:** Table 6 shows that infant mortality is lowest (12.95 per cent), in case of 2.1+ years birth interval and highest (17.52 per cent) in case of one year birth interval. The result of λ^2 analysis shows that there exists no significant association between birth interval and infant mortality.
7. **Medical check-up of mothers:** Table 7 shows that negative relationship exist between medical check-up of mothers before delivery and infant mortality, which is found to be higher (14.95 per cent) among the women who have not opted for medical check-up before delivery. The result of λ^2 analysis shows that there exists no significant association between medical check-up of mothers and infant mortality.
8. **Delivery care:** Table 8 exhibits that infant morality is lower (13.63 per cent) among the mothers whose babies were delivered by indigenous Dais. Side by side, a higher incidence of this mortality is noticed in case of deliveries attended by medical person. When λ^2 test is performed it is found that there exists no significant association between delivery care and infant mortality.
9. **Immunization of mothers:** Table 9 shows that a positive relationship exists between immunizations of mothers and infant mortality. Infant mortality is lower (13.71 per cent) among the women who were immunized. When λ^2 test is performed it is found that there exists no significant association between immunization of mothers and infant mortality.
10. **Place of delivery:** Table 10 shows that infant mortality is lowest (8.33 per cent) in case of the deliveries taking place at other places. However, the small number of cases in PHC and other place delivery does not permit us to draw any inference in detail in this respect.
11. **Auxiliary Nurse Midwife (ANM) check-up:** Table 11 shows that no definite relationship exists between ANM check-up and infant and child mortality. Infant mortality is found to be higher among the mothers who have not opted for auxiliary nurse midwife check-up before delivery. When λ^2 test is performed it is found that there exists no significant association between ANM check-up and infant mortality.
12. **Family planning:** Table 12 shows that there exist an inverse relationship between family planning and infant mortality which is found to be highest (14.51 per cent) among the parents who are not adopting any family planning methods.

Table 1 *Infant mortality and sex differences*

Population	*No. of mothers*	*Sex*	*No. of live births*	*Neo-natal death*		*Post neo-natal death*		*Infant death*	
				No.	*%*	*No.*	*%*	*No.*	*%*
		Male	973	63	6.47	70	7.19	133	13.67
Kol	444	Female	908	50	5.51	76	8.39	126	13.88
Total			1881	113	6.01	146	7.76	259	13.77

* Result of binomial test of equality of proportion: male vs female: T1=0.0021, T2=0.0141

* Inference: Insignificant

Table 2 *Age at marriage*

Age at marriage	*No. of mothers*	*No. of live births*	*Infant mortality*	
			No.	*%*
<12	20	127	23	18.11
13–15	365	1591	217	15.27
16–17	48	137	18	12.78
18=	11	26	01	12.36

$\lambda^2 = 3.4802 < \lambda^2$ 0.05, 3: insignificant

Table 3 *Duration of breast feeding of the first child*

Duration of breast feeding	*No. of mothers*	*No. of live births*	*Infant mortality*	
			No.	*%*
<2 years 191	724	107	14.78	
2–2.6 years	193	885	109	12.32
2.6–3 years	34	159	28	17.61
3 + years 26	113	15	13.27	

$\lambda^2 = 3.0957 < \lambda^2$ 0.05, 3: insignificant

Table 4 *Infant mortality by birth order*

Birth order	*No. of live births*	*Infant mortality*	
		No.	*%*
1–3	1095	173	15.79
4–6	589	60	10.19
7–9	180	22	12.22
10+	17	4	23.53

$\lambda^2 = 9.0147 > \lambda^2$ 0.05, 3: insignificant

Table 5 *Material applied to the umbilical cord*

Response	*No. of mothers*	*No. of live births*	*Infant mortality*	
			No.	*%*
Ash	348	1524	216	14.17
Oil	79	314	39	12.42
Medicated powder	17	73	04	9.30

$\lambda^2 = 3.9814 < \lambda^2$ 0.05, 2: insignificant

Table 6 *Birth interval*

Interval	*No. of mothers*	*No. of live births*	*Infant mortality*	
			No.	*%*
1 Year	25	97	17	17.52
1.1 to 1.6 years	101	460	61	13.36
1.7 to 2 years	185	830	117	14.09
2.1 years +	133	494	64	12.95

$\lambda^2 = 1.1889 < \lambda^2$ 0.05, 3: insignificant

Table 7 *Medical check-up for mothers*

Response	*No. of mothers*	*No. of live births*	*Infant mortality*	
			No.	*%*
Yes	312	1346	179	13.29
No	132	535	80	14.95

$\lambda^2 = .6654 < \lambda^2$ 0.05, 1: insignificant

Table 8 *Delivery attendant*

Response	*No. of mothers*	*No. of live births*	*Infant mortality*	
			No.	*%*
Indigenous	420	1789	244	13.63
Medicals	24	92	15	16.30

$\lambda^2 = .3881 < \lambda^2$ 0.05, 1: insignificant

Table 9 *Immunization of mothers*

Interval	*No. of mothers*	*No. of live births*	*Infant mortality*	
			No.	*%*
Yes	179	722	99	13.71
No	265	1159	160	13.80

$\lambda^2 = 0.0024 < \lambda^2\ 0.05, 1$: insignificant

Table 10 *Place of delivery*

Place of delivery	*No. of mothers*	*No. of live births*	*Infant mortality*	
			No.	*%*
Home	434	1851	225	13.78
PHC	06	18	03	16.67
Other places	04	12	01	8.33

$\lambda^2 = 1.2612 < \lambda^2\ 0.05, 2$: insignificant

Table 11 *Auxiliary nurse midwife (ANM) check-up*

Response	*No. of mothers*	*No. of live births*	*Infant mortality*	
			No.	*%*
Yes	396	1732	237	13.68
No	48	149	22	14.76

$\lambda^2 = 0.1021 < \lambda^2\ 0.05, 1$: insignificant

Table 12 *Family planning*

Name of family welfare devices	*No. of mothers*	*No. of live births*	*Infant mortality*	
			No.	*%*
No	393	1620	235	14.51
TT	39	197	18	9.14
Condom	05	28	03	10.71
Others	07	36	03	8.33

$\lambda^2 = 4.2535 < \lambda^2\ 0.05, 3$: insignificant

Path analysis

In order to find out the causal model to depict the relationship among different variable with infant mortality, the path analysis is performed using multiple regression equation. For this purpose, the method suggested by Wonnacott and Wonnacott (1990) is followed using SPSS the following structural equations were evolved:

Biological Variables (Path Diagram Figure No. 1)

$$Y0 = al - .036\,(X1) - .018\,(X2) - .26\,(X3) + .411\,(X4) + .106\,(X5) - .053\,(X6)$$

$$X6 = al + .007\,(X1) + .189\,(X2) - .0163\,(X3) + .496\,(X4) + .150\,(X5)$$

$$X5 = al - .079\,(X1) + .318\,(X2) - .096\,(X3) + .173\,(X4)$$

$$X4 = al - .252\,(X1) + .130\,(X2) - .080\,(X3)$$

$$X3 = al - .006\,(X1) + .162\,(X2)$$

$$X2 = al - .080\,(X1)$$

Other Variables (Path Diagram Figure No. 2)

$$Y0 = al - .068\,(X1) - .024(X2) - .004\,(X3) + .049\,(X4) + .121\,(X5) - .036\,(X6)$$

$$X6 = al + .027\,(X1) + .027\,(X2) - .052\,(X3) + .015\,(X4) + .096\,(X5)$$

$$X5 = al - .258\,(X1) + .001\,(X2) - .223\,(X3) + .032\,(X4)$$

$$X4 = al - .048\,(X1) + .111\,(X2) - .039\,(X3)$$

$$X3 = al - .394\,(X1) + .096\,(X2)$$

$$X2 = al - .080\,(X1)$$

Based on the structural equations, the direction of causal relationship between six independent variables for biological variables, five independent variables for social variables and six independent variables for other variables and one dependent variable (i.e., infant mortality) have been conceptualized and presented in path diagrams (Figs., 1&2). Further on the basis of path coefficient the results on the direct, indirect and total effect have been worked out separately for biological (Table 13) and other

Table 13 *Direct, indirect and total effect of the biological variables on infant mortality*

	Variables	*Direct effect*	*Indirect effect*	*Total effect*
X1	Mother's age at marriage	−.036	.1146	.0786
X2	Breast feeding duration	−.018	.1574	.1394
X3	Material applied in cord	−.0260	.0016	.0244
X4	Birth order	.411	.0594	.3516
X5	Birth interval	.106	−.090	.016
X6	Mother's age	.053	.2239	.1709

Table 14 *Direct, indirect and total effect of the other's variables on infant mortality*

	Variables	*Direct effect*	*Indirect effect*	*Total effect*
X1	Medical check-up of mother	−.068	−.0381	−.1061
X2	Delivery attendant	−.0240	.012	−.012
X3	Immunization of child	−.0040	.0573	0.0533
X4	Place of delivery	−.044	.0259	−.0181
X5	ANM check-up	−.1210	.0234	.0976
X6	Family planning	−.0360	−.0166	−.0194

variables (Table 14). It reveals from Table 13 that there is a positive effect of mother's age at marriage on infant mortality (+.0786). The effect of this variable is, however, found to be mostly indirect (+.1146) with negligible direct effect (−.036). The effect of breast feeding is found to be mostly indirect (+.1574) with direct effect (−.018) which is negative. The total effect of this variable is also considerable (+.1394). In case of material applied in umbilical cord the total effect is found to be negligible (±.0244) with negligible direct and indirect effects. Total effect is found to be considerably high in case of birth order (+.3516), which is highest among all the variables. Effect of this variable is, however, mostly direct (+.411) with negligible indirect effect (.0594). Though the total effect of live birth interval is negligible (+.0160) with infant mortality its direct effect is found to be high

(+.0160) than that of the indirect effect (−.090). In case of mothers' age, the total effect is found to be comparatively higher (+.1709) than that of the earlier variables. Effect variable is mostly indirect (+.2239) with negligible direct effect (+.053).

Table 14 shows that total effect of medical check-up of mothers on infant mortality (−.1057) is negative.The effect of this variable is, however, found to be direct (−.068) with negligible indirect (−.0377) effect. The effect of delivery attendant is found to be mostly indirect (+.012) with lower direct effect (−.0240). The total effect to this variable is negative (−.012).

Table 15 shows six variable correlations matrix is set out for biological variables. Material applied on the cord (r = +0.417), and mother's age (r = + 0.223) shows highest correlation with infant mortality. Other two variable live birth interval (r = + 0.195) and breast feeding duration (r = +0.076) also show a positive relationship with infant mortality. But mother's age at marriage (r = 0.152) and birth order (r = −0.076) show inverse

Table 15 *Correlation matrix of biological variables*

	Infant mortality	*Mother's age at marriage*	*Breast feeding duration*	*Birth order*	*Material applied on the cord*	*Birth interval*	*Mother's age*
	Y1	*X1*	*X2*	*X3*	*X4*	*X5*	*X6*
Y1	1.000						
X1	−.152	1.000					
X2	.076	−.084	1.000				
X3	−.076	.018	−.164	1.000			
X4	.417	−.266	.160	−.107	1.000		
X5	.195	−.155	.364	−.169	.253	1.000	
X6	.223	−.165	.332	−.172	.569	.353	1.000

relationship with infant mortality.

It appears from correlation matrix that relationship among these variables is mostly negative excepting immunization of child (+.006) in which the relationship is found to be positive with other variables (Table 16).

Table 17 is showing regression coefficient for biological variables. Birth order and live birth interval are statistically significant with infant mortality but mother's age at marriage, breast feeding duration, material applied to the cord and mother's age are not statistically significant.

Table 16 *Correlation matrix of other variables*

	Infant mortality of mother	*Medical check-up*	*Delivery attendant*	*Immunization of child*	*Place of delivery*	*ANM check-up*	*Family planning*
	Y01	*X01*	*X02*	*X03*	*X04*	*X05*	*X06*
Y01	1.000						
X01	–.0029	1.000					
X02	.020	.083	1.000				
X03	.006	.402	.129	1.000			
X04	–.038	.023	–.112	. –.34	1.000		
X05	–.097	–.348	.047	–.325	–.030	1.000	
X06	–.044	–.038	.028	.024	–.023	.088	1.000

Table 17 *Regression coefficients of biological variables*

Variables	*Regression coefficients*	*t-value*	*Inference*
Mother's age at marriage	–.036	–.803	.423
Breast feeding direction X2	–.018	–.382	.702
Material applied on the cord X3	–.026	–.584	.560
Birth order X4	.411	7.614	.001*
Birth interval X5	–106	2.182	.030*
Mother's age X6	–.053	–.941	.347

* Significant

Table 18 *Regression of other variables*

Variables	*Regression coefficients*	*t-value*	*Inference*
Medical check-up of mother X01	–.068	–1.264	.207
Delivery attendant X02	–.024	–.496	.620
Immunization of child X03	–.004	–.069	.945
Place of delivery X04	–.044	–.922	.357
ANM check-up X05	–.121	–2.329	.020
Family planning X06	–.036	–.751	.453

It reveals the regression coefficient for other variables. Only ANM check-up is statistically significant with infant mortality. However, other five variables do show insignificant relationship in this respect (Table 18).

Conclusion

It is generally believed that lower the level of socio-economic development, the higher will be the proportion of infant deaths.

Rate of infant mortality among them is found to be 139 per 1,000 live births. This is higher than Madhya Pradesh state level data (86 per 1,000 live births) and much higher than national level (70 per 1,000 live births). Type and number of determinants of infant mortality is so innumerable and diverse in nature that it is indeed difficult for a single researcher to do justice in this field. There prevails confusion regarding the nature and number of determinants of infant mortality. In the present study, a wide spectrum of determination on infant and child mortality are covered.

The present study is based on the data collected form the Kol tribe of Satna district, Madhya Pradesh. The study reveals that mothers who opted for regular medical check-up before delivery show lower number of infant deaths. Side by side, the mothers who received medical care during delivery also experienced lower infant deaths, babies with higher birth interval and medium birth order experienced lower infant deaths. This mortality is higher in cases of the babies with lower duration of breast feeding. Side by side, incidence of these deaths increase with lower ANM check-up. These observations corroborate with the findings of rate of infant mortality in the present study.

The Kol represent the first stage of demographic transition, characterizing with high level of fertility and infant mortality. It is apparent from the present findings that the Kol couples are motivated for keeping the level of fertility high in order to cope with the high level of infant mortality due to their low level of socio-economic development.

From the results of multivariate analysis it, however, reveals that type and size of family, birth order, birth interval and ANM check-up emerged as important determinants of infant mortality differentials among the Kol.

On the whole, analysis shows that cultured practices, availability and utilization of mother and child health service have strong influence on infant mortality among the Kol. The analysis indicates that effective implementation of Mother Child Health Programme is bound to reduce infant mortality among the Kol, it also reveals that more improvements in infrastructure facilities for MCH services is not enough to bring down the infant mortality in the studied population but appropriate delivery of MCH services within the easy reach of the Kol people will certainly reduce high infant mortality.

■ References

Adak, D.K. 2001 "A Study of the Phenomenon of Demographic Transition Among the Ladiya of Madhya Pradesh, India", *Anthrophologie*, XXXIX (2–3): 241–42.

Basu, S.K. 1989 "Factors Affecting Fertility and Mortality Behaviour Among Tribal Population Groups of Bastar District (Madhya Pradesh)", in B. Jena and R.N. Pati (eds), *Health and Family Welfare Services in India*, Ashish Publishing House, New Delhi.

Gubhaju, B., K. Streatfield and A. Majumdar 1991 "Socio-economic, Demographic and Environmental Determinants of Infant Mortality in Nepal", *J. Biosoc. Sci.*, 23: 425–35.

Jain, K. 2000 "Infant Mortality Rate Rising in Most States", *Times of India*, New Delhi , 5 March, 2000.

Mahadevan, K. 1986b "Mortality, Biology and Society: Analytical Framework and Conceptual Model", in K. Mahadeban et al. (eds), *Fertility and Mortality: Theory, Methodology and Empirical Issues,* Sage Publications, New Delhi, 241.

Pandey, C.D., Arvind Verma and R.S. Tiwary 2001 "Some Correlates of Infant Mortality in a Primitive Tribe of Madhya Pradesh", *Journal of South Asian Anthropologist,* 1(1), New Series, 107–20.

Sandhya, S. 1991 *Socio-economic and Cultural Correlates of Infant Mortality*, Concept Publishing Company, New Delhi.

Sharma, K.K.N. 1999 *The Khairwars*, Northern Book Centre, New Delhi.

Talwar, P.P. 1988 "Infant Mortality: Some Evidence From Rural Madhya Pradesh", in A.K. Jain and P. Visaria (eds), *Infant Mortality in India: Differential and Determinants*, Sage Publications, New Delhi.

Wonnacott, T.H. and R.J. Wonnacott 1990 *Introductory Statistics*, Wiley and Sons, New York.

11

Disability among the Scheduled Tribes: Observations for policy towards the disabled

Udita Rathi and B.V. Sharma

Disability, either physical or mental, forces the persons affected to face challenges in adjusting to normal features of life. The disabled have special needs and in order to lead a life which in no manner is less dignified than the people around them, there has to be made adequate and specific provisions. The civil society and the state have to derive at policies and programmes that will assist the disabled in leading a life of dignity and self-dependency. Herein, it is also required that the marginalised groups be recognised and be given prominence since it is they who are truly in need and ought to be specially targeted. Evaluating the census data of 2001 for disability and the Scheduled Tribes (STs) among the disabled of Andhra Pradesh, it is highlighted how the policies have failed to address the special needs of the ST disabled. The paper seeks to discuss the following issues—extent of disability among the STs (in terms of age group, sex and type of disability), educational and employment challenges, the policy of welfare for the STs and for the disabled and its consequences.

Extent of disability among the STs of Andhra Pradesh

Among the total disabled, ST disabled in AP constitute 6.6 per cent which is equal to the proportion of the ST population to the total population of AP (6.6%). Maximum disabled among the STs are seen in the age group of 0–19 years in all the types of disabilities.

The distribution of the disabled is also not even among the different types of disabilities (Table 1). The seeing disability is the highest with 45.1 per cent. Second is movement disability (31%). Hearing disability is seen as the least (5.4%) (Table 2).

Table 1 *Distribution of ST disabled by the type of disability and age group*

Age group	*Total persons*	*Seeing disabled*	*Speech disabled*	*Hearing disabled*	*Movement disabled*	*Mental disabled*
0–19	34801	11517	4855	1470	13002	3957
20–39	22895	10195	2217	847	6760	2776
40–59	17442	9352	930	1155	4696	1309
60–79	14122	8801	420	1244	3201	456
Above 80	2091	1344	57	163	479	48
Total	91351	41209	8479	4979	28138	8546

Table 2 *Distribution of disabled among STs and total disabled by the type of disability*

	Seeing	*Speech*	*Hearing*	*Movement*	*Mental*
STs disabled	45.1%	9.2%	5.4%	31%	9.3%
Total disabled	42.6%	10.1%	5.3%	30.4%	11.3%

Distribution of disabled by the type of disability among the STs when compared to the general disabled brings to notice certain differences. The difference in the case of seeing disability is quite clear between the STs disabled (45.1%) and the total disabled (42.6%). The difference could be due to malnutrition among the tribals that causes a higher number of seeing disabled. Tribals have enjoyed for centuries food diversity and ample supply of vitamin through green leafy vegetables. Since their increased contact with the urban world, processes of acculturation and policies leading to food change, there are noticed trends of disguised malnutrition which may account high seeing disability among them.

For mental disability too there are two kinds of opinions. It is presumed by some that the number of mental disabled is under-reported due to differential understanding in mental illness amongst the tribals. According to this opinion, the number should be higher than 9.3 per cent. The other opinion is that the 9.3 per cent in itself is a high number. The reasons for this are explained as pressures of change and competition with outsiders, loss of traditional livelihoods, contact change and competition, contact with urban sector leading to culture shock, breakdown of traditional set-ups, weakening kin solidarity. The tribal societies facing transition are unable to cope up with the pressures and make the required adjustments leading to more stress and mental ailments.

Table 3 *Distribution of ST disabled by age group (sex-wise)*

Age (in years)	*Persons*	*Male*	*%*	*Female*	*%*
0–19	34801	19686	56.5%	15115	43.43%
20 to 39	22895	14033	16.3%	8862	38.7%
40 to 59	17442	10285	59%	7157	41%
60 to 79	14122	7110	50.3%	7012	49.7%
Above 80	2091	1013	48.4%	1078	51.6%
Total	91351	52127	57.1%	39224	42.9%

The sex-wise distribution among the ST disabled points out the proportion of 42.9 per cent women and 57.1 per cent men (Table 3). The difference in distribution according to sex and age group brings out that more females are disabled in the age group of above 80 (males 48.4% and females 51.6%). Also it is noted that the difference between men and women is much, i.e., 14.2 per cent. This trend is especially noticed in the age group of 20–39 years where males are 61.3 per cent and females 38.7 per cent and the difference is 22.6 per cent. This raises the scope for relevant inquiries.

Variation in sex-wise distribution can also be seen in the distribution according to types of disability (Table 4). When compared to the total male and female proportion, amongst the ST disabled the female ratio is higher in almost all disabilities except movement (39.6%). We also find that in hearing the percentage of females is much more than the average (47.9%) with a difference of 5 per cent.

Table 4 *Distribution of type of disability and sex*

	Seeing	*Speech*	*Hearing*	*Movement*	*Mental*	*Total*
Male	56%	55%	52.1%	60.4%	55.6%	57.1%
Female	44%	45%	47.9%	39.6%	44.4%	42.9%

Though the gap between the male and female proportion in different types of disabilities can be explained as due to higher sex ratio in population, yet the difference in case of movement blaringly stands out. 60.4 per cent male members are found to be with movement disability and 39.6 per cent females. There is thus a gap of 20.8 per cent. More than average proportion of male members as movement disabled could be understood as due to greater exposure to occupational risks and injuries.

Educational and employment challenges for ST disabled

One of the main problems in India is poor rate of literacy. The problem is more acute in case of people living in rural areas and especially for the females. The reasons for low literacy are many, but poverty is said to be the most important one. It is important to know if the disabled face greater challenges for attainment of education. The challenges faced are different for the different categories of the disabled too. The members with seeing disability and mental disability require special institutions and facilities for educational attainments. Those suffering moving disability require educational institutions that are very easily accessible and with some special provisions.

The data about the education level among the ST disabled is unavailable in the census details which itself raises certain pertinent questions. The whole issue is neglected giving no significance to the challenges faced by the ST disabled and thus falls short to equip either the Ministry for STs or the Ministry of Social Justice and Welfare in understanding the gravity of the matter. Estimating the educational level of the ST disabled on the basis of the proportion of literates in the total population, ST literates and disabled literates, the percentage of ST disabled literates shows a huge gap. Whereas the level of literates amongst the general disabled is 32 per cent, the percentage of ST disabled literates is estimated to be around 10.3 per cent.

Table 5 *Percentage of literacy among general, ST, disabled and ST disabled*

	General Population	*ST Population*	*Disabled Population*	*ST Disabled Population**
Literates	52.4%	30.7%	32%	10.3%
Illiterates	47.6%	69.3%	68%	89.7%

*Estimated on the basis of figures available for general, ST and disabled populations.

The ST disabled with such low literacy are definitely inhibited from undertaking many employment opportunities that are offered to them, the right to education for all for a dignified life by Article 21A only remains an ideal without any real implementation. The disabled and ST population already face immense educational challenges and lack of schools in remote areas only adds to their disadvantaged situation. In the light of this it is imperative to acknowledge the lack of special schools for the disabled among the STs and its consequences on the level of literacy for them. Similarly, it is to be recognised that in areas where the parents are illiterate the first generation school goers have to struggle a lot, the situation would be much more difficult for the disabled children. The use of braille for the blind and special techniques for the spastic or mentally challenged needs first the IEC for the parents and community. There is also a specific need of vocational institutes that shall seek to train the disabled in activities or skills possible for them and at the same time not neglect the local traditions so as to equip the disabled to remain a part of their society while learning to become self-dependent.

Similar to education, the data for the employment among the ST disabled is not available in census details. Employment plays a significant role in becoming self-dependent and enhances economic as well as social well being. An estimation on the basis of data available of the proportions of working population amongst the general population, ST population and disabled population present the following (Table 6).

In case of STs, the main work is of agriculture or agricultural labour. There is very limited workforce from amongst the STs employed outside agrarian work or employed in secondary sector. Thereby, it has to be taken into account that the ST population having a higher employment rate is due to their employment in agriculture wherein the disabled cannot be employed. The figures based on estimation therefore mislead us to believe that 34.2 per cent of ST disabled are engaged in work whereas the figure would be much lower. This leaves the ST disabled completely dependent on their families and the community.

Table 6 *Percentage of main, marginal and non-workers among general, ST, disabled and ST disabled populations*

	General Population	*ST Population*	*Disabled Population*	*ST Disabled Population**
Main workers	38.1%	42.7%	29.68%	34.28%
Marginal workers	7.6%	11.1%	6.68%	10.18%
Non-workers	54.2%	46.2%	63.6%	55.6%

* Estimated on the basis of figures available for general, ST and disabled populations.

Policies of welfare for disabled

Following the guidelines at the central level, the Government of Andhra Pradesh has also established Directorate for the Welfare of Handicapped in February 1983. This department is functioning under the administrative control of the Principal Secretary, Women Development, Child Welfare and Disabled Welfare Department. A comprehensive law, namely, Persons with Disabilities (Equal Opportunities, Protection of Rights and Full Participation) Act, 1995 has been enacted and enforced in February 1996. The law deals with both prevention and promotional aspects of the rehabilitation such as education, employment and vocational training, creation of barrier-free environment, provision of rehabilitation service for persons with disabilities, institutional services and supportive social security measures.

There are various policies being undertaken. At present there are 41 (38 hostels and 3 homes) functioning in the state with a sanctioned strength of 3,700 boarders/inmates. Their education and stay is subsidised by the government. All provisions are made free or given at very low rates.

There are 10 special schools for visually disabled persons in the state but sufficient special teachers to teach these visually disabled are not available. Other provisions include pre-metric scholarships from I to VIII classes, supply of nationalised textbooks to pre-metric students, scholarships to mentally retarded children (the mentally retarded children admitted into specialised schools meant for them are sanctioned scholarship of Rs 1,000 per annum per child. This scheme is limited to such mentally retarded children as those who have been admitted into the special schools run by non-governmental organizations which do not get grant-in-aid from Government of India), junior college for hearing impaired, residential schools for disabled, tuition fees to the students studying professional courses, financial assistance to unemployed disabled, creation of corpus fund for disabled persons (government has sanctioned Rs 20 lakhs towards corpus fund for the purpose of vocational training to mentally retarded children), etc.

The policies for the disabled foremost ignore the lack of manpower, and infrastructure in the remote areas of the country and especially the tribal areas where regular schools are also not there. Only 10 special schools for the visually challenged are in any case insufficient for 5,06,651 visually challenged persons in the state. Further, most of the facilities remain distributed only in the urban sector. The very implementation of special schools in remote areas is far from reality. Secondly, there are no special provisions made for the disabled among the STs. There are no specific clauses for the ST disabled to enhance their development and encourage them towards education or skills to become self-dependent. The reservations in educational institutes and for employment for disabled is 3 per cent with 1 per cent for visually challenged, 1 per cent for hearing disabled and 1 per cent for locomotor disabled or cerebral palasy. The intake of disabled in the institutes is from amongst the general disabled population and that too from the urban sector. The benefits of the reservations do not reach the ST disabled.

"The Disability Act, which promises equal opportunities to the disabled, provides for three per cent job reservations for disabled people. However, the shadow report reveals that, for the past four years, the annual reports of the Chief Commissioner for Persons with Disabilities, the Ministry of Social Justice and Empowerment and the Ministry of Labour do not provide any information on the implementation status of the three per cent reservation in government jobs" (http://www.infochangeindia.org/Disabilities1top).

Policies of welfare for the Scheduled Tribes

The Ministry for Scheduled Tribes under their budget for education and employment have made allocations for educational institutions, residential schools, College of Teacher Education (TW), Bhadrachalam ITDA, post-metric scholarships, pre-metric scholarships, buildings for educational institutions, buildings for school complexes, establishment of ashram-type school building, Integrated Area Development Programme, schemes under Tribal Area Sub-Plan, etc. There is no fund for the ST disabled under their budget. Among the engineering trades—electrician, fitter machinist, motor vehicle mechanic, turner and wiremen and among the non-engineering trades hand composing and proofreading, printing machine operator, cutting and tailoring, and stenography are the most popular trades. These very clearly give almost no scope to the disabled to partake in vocational education (http://education.nic.in). The 6 per cent reservation for STs in government-aided institutions for education and in jobs (for Andhra Pradesh) does not percolate to the disabled amongst the STs and is utilised by the general ST population.

The problem of the ST disabled

The Scheduled Tribes are already disadvantaged and those suffering from disability are doubly so. Because of the lack of avenues, the disabled amongst STs are more dependent upon their families for their sustenance. Due to lack of special schools in these remote areas, the disabled amongst the STs are left bereft of the benefits of the policies for the disabled. Similarly, there are no vocational institutes targeted at the ST disabled which would allow them to continue to survive in their traditional set-up as self-dependent. The high number in the 0–19 age group too raises the alarming need for intervention. This group will remain a dependent category for a longer time upon those around them. Perpetual dependency on family and community gradually leads to depletion of resources for all associated. The tribals already face difficulty in managing basic sustenance for their family. Faced with disability they have to turn to moneylenders. With high interest loans they find themselves under heavy debts. The resources being spent on the disabled child would compromise with the resources that can be allocated for other children and their education and social development. This definitely impacts their growth and limits them from reaching the economic level of non-tribals around them. This in itself defeats the very purpose of the policies undertaken for the tribals and the disabled.

"Some groups among the STs are able to politically organise themselves and are able to put pressure in demanding more benefits whereas the disabled are unable to do so. All the reservations for jobs and seats in educational institutions are for the SC/ST category, because they serve as a potential vote bank. Although there are reservations for disabled people, no ministry seems to take them seriously", says Abidi (http://www.infochangeindia.org/Disabilities1top). To add to this, the ST disabled are actually the ones who are left out of the assistance made available to both the STs and the disabled.

Conclusion

There is a significant number of disabled among the ST population. They are faced with educational and employment challenges that restrict them from pursuing a life of self-dependency. There has been unequal distribution of resources with major shares reaching urban areas and others being ignored especially remote areas with considerable ST population. Along with that the policies of welfare under ST Ministry and for the disabled are found to ignore the special needs of the ST that are disabled. Being doubly disadvantaged, they should be specially targeted for the programmes yet it is this category which is completely overlooked. There is thus shifting of responsibilities in between the two departments and disabled among the STs are left to struggle to lead a life of dignity.

Reference

Census of India 2001, B Series (Economic Tables) and C Series (Socio-cultural Tables), Office of the Registrar General of India, New Delhi.

Appendix

Table 4.1 *Proportion of males and females among the seeing disabled among the ST communities*

Age groups	*ST Female*	*ST Male*
0–19	53.8%	46.2%
20–39	64%	36%
40–59	58.7%	41.3%
60–79	48.4%	51.6%
Above 80	46.8%	53.2%
Total	56%	44%

Table 4.2 *Proportion of males and females among the speech disabled in case of ST*

Age groups	*ST Female*	*ST Male*
0–19	56.2%	43.8%
20–39	54.9%	45.1%
40–59	52.2%	47.8%
60–79	47.6%	52.4%
Above 80	49.1%	50.9%
Total	55%	45%

Table 4.3 *Proportion of males and females among the hearing disabled in case of ST*

Age groups	*ST Female*	*ST Male*
0–19	59.3%	40.7%
20–39	51.8%	48.2%
40–59	49.6%	50.4%
60–79	46.7%	53.3%
Above 80	47.2%	52.8%
Total	52.1%	47.9%

Table 4.4 *Proportion of males and females among the movement disabled in case of ST*

Age groups	*ST Female*	*ST Male*
0–19	59%	41%
20–39	63.1%	36.9%
40–59	63.3%	36.7%
60–79	56.9%	43.1%
Above 80	52.8%	47.2%
Total	60.4%	39.6%

Table 4.5 *Proportion of males and females among the mentally disabled in case of ST*

Age groups	*ST Female*	*ST Male*
0–19	55.6%	44.4%
20–39	55%	45%
40–59	58.2%	41.8%
60–79	52.8%	41.8%
Above 80	52%	48%
Total	55.6%	44.4%

12

The Betta Kuruba of Karnataka: Struggle for existence

B.R. Vijayendra

The Betta Kuruba is a Scheduled Tribe of Karnataka and is mainly concentrated in the forest areas of Heggadadevanakote and Hunsur taluks of Mysore District. This area is bound on the north and the east by Hassan, and Mandya districts of Karnataka; on the south it is bound by Kannur district of Kerala and the Nilgiris and Coimbatore districts of Tamil Nadu and on the west by Madikeri district of Karnataka. The habitat of the Kadu Kuruba lies with the natural vegetation ranging from the wet evergreen to the dry deciduous, with profuse bamboo brakes and grasslands. It is rich in wildlife including tigers and leopards, bisons, elephants, deers, monkeys and a variety of birds.

Regarding human origin based on some strong evidences, Suresh Patil and Ramji Gupta (2001) reported: "History of tribes is obscure and scanty. However other hard evidences suggest that these tribes are most ancient people of this region. Evolutionary anthropologists and other authorities on human origins agree that the entire present day population on earth belongs to six lineages in Africa which grew and populated the globe since one lakh to one-and-a-half lakh years ago. Based on mitochondrial DNA and Y chromosome DNA analysis, the researchers suggest that human populations entered Indian subcontinent around 73 to 50 thousand years, and those populations were the parental populations to our many present day tribes. A large number of these tribes lived in mosquito-infested forest for hundreds of generations, if not for thousands—in fact long enough to adapt genetically to forest eco-niche. A good example of such adaptation is against malaria—a dreaded disease so widespread in the area. As such, one can see among many Indian tribal communities a 'very-high' to 'high' frequencies of haemoglobinopathies (sickle cell) and G6PD deficiency. It is not at all far fetched to say that the genetic make up and social institutions of these tribes are fine-tuned to the forest environment and forest-based livelihood. In the last fifty years they are being willy-nilly, by persuasion and sometimes by force, shifted from forest to fringe areas and have been persuaded to adopt agriculture, educate their children and participate in political affairs. It has not been a smooth affair for these tribes to give up their traditional life, followed meticulously generation after generation, and now adopt to something which they never knew, in just one or two generations. Their view of life is not conducive to carry out agriculture that requires some investment and a different skill set".

Regarding the early history of the Betta Kuruba, H.V. Nanjundayya and L.K.A. Iyer quoting the Madras Census Report 1891 write, "the Kurubas or Kurumbas are said to be the modern representative of the ancient Kurumbas or Pallavas who were once very powerful in south India; but there is very little trace left of their former greatness anywhere. In the seventh century, the power of the Pallava kings was at its zenith. It gradually declined owing to the rise of Kongu, Chola and Chalukya chiefs. The final overthrow of the Kurumba sovereignty was affected by the Chola King Adoni about the seventh or the eighth century A.D. This led to the dispersion of the Kurumbas far and wide. Many fled to the hills of Malabar, Nilgiris, Coorg, Wynad and Mysore. Thus during the long lapse of time, they have become wild and uncivilized and have owing to their comparative isolation lost their ancient culture" (1988: 68). Indeed, Kurumbas must be regarded as very old inhabitants of this land, who can contest with their Dravidian kinsmen for the priority of occupation of the soil. Whereas they have also stated that at least physically all the groups do not resemble, and some of them show similarity with some other tribes.

Besides they state based on their observation, "the assumption that the Kurubas who are found in towns and villages are of the same stock as the uncivilized jungle tribes of Kadu Kurubas, is, not withstanding the traditionary story, highly doubtful. In customs, beliefs and other vital matters, the two communities differ from one another very much" (1988: 31). Actually, the Kadu Kuruba are divided into two endogamous groups, namely, the Betta Kuruba and the Jenu Kuruba. The Census of India, while giving population figures, listed the Betta Kurubas' population under the name 'Kadu Kuruba'. This anomaly continued for decades and was not rectified. Now the Betta Kurubas identify themselves as Kadu Kuruba in order to get welfare benefits.

The word *kadu* means forest, *betta* means hill and *kuruba* is the one who tends sheep in Kannada. The term *kuruba* is somehow connected with the kadu, because they live in forest and have nothing to do with sheep rearing. Their mother tongue *kuruba basha* is an admixture of Kannada, Malayalam, Kodava and Tamil words. Their population is 63,218 (1991 census). According to the 1971 census their population was only 8,192. There was a sudden increase of 201,485 people during the decade 1971-1981 census, which could be owing to the inclusion of some other non-scheduled communities having a similar nomenclature (Singh, 1994). Again there was a sudden fall of 146,459 people of Kadu Kuruba during the decade 1981-1991 as per 1991 census (63,218). The total population of Karnataka, as per 2001 census was 52,850,562. Of this 3,463,986 were Scheduled Tribes (STs). The ST population constitutes 6.6 per cent of the state population and 4.1 per cent of the country's ST population. Forty-nine STs have been notified in Karnataka by the Scheduled Castes and Scheduled Tribes Order (Amendment) Act, 1976 and by the Act 39 of 1991. This is the second highest number, next to Orissa (64) if compared with the number of STs notified in any other states/UTs of the country.

According to H.V. Nanjundayya and L.K.A. Iyer, the Kadu Kuruba had three minor groups, namely Ane, Bevina and Kolli (1988: 69), but K.S. Singh states, "at present these groups are not identifiable" (1994: 677). The present study succeeded in finding out their social divisions and based on that the Betta Kuruba are mainly divided into two moieties, namely, aidel and Murel and each moiety has several clans. Aidel is again divided into a number of moges, i.e., clans such as Sogum moge, Admel moge, Koleer moge, Kupoose moge, Konjir moge, Jeergal moge, Yanal moge, Balkir moge, Mazal moge, Sambal moge and so on. In the same way Murel is also divided into a number of moges, such as Nimal moge, Nancy moge, Bagler moge, Kalkar moge, Jedal moge, Tholpat moge, Shilleer moge, Bonvat moge, Charkal moge, Chinkiral moge, Adser moge, Vadgal moge and so on.

The primary occupations of Kadu Kuruba are cultivation, agricultural labour and basket making. Some of them have received agricultural land from the government. They cultivate cotton and millets (ragi). Rice and ragi comprise their staple food. In the past they took part in Khedda operations to trap wild elephants, and are generally skillful at handling and riding them. The women are experts in basket-making and most of the time they are engaged in making winnowing fans and small baskets. The farmers and others utilise the baskets and winnowing fans made by them.

The area

The study was conducted in Jaganakote settlement of Heggadadevanakote situated about 34 kms from the taluk headquarters. The *haadi* is inhabited by 46 families and there are 169 persons (87 males and 82 females). The river Kapila flows at a distance of one kilometre from their habitat. Usually most of them go to this river for taking bath and washing clothes. The *haadi* is electrified but only streetlights have been provided. The primary health unit is situated about half a kilometre from the *haadi.* In addition to this, there is a well-developed hospital situated at about three kilometers and is maintained by a voluntary organization. The *haadi* is accessible by bus. Two government buses and one private bus ply in this road.

Forest and tribals are interdependent. The forest has played a significant role in shaping the social, economic, religious, political and cultural systems of tribal societies. The Betta Kuruba lived in hilly and forested areas for many years happily but nowadays they have to struggle much to survive. The problems they face are discussed under the following headings:

1. Housing
2. Malnutrition

3. Unemployment
4. Indebtedness
5. Removal of area restriction
6. Education
7. Health
8. Consumption of alcohol

Housing: In hilly and forest areas they were happily living in their huts made of mud, wood, grass, leaves, bamboos, etc. Though these huts were not strong yet they did not face any difficulties as they were capable of repairing those huts. Whereas now the government has provided them with tiled houses, which they cannot repair themselves. Further they experience the following problems:

- Leakage through roof during rainy season.
- Smoke accumulation inside the house.
- As there is no proper security for their domestic animals, they prefer to keep the animals inside their houses and they themselves sleep outside.
- They feel insecure because of poor quality of wooden reapers used for roofing.
- The houses do not have proper drainage connection.
- The windows of the houses are of very poor quality which cannot be operated. There is no other source of ventilation.
- Houses are neither repaired nor whitewashed.

Malnutrition: Hunting and food gathering represented the early stage of the economy of mankind. Human beings were dependent upon the nature particularly forest for their livelihood and survival. People are of the opinion that previously, there was no scarcity of food among food gatherers and hunters, as forest was rich in flora and fauna. They moved in search of honey, yams, edible roots, fruits and edible leaves called soppu (such as *Kirkire soppu, Agase soppu, Hongane soppu, Kumbala soppu, Mulugere soppu, Elavari soppu, Tumbe soppu, Anne soppu, Togate soppu, Kalasige soppu, Sige soppu*, etc.). However, of late, their movements in the forest have been very much restricted and hence it has become difficult for them to collect those leafy vegetables from the forest. Presently, they are depending on small agriculture or wage earning, which is not sufficient to meet the requirements of a balanced diet.

Unemployment: The areas in which they live do not provide employment round the year. In summers they get employment as firewatcher for about 30 to 45 days in a year with the daily wage of Rs 83.80. With the increasing restrictions imposed by forest department on movement and collection of forest produce, the tribes are left with a few options. One has to work for daily wages in forests or in the fields of other communities. The minimum requirement is of two adults to do agricultural work for one full cycle of cultivation on a land of two acres and more labour is required at the time of harvesting, threshing, cleaning and storing the yield. But, it is impossible for them to hire labourers during the harvesting season. In fact, the land given to them in the fringes of forest is not sufficient enough to make the family solely dependent on agriculture. When elephants and wild boars attack their fields they suffer heavy losses. During the agricultural season, they get employment as agriculture labour. Otherwise they have to migrate to Kodagu district to work as farm labourers. It is reported that wages for women is about Rs 40 to 50 and for men it is Rs 80 to 90. However, if they move out to far off places like Kodagu, where plantation requires intense labour input, they get around Rs 60 for women and Rs 80 for men as wage labour per day. Normally, the labourers stay at least for one month in plantations, and in which case they get free bus fare back to their hamlets. In case they return quickly, they themselves have to spend for the fare. They make a few such trips in a year to earn wages to support the family. The forest department has hired some of them as forest watchers, firewatchers, and so on. A few of them have been given permanent appointment.

Indebtedness: Poverty and indebtedness are interrelated. In the settlement, majority of them are indebted to the moneylenders. They take loans to perform marriages, rituals associated with festivals, worship of gods and goddesses, and death. They also take loans for treatment of diseases. They find it difficult to repay the loans and hence often they have to mortgage their lands or work as labourers for the moneylenders.

Removal of area restriction: The removal of area restriction by the government caused a setback for the actual Betta Kuruba tribe. According to the 1971 census, their population was only 8,192. There was a sudden increase of 201,485 people during the decade 1971-1981 census, which was due to the removal of area restriction and some non-scheduled communities having a similar nomenclature availed the opportunity and started claiming the Scheduled Tribe status. Thus, they derive the benefits to which they are not entitled.

Education: As far as education is concerned it is closely related to their cultural practices and economy. The children are enrolled in the schools, but they drop out owing to their poverty. They work as labourers during peak agricultural seasons. Besides, the school environment is not attractive for them as the syllabus does not reflect tribal environment, medium of instruction is not in their language and often teachers are absent.

Health: They suffer from many chronic diseases owing to poor drinking water supply and poor sanitation. Hence diarrhoea, dysentery, cholera, worms and skin diseases are the most common ailments among them. However they believe that diseases are caused by evil spirits, the spirits of the dead ancestors not being satisfied or casting of evil eye or witchcraft performed by their enemies, etc. Their medicine men have knowledge of medicinal plants, but due to the restrictions of entering inside the forest they had to give up the use of herbal medicines. On the other hand, modern treatment is not easily available to them.

Consumption of alcohol: Drinking arrack is widely prevalent among them. They have strong weakness for arrack and it makes them an easy victim of liquor peddlers. Hence, the government has taken strong steps regarding the imposing of ban on selling arrack in the surrounding areas of tribal settlements.

Conclusion

The Kadu Kuruba is a Scheduled Tribe of Karnataka. Formerly, their habitat was within the forest which was rich in wildlife as well as in vegetation and bamboo brakes. Later, they were shifted to Jaganakote where 46 tiled houses were constructed, situated in the outskirts of N. Begur village. They occupied these houses with lots of hopes of getting land with agricultural implements, etc. but they were disappointed as most of the promises were not fully met and also the National Park rules were imposed on them. People are of the opinion that they had a better life when they were living in the forest. They were dependent on forest for their livelihood. The forest not only provided food, material to build houses, fuel for cooking, but also satisfied their deep-rooted sentiments. With the increasing restrictions imposed by forest department on their movement, either they have to give up their traditional occupation of basket making or collect bamboo from the forest illegally for which they have to be ready for harsh punishment. From the survival point of view, the Betta Kurubas are struggling hard. The concerned departments have to take strong steps to save them from disintegrating.

■ References

Kurup, A.M. and B.K. Roy Burman 1961 *Jenu Kuruba and Kadu (Betta) Kuruba,* Census of India, Part V-B(i), Ethnographic Series, Manager of Publications, Delhi.

Nanjundayya H.V. and L.K.A. Iyer 1988 "Kadu Kuruba", in *The Mysore Tribes and Castes,* Vol.IV, Mittal Publications, Delhi, 68-73 and 31.

Patil, Suresh and Ramji Gupta 2001 *Cultural Dimension of Tourism: Nilgiri Biosphere Survival Strategies of the Jenu Kuruba, Betta Kuruba and Soliga of Mysore and Chamarajnagar Districts in Karnataka (India),* Unpublished report submitted to an S.I., Kolkata.

Singh, K.S. 1994 *People of India: The Scheduled Tribes,* Vol. 3, Oxford University Press, New Delhi.

Thurston, E. 1909 "Kadu Kuruba" in *Castes and Tribes of Southern India,* Government Press, Madras.

13

Impact of the *Velugu* programme and changes in lifestyle of the Yanadi tribe of Rayalaseema region of Andhra Pradesh

S.A.A. Saheb

Despite the initiation of several welfare and development progammes, wide rural–urban differences and poverty in rural areas persist. For the speedy upliftment of the rural people, the Andhra Pradesh government has launched a massive rural poverty alleviation programme popularly known by its Telugu name *Velugu*, which literally means light. The objectives of the programme are to improve and increase socio-economic opportunities for the poorest of the poor, including the tribals, to develop their capacities, organise institutions for them and support economic development activities. Eradication of child labour and promotion of female education too are part of the programme. In villages which have access to forests, biodiversity programmes have been added as well. The *Velugu* programme is funded by the World Bank and it came into effect on 18 April 2000 and is in operation in 22 districts of Andhra Pradesh.

The Yanadi tribe is one of the major tribes of Andhra Pradesh, mainly concentrated in the districts of Chittoor, Nellore and Guntur. According to 1991 census, the total Scheduled Tribes population in India is 41,99,481, which includes 21,42,817 males and 20,56,664 females, out of which the total Yanadi tribal population is 3,95,739 (9.4%), which includes 2,03,945 (9.5%) males and 1,91,794 (9.3%) females. The Yanadis who are classified as a Scheduled Tribe form 39.68 per cent of the total Scheduled Tribe population of Andhra Pradesh. It is found that 72.38 per cent of the Yanadi population lives in rural areas, while 27.62 per cent are in urban areas.

The Yanadi of Chittoor district, Andhra Pradesh inhabits the Deccan tableland characterised by rolling uplands, a few perennial streams and a wide range of temples. The present study is focused on the Yanadis who once upon a time were in the jungle and ran down the hill to plains in search of food. An attempt is made here to describe how *Velugu* programme and Self-Help Groups (SHGs) play an important role in their distribution, density in natural habitat, settlement pattern, house structure, food habits and lastly how their subsistence economy of food gathering has changed to settled agriculture. The study also would analyse the implications of these changes in their life. With this objective, two different ecological zones of the Yanadi and two different Yanadi sub-divisions were selected for the study. One was *Manchi* Yanadi who live in rural settings, and have shifted from nomadic stage to food gathering and finally to settled agriculture stage growing cash crops.The other was *Challa* Yanadi who live in urban settings, and have voluntarily accepted to change their location, occupation and have raised their social and economic status.

Ethno-history of the Yanadi

The origin of the Yanadi tribe has much etymological speculation. Thurston (1909) states that the tribe is derived from *nathu* (lord or protector) and it may see those who are not included in the ruling or principal caste. Again it has been derived from boat (*yanam*) and *adi* (means). The word would seem to be derived from the Sanskrit *anadi*, i.e., those whose origin is not traceable. The people perhaps elongated the vowel sound, so that it became Yanadi. The Yanadi speak Telugu at home and with outsiders, and use the same script, whereas their counterparts (Irular) in Tamil Nadu speak Tamil at home and with outsiders, and use the same script. They are referred to as Tamil Yanadi, Irular and Irulan. In the border areas of Andhra Pradesh and Tamil Nadu, marriages are allowed between Telugu speaking and Tamil-speaking Yanadi, whereas marital relations are not allowed with Tamil speaking Irular and Irulan.

The local social hierarchy of the Yanadi

The present paper is based on the data collected from two different locations, viz., rural and urban areas. One sub-division from each location, that is *Manchi* Yanadi (pure) and *Challa* or *Pullekula* (scavenging) Yanadi is selected. The data was collected from 200 households of the Yanadis in each location.

Table 1 *Sex-wise Yanadi population in the two ecological locations*

Name of the Yanadi sub-division	*Yanadi Population*						
	Total no of households	*Male*	*%*	*Female*	*%*	*Total*	*%*
Manchi Yanadi	200	476	49.79	392	44.75	868	47.38
Challa Yanadi	200	480	50.21	484	55.25	964	52.62
Total	400	956	100	876	100	1832	100

Table 1 shows the total Yanadi population is 1832, which has 956 males and 876 females in the present study, out of which total population of *Manchi* Yanadi is 868 (47.38%) which has 476 (49.79%) males and 392 (44.75%) females. The total population of the *Challa* Yanadi is 964 (52.62%) which has 480 (50.21%) males and 484 (55.25%) females.

The Yanadi are broadly classified into three categories, based on their ecological settings, occupation and social status, viz., *Manchi* (Pure) Yanadi, *Challa* or *Pullekula* (Scavenging) Yanadi and *Adavi* (Forest) Yanadi.

The local social hierarchy of the Yanadis is as follows:
Manchi (Pure) Yanadi
Challa/*Pullekula* (Scavenging) Yanadi

Adavi *(Forest) Yanadi*

The Yanadi strictly maintain the social hierarchy even today, in respect of marriage rules, commensal norms, occupation pattern and habitations. The Manchi Yanadi are treated as clean caste by the Hindus and allow them into their houses and appoint them as cooks and cattle caretakers.

They are called Pure Yanadi. Some of the Hindus whose family deity is *Chenchulaxmi* (Yanadi clan deity) consider the Manchi Yanadi as their priests who conduct rituals for them. They are allowed to interdine with the members of some Hindu castes. They do not accept cooked food and water from the Challa and Adavi Yanadi. They strictly avoid the connubial relations with the other two divisions, though they are economically poor and live in rural areas.

The second sub-division in the social hierarchy is Challa/Pullekula (scavenging) Yanadi, which is superior to the Adavi Yanadi, who have shifted their occupation of collection of minor forest produce to scavenging work on wages. They live amidst other populations such as *Arwamalas* (Tamil-speaking Scheduled Castes) and *Mala* and *Madiga* (Telugu-speaking Scheduled Castes). Majority of them work in the Tirumala Tirupati Devasthanam and Tirupati Municipality as scavengers. Some of them work as daily wage labourers in construction work, some others are engaged in collection of plastics and scrap iron. A few have learnt the technique of *Kaluvapani* that is cleaning of the dust for gold. Owing to their being engaged in works considered to be unclean, they are neither allowed into the Hindu castes houses nor allowed to interdine with them. Even the Manchi Yanadi avoid contacts with them and maintain a certain social distance. They accept cooked food and water from the Manchi Yanadi. But Manchi Yanadi do not accept water and food from them. They accept bride from Manchi Yanadi but Manchi Yanadi do not make matrimonial alliance with them because they eat left over meals and their profession of scavenging work. They are comparatively better in economic position than the Manchi Yanadi sub-division.

The Adavi Yanadi is placed in the bottom of the social hierarchy, who mainly live in the hills and whose means of livelihood is through collection of minor forest produce like *pandlu* (fruits), *iumpalu* (tubers), *verlu* (roots) and *tene* (honey). They hunt small games like *kundelu* (rabbit), *udumu* (lizard), *adavi gorre* (wild sheep) and *adavi kodi* (wild cock). They seldom consume rice. If they do, they make a kind of gruel called *ganji* .Often they exchange what they collect in forest for their essential commodities. They try to avoid any relations with the people of plains and even do not mix with the Manchi Yanadi and Challa Yanadi.

The subsistence economy of the Manchi Yanadi

The data on the Manchi Yanadi is collected from four villages, namely, Dodla metta, Verapareddy palem, Kalyanapuram, and Gopalakrishna puram. Dodla metta is near to Karkamabadi village, which is amidst the Sadasiva Kona Hills and linked to Tirupati town by road. It is on the way to Cuddapah and comes under the Renigunta Mandalam jurisdiction. The other three villages are about 25 kms away from Tirupati town and come under the jurisdiction of Puttur Mandalam. There is no pucca road connection to Gopalakrishnapuram village and no bus services either. There are Manchi Yanadi, Vadde, Mala and Reddy castes inhabiting the village but is dominated by Manchi Yanadis.

Table 2 shows sources of income and various occupational categories of the Manchi Yanadi of the rural location. Table 3 shows that the Manchi Yanadi are mainly dependent on agriculture. A few of them depend on the forest produce, which is collected from the Sadasivakona Hills, the abode of their economy and religious deities. 36.77 per cent of Manchi Yanadis are mainly dependent on agriculture and 0.67 per cent of them are engaged in rickshaw pulling. The rest of them depend on both primary and secondary occupations.

Table 2 *Source of income and the various occupational categories of the Manchi Yanadi of the rural location*

Primary source	*Secondary source*
Agriculture	
Rat hunting	
Snake catching	Rat hunt
Rickshaw pulling	Agricultural labour
Coolie (Agricultural labour)	
Coolie (forest labour)	Collection of firewood and selling and hunting
Collection of forest produce and selling	Agricultural labour
Collection of firewood and selling and hunting	
Honey collection	Rat hunt
Fishing Agricultural labour	

Table 3 *Sex-wise distribution of the Manchi Yanadi population and their occupational activities in the rural location*

Occupational activities	*Yanadi Population*					
	Male	*%*	*Female*	*%*	*Total*	*%*
Agriculture	79	32.78	85	1.46	164	36.77
Rat hunt	25	10.37	10	4.87	35	7.84
Snake catching	10	4.15	0	0	10	4.15
Rickshaw pulling	3	1.24	0	0	3	1.24
Coolie (agricultural labour)	29	12.83	30	14.63	59	13.22
Collection of minor forest produce and selling	30	12.45	26	12.68	56	12.55
Coolie (forest department)	17	7.05	26	12.68	43	9.64
Collection of fire wood and selling	26	10.78	15	7.31	41	9.19
Honey collection	7	2.90	9	4.39	16	3.58
Fishing	15	6.22	4	1.95	19	4.26

Training programme on sustainable biodiversity

Prior to the introduction of *Velugu*, the government used to auction the forest products to forest contractors, who made use of the services of the Manchi Yanadi, and paid them meagre wages. The contractors also used to illegally fell huge forest trees. The poor people living near the forest did so as well, but only to eke out their livelihood. The *Velugu* programme has initiated several strategies for sustainable biodiversity and conservation of forests, such as creation of awareness about conservation, extraction and marketing of minor forest produces, their economic value, visits to different places and markets where the products have great commercial possibilities, under *Velugu* programme villagers were formed into groups. Institutional support was provided to them for maintenance, collection and sale of forest produces. Manda *Velugu* training centres have been established, to impart training to the villagers for a period of 3 years, for both men and women. Every year for about 40 days, training is given to them. In this programme botanists have been appointed to provide expertise on biodiversity, conservation and better techniques for extraction of forest products in such a way that plants, trees and herbs and roots are not damaged. A bare foot botanist from the Yanadi tribe is also appointed to get trained. As a result of the training, the Yanadi are now able to preserve seeds and sow them during the rainy season.

After the *Velugu* programme came into operation, a few Manchi Yanadi were taken to different towns and cities within Andhra Pradesh and also to other neighbouring states, where there was great demand for the forest products. They were also introduced to the merchants who deal in their products. These visits helped them to get acquainted with the merchants and know the prices of each forest product in different places. As a consequence, they have realised that they had been selling the products at throw-away prices, and that they could benefit by taking the forest produce to these places where they would get better prices.

The *Velugu* programme has been providing support to the Manchi Yanadi also in the collection and sale of forest products. For instance, formerly, for each sack of 20 kg gooseberry (amla), they were getting only Rs 15. Now, they are able to sell each kg of amla for Rs 2 and wholesale merchants come to their habitations and lift the forest products by paying cash. Earlier, merchants and contractors used to deceive them while weighing the forest products. Now, the Yanadi as a group has purchased weighing scales with their savings to weigh the products correctly, so that none dare to cheat them in weight. They have even built a small hut to store and preserve collected forest products, and they are able to bargain with their customers for a fair price, as they know the actual market value of each product.

Training programme on women empowerment

The Yanadi generally fear and do not trust government official. When the community coordinator of *Velugu* assumed charge, the Manchi Yanadi ran away into the forest. However, the community coordinator endeared himself to them by cultivating friendship with the key leaders of the tribe and built up rapport with them. As a result, he became their friend and could successfully implement various programmes of *Velugu* over the last three years. The *Velugu* programme has organised two Self-Help Groups (SHGs) among the Yanadi, one for men and another for women. Under the SHGs programme, every week, each member has to save Rs 5. To date, a sum of Rs 20,000 has been saved by the two SHGs , which is indeed a great achievement. In the past, the Yanadi used to pay moneylenders an interest of Rs 5 per one hundred per month. They have now stopped borrowing from moneylenders. Instead, they borrow money only from SHGs on grounds of urgent priority needs like health, children's education and purchase of rice. Usually, they give a loan of Rs 100 to each member, which has to be repaid in 10 installments. The new loan programme arranged by the SHGs have liberated the tribals from the clutches of moneylenders and has inculcated a certain financial discipline among them.

The Manchi Yanadi women have developed habit of saving and use their meagre resources judiciously. On the social front, they have succeeded to a great extent in weaning their husbands from alcoholism.They sat along with their husbands and explained all their achievements to the research team. Now, all their children go to school. None are engaged as a child labourer which was openly done in the past. In the past, tribal children had to look after the children of their employers, mostly agriculturists and their cattle. All that has stopped. As a result of their social development, the Yanadi have started demanding more amenities, introduction and implementation of development schemes. For instance, they had sought the help of the Sarpanch to improve their roads and provide electricity and street lights in their areas. Similarly, they obtained certain man-days of work under the "food for work" programme in the drought period. Most of their demands, collectively made were granted without delay.

The main economic resources of Manchi Yanadi

Vyavasayam (Agriculture)

Many special schemes have been adopted by the State Government to persuade the food gathering Yanadis to take to plough cultivation. One of such programmes that is Chethana Scheme was undertaken by the then Tahsildar of Puttur who formed that village, which was named after him, as Gopalakrishnapuram. They have been provided with land, bullocks, bullock carts, sheep, fishing nets, seeds and borewells free of cost. The government has developed the *Porumboku bhoom*i (a piece of land over which no particular individual has any right) located at the foot of the Sadasiva

Kona Hills into irrigated land which were allotted to them on some terms and conditions but exempted them from tax. All the Yanadis in and around Gopalakrishnapuram have settled there and practice agriculture. Everybody has been granted one acre of land and electric borewells are supplied to them for irrigational purpose. Rainfall is low, borewells do not yield much water. Therefore, they mainly grow rain-fed crops like groundnuts and *ragi.* Some of them grow paddy, chillies and *resami* (mulberry). They give their land to other non-tribal people on share cropping basis.

Yata (Rat Hunt)

It is locally known as *yata* or *veta.*Yanadi spend the whole day, from dawn to dusk happily in search of field rats. Usually husband and wife go together for rat hunt. The main devices used for rat hunt are *toliki* (wooden digging stick), *kunda* (old mud pot with one small hole in the back side), *gaddi* (dried grass) and *kodavali* (sickle). *Toliki* is used to dig the rat hole. *Kunda* which has one small hole in the backside of it is filled with grass and used for making smoke. The *kodavali* is used to clean the bushes and shrubs near the rat hole. Before starting the rat hunt, the Yanadi first study the situation and position of the rat hole. They first fix the pot mouth into one end of the rat hole and on the other side they make fire (*nippu*). It takes approximately 30 minutes to smoke out the rats. They come to the mouth of the pot and die near it. They collect the rats and search paddy stored by the rats. Paddy collected from the rat hole and rats are used for self consumption and also in selling them. They get Rs 5 per rat in cash or one *seeru dhanyam* (equivalent to 1 kg of paddy) in kind. At present, the Yanadi use the *gaddapara* (iron crowbar) as digging stick instead *toliki.* There are 34 persons who mainly depend on this source of income.

Thenethiyuta (Collection of Honey)

It is a skilled performance and at the same time dangerous. It is learnt that the Yanadi are experts in honey collection that is why they are wanted by the forest department for this specific job. For their work they are paid Rs 36 per day as wage labour. Generally, the season for honey collection starts in March–April and lasts till June. There is a saying that Yanadi prefer to go for honey collection with his *bava-maridi* (wife's own brother) because they believe that the wife's brother always wishes welfare of his sister and sister's husband. *Theeneputta* (beehive) is found on the trees, bushes, gorges and ravines. Generally, they go for honey collection during full moon day. The honey is collected by the honey collector, from the bee-hive after driving away the bees through smoke. The honey is sold to the plains people, which is one of the means on supplementing their income. Generally one bottle of honey is sold for Rs 30 to the plains people. There are 16 persons who make their living through this profession.

Apart from agriculture, 59 Yanadi work on daily wages in the fields of neighbouring Hindu castes; 43 persons as forest labourers and to some extent 56 persons depend on forest produce like roots, fruits, tubers and leaves. As their settlement is nearer to the foot of the hills of Sadasivakona, they are aware of the forest medicinal herbs and shrubs. They have their own remedies for snakebite and scorpion stings. Among them there are16 experts in honey collection, 10 in snake catching and rat hunt, 3 have switched over to new avenue of rickshaw pulling and 19 continue in fishing profession.

The economic activities of the Challa Yanadi

Table 4 shows sources of income and the various occupational categories of the Challa Yanadi of the urban location. The data for the Challa Yanadi was collected from the scavengers of Tirupati urban centre. There are 48.76 per cent of Challa Yanadi who work as scavengers in Tirupati Municipality and 37.31 per cent of them in Tirupati Tirumala Devasthanams on regular basis. Barring the permanent scavengers, 20 persons are dependent on secondary sources of income. Both men and women are employed as scavengers. Challa Yanadi begin their work by 6.00 am and remain on duty till midday. They are paid monthly salary of Rs 1,000 per head. The TTD has given them free houses and provide them all facilities like electricity, borewell for drinking water and anganwadi school for their children. Though they get good income in cash, most of them are addicted to arrack on account of which their economic condition has not improved much.

There are six persons who are mainly dependent on collection of selected items of garbage. Since they live in the urban centres it is not possible for them to go to forest which is 15–20 kms away to their habitat. They collect glass pieces, iron scrap and plastics which they sell to the *gujary* (iron scrap traders) and get cash payment from them. One may get Rs 30–40 per day. Though it looks like an easy work, one has to go round each and every

Table 4 *Source of income and the various occupational categories of the Challa Yanadi of the urban location*

Primary source	*Secondary source*
Permanent scavengers (municipality)	
Permanent scavengers (TTD)	
Daily wage scavengers and working in private houses	Collection of glass pieces, plastics and iron scrap
Collection of glass pieces, plastics and iron scrap	Coolie (building works)
Kaluvapani (cleaning of gold dust)	Collection of glass pieces, plastics and iron scrap
Coolie (building works)	

Table 5 *Sex-wise distribution of the Challa Yanadi population and their occupational activities in the urban location*

Occupational activities	*Yanadi Population*					
	Male	*%*	*Female*	*%*	*Total*	*%*
Permanent scavengers (municipality)	96	48.73	99	48.29	196	48.76
Permanent scavengers (TT Devasthanam)	74	37.56	76	37.07	150	37.31
Daily wage scavengers and working in private houses	9	4.57	12	5.85	20	4.98
Collection of glass pieces, plastics nd iron scrap	4	2.03	02	0.99	6	1.48
Kaluvapani (collection of gold dust and cleaning)	6	3.05	04	1.95	10	2.49
Coolie (building workers)	8	4.06	12	5.85	20	4.98

corner of the city to collect. There are 20 persons depending on daily wage (Table 5) labour of either scavenging or building works. There are 10 persons who are mainly dependent on this work. It is also locally known as *jala kaduguta* (cleaning of the gold dust). They collect the raw material either from the goldsmith's *poyyi* (hearth) or by sweeping the goldsmith's streets. Then it is cleaned in the drainage canal water. After cleaning the dust the gold pieces are sold to the patrons only. Through this work they are able to earn Rs 25–35 per day.

Problems and propects

The sub-divisions Manchi Yanadi and Challa Yanadi though belong to the same stock, due to their location in two different ecological settings and their occupational pattern, they appear to be distinctive in their food getting techniques and economic pursuits. Manchi Yanadi though they live in the rural areas, maintain their social distance and hierarchy in respect of their traditional occupation, commensal and connubial norms with Challa Yanadi.

In the first instance Manchi Yanadi are based on forest that is on the forest produce, secondly the government has also helped them by giving free training, free irrigated lands and other livestock, etc. The influence of the plains people and the restrictions imposed by the forest department have curtailed their free movement in the forest. They have been forced to switch over from collection of forest produce to settled agriculture. In case of Challa Yanadi, their scavenging work has taken them to urban setting where they draw regular salary.

We can find a kind of symbiotic relationship among the rural Yanadi and Reddy caste regarding their activities of agriculture, coolie and rat hunt. The rural Yanadi to some extent still practise barter to obtain the items for their consumption, but all the transactions of urbanised Yanadis are purely on cash basis. Rearing of livestock is an important source for the Manchi Yanadi to supplement their economy. For the Challa Yanadi, men and women equally participate in scavenging work. The division of labour in case of the Manchi Yanadi is clearly demarcated. Men do ploughing, transportation and thrashing, whereas women do weeding, cleaning and harvesting.

If we compare the standard of living of both the Manchi and the Challa Yanadi, it is observed that the Challa Yanadi enjoy better food because of their regular income on monthly basis. The Manchi Yanadi do not have regular income and often they have to sometimes depend on forest to supplement their food requirement. Challa Yanadi have full control over their capital, whereas the Manchi Yanadi have to depend on others for money, and have no power on agricultural labourers. The economy cannot provide them that sort of security as it has been observed among the Challa, who are salary-based government or Tirumala Tirupati Devasthanam employees. Though the Manchi Yanadi are considered to be higher in social hierarchy they find it difficult to manage their livelihood.

Agricultural economy has to depend upon many factors like good knowledge of agriculture, availability of labour, supply of proper seeds, money to afford irrigation and skills in marketing products. Above all the weather has to be kind. The Yanadi are very poor, for money they have to depend on Reddy and Naidu (agricultural castes) to continue their agricultural operations. As many of them are not able to cope up with the demands of agriculture, they gave up their lands to the Reddys or Naidus on lease and on crop sharing basis. Some of them mortgage their lands for loans. Though the Yanadi have been provided with free lands and irrigational facilities they are not successful in agricultural operations. They have to compete with castes who have generations of experience in agricultural works.

Impact of *Velugu* programme

As a result of the continuous *Velugu* training progammes with the help of the botanist—the resident botanist and his colleague, the barefoot botanist—the Manchi Yanadi are able to maintain biodiversity and have managed to minimise damage to the forests. In addition, the Manchi Yanadi have put up a shed with their own savings to store and preserve forest products and lift them in huge quantities at one go to far away markets or sell them in bulk to the wholesale merchants who approach them.

Prior to the launching of the *Velugu*, the Manchi Yanadi children were never sent to school. They approached the government officials to open a school in their village. Now, all the children are attending the school. Whenever they have any problem, they meet the concerned officials and get their problems resolved. This way, they are able to get house sites, material and money to construct houses, dig borewells, and improve their lands. Their women are now emancipated. Under the aegis of *Velugu*, they attend meetings, visit different places to see the markets there. Earlier, Manchi Yanadi women were shy and their husbands never permitted them to leave their houses alone. The biodiversity programme has enhanced unity among the people and facilitated economic prosperity and conservation and development of the forest. By and large, it also has eliminated the illegal felling of trees. It has become a good source of employment to these tribals. The role of middlemen and contractors in the collection and sale of forest products has been totally eliminated.

References

Government of AP 2002 *Sarvatomukhabhivruddhi to Swarnandra Pradesh Vypu*, Hyderabad: Government Press.

Gousia Begum, S. 1986 The Yanadis: A Study in Marriage, Family and Intercommunity Linkages, Dissertation submitted to S.V. University, Tirupati, AP, (unpublished dissertation).

Pulla Reddy, A. 1984 "Ethnographic Note on the Yanadi Tribe of Andhra Pradesh", *Vanyajathi*, Vol. XXXII, Delhi: Bharatiya Adimajathi Sevak Sangh.

Pratap, D.R. n.d. *Andhra Pradesh Adimajathulu* (in Telugu), Hyderabad: Tribal Central Research and Training Institute.

Raghavaiah, V. 1962 *The Yanadi*, Delhi: Bharatiya Adimajathi Sevak Sangh.

Rameshan 1991 *Andhra Pradesh District Gazetteers*, Chittoor: The Director, Andhra Pradesh: Government Press.

Saheb, S.A.A. 1985 *Tribal Motivation and the Voting Behaviour of Yanadis*, Mysore: Anthropological Survey of India (unpublished report).

——. 1993 *Shamanism Mother Goddess Cult among the Irulas of Tamil Nadu*, Mysore: Anthropological Survey of India (unpublished report).

——. 2004 "Yanadis: Ethnographic Profile of the Scheduled Tribes", in K.S. Singh (ed.), *People of India*, Vol. 2, Tamil Nadu, Kolkata: Anthropological Survey of India.

Subramanian, V. 2002 *A Text Book in Environment Science*, New Delhi: Norosa Publishing House.

Thurston, E. 1909 *Castes and Tribes of Southern India*, Madras: Government Press.

Vasulu, T.S. 1980 *Demographic Study of a Genetic Isolate: Genetic Implications of Demography of Yanadis*, Mysore: Anthropological Survey of India (unpublished report).

14

Policies and issues in the education of Scheduled Tribes

B.V. Raviprasad

The Scheduled Tribes constitute 8.1 per cent of the Indian population which comes to 83.6 million people (2001). They are distributed all over the country but are found in majority in central, eastern and north-eastern India. Two broad types of scheduling exists for tribes, viz., area-based (fifth and sixth schedules) and community-based. Area under fifth schedule belongs to nine major states (Andhra Pradesh, Jharkhand, Gujarat, Himachal Pradesh, Maharashtra, Madhya Pradesh, Chhattisgarh, Orissa and Rajasthan) extending from Maharashtra on the west to Jharkhand in the east. The sixth schedule applies to tribal areas in the north-eastern states. More than 50 per cent of Scheduled Tribes live in parliamentary constituencies, where they form the majority. They occupy a belt stretching from Bhil region of western India through Gond districts of central India to Jharkhand and West Bengal where Mundas, Oraons and Santhals are predominant (Sundar, 2006). The community-based tribes in West Bengal, Karnataka, Tamil Nadu and Kerala are not covered by fifth schedule. All these tribes defined are on the basis of social, religious, linguistic, cultural distinctiveness and partly, on habitat and geographical isolation.

Colonialism marked a turning point in the history of tribes. Economic interests of the colonists required large-scale acquisition of natural resources, reducing tribes to positions of economic and cultural subservience to non-tribal communities. Desai (1969) classifies tribes according to various stages of cultural development which gives some broad idea of the variation:

Class I	The purest of pure groups.
Class II	Those having contact with plains.
Class III	Those in the stage of transition, mostly backward Hindus, Scheduled Tribes by name.
Class IV	Tribes who won historical battles.

Christian missionaries have done commendable job of spreading education among tribes in various parts of the country—a development which had diverse social and political consequences for the tribes, but the magnitude of Christian impact 'as a motive force to modernisation' varied between these tribal regions (Ahmad, 2003; Bara, 1997). Overall, small sections of tribal groups benefited while majority remain impoverished. In recent years, national and global business interests and capitalism have further ruined tribal way of life and their economies. Large-scale displacement of tribal families due to construction of big dams and power plants; land alienations and depletion of natural resources have pushed the tribes into economic deprivation. Those who once led a bountiful existence now struggle for basic livelihood. How these processes worked in tribal regions have been discussed in several studies (Pathy, 2000; Punalekar, 2000; Sundar, 2006). After 1990s the flow of funds for Tribal Sub-Plans declined; faulty implementation strategy further worsened, the bad situation created, since its inception in the Fifth Five-Year Plan (Sharma, 1994).

Present educational status of Scheduled Tribes

The constitutional commitments accorded priority to the welfare and development of Scheduled Tribes from the beginning of 1951. Elementary education is a priority area in the Tribal Sub-Plans from the Fifth Five-Year Plan. Education of tribal children is important, for total development of tribal communities. Education is in the concurrent list, therefore, both state and central governments have equal responsibilities in providing basic educational facilities such as schools, scholarships, books, etc. The second important development towards education of tribe came with recommendations of the National Policy on Education (NPE, 1986) which specified, among other things, the following objectives:

- Priority will be accorded to opening primary schools in tribal areas.
- There is a need to develop curricula and devise instructional material in tribal language at the initial stages with arrangements for switchover to regional languages.
- Promising ST youths will be encouraged to take up teaching in tribal areas.
- Ashram schools/residential schools will be established on a large-scale in tribal areas.
- Incentive schemes will be formulated for the Scheduled Tribes, keeping in view their special needs and lifestyle.

Schemes for Scheduled Tribe children include:

- Free education for all levels.
- Free supply of textbooks and stationary at all stages of school education.
- Free uniform for children in ashram schools and for children in government approved hostels and for children in regular schools in some states.
- Pre-metric stipends and scholarships to students at middle and high school stage.
- Girls and boys hostels for students.

Several studies were carried out which suggested remedial measures for improvement of these schemes in the initial decades after independence, however the landmark report of the Commissioner of SCs/STs of 1986–87 showed that educational progress till the mid-80s was slow and uneven (Srivastava, 1971; Kamat, 1985; Government of India, 1990, 1998; Velaskar, 1986; Chatterjee, 2000).

School participation

Enrolment, attendance and drop-out are the main criteria for understanding the magnitude of school participation of Scheduled Tribe children. Although a lot of data was generated, still the main sources are census statistics published by of the Ministry of Human Resource Development, the National Sample Survey Organisation and reports of the Commission for SCs/STs and a few existing studies (Nambissan, 2000; Sujatha, 1987, 1994, 1996, 2002; Aggarwal and Sibou, 1994; Chatterjee, 2000).

A nation-wide study of educational progress of the Scheduled Castes and Scheduled Tribes conducted, in mid-70s concluded that though a significant overall educational progress had been made (Figs. 1, 2, 3 & 4) there was still a long way to go as far as their educational progress was concerned (Chitnis, 1981). No such study was repeated in recent years. It is also evident from figures that the rural female Scheduled Tribe literacy rate has doubled since 1991 but is still the lowest at 32.4 per cent and sharp differences persist between the general population and SC/ST population in rural areas.

Figure 1 Literacy for STs in India : Trends

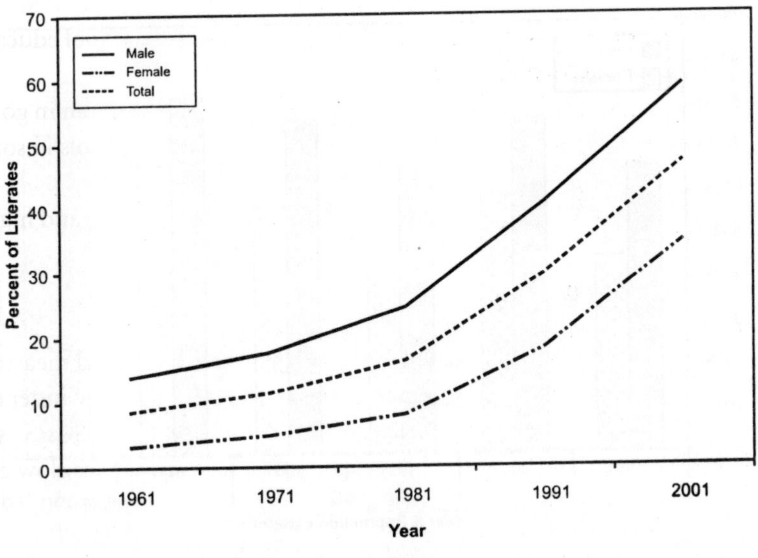

Figure 2 Literacy Gains during 1991-2001 (Rural)

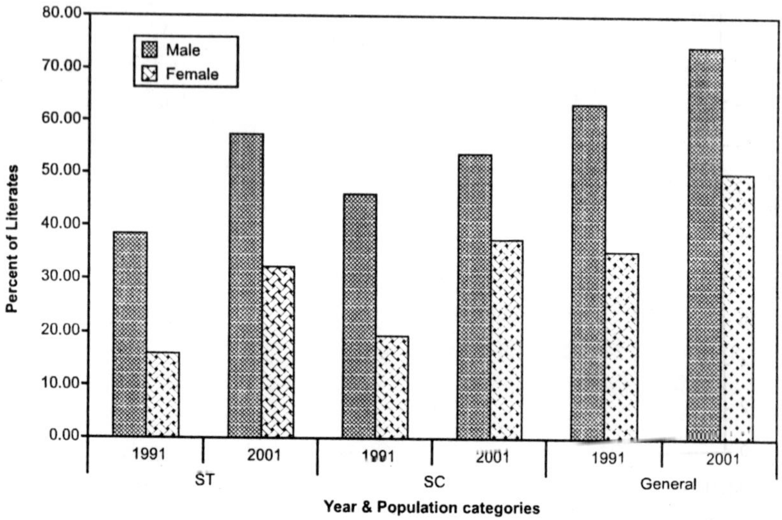

Figure 3 Literacy Gains during 1991-2001 (Urban)

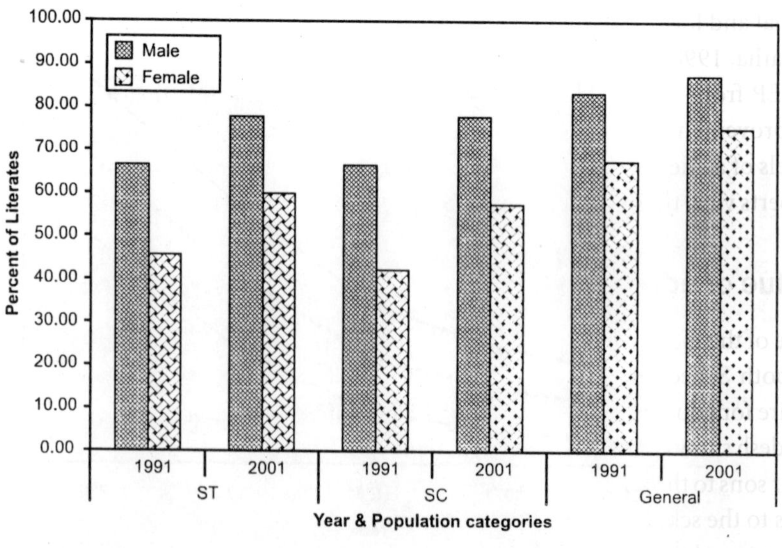

Figure 4 Enrolment of SC & ST Children

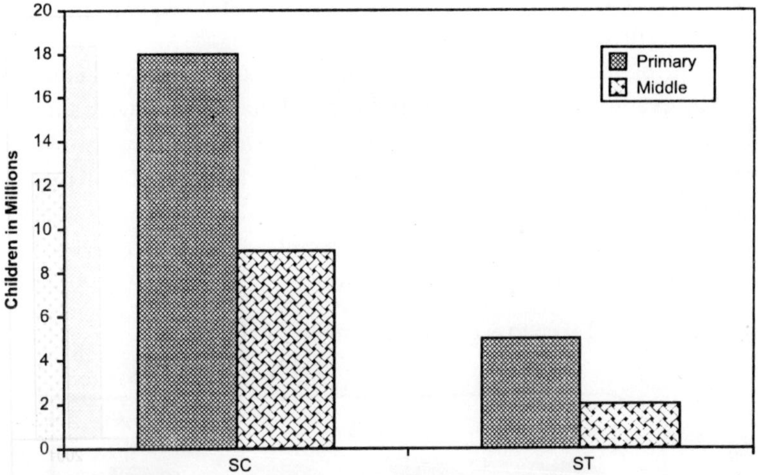

Source: MHRD 1997

Learning skills

Studies on learner achievement skills have shown that tribal students in primary classes have lower achievement compared to non-tribes. The low achievement levels were attributed to disadvantages arising out of social and location factors (Govinda and Varghese, 1993; Varghese, 1994; Sujatha, 1998; Prasad, 1993). However, baseline studies conducted under DPEP from 1993 to1998 showed slight improvement, but this marginal improvement is not sufficient to achieve educational parity in terms of levels of achievement between tribal and non-tribal students. Educational experts view this is a major concern and requires strategic intervention.

Value of education

One of the major impacts of schemes is an unprecedented rise in enrolment of both Scheduled Castes and Scheduled Tribes, which indicate a strong desire for education. However, a micro-level study among tribes in Andhra Pradesh shows that 61 per cent of parents expressed their willingness to send their sons to the school while 39 per cent of them are not willing to send their sons to the school. A total of 32 per cent of the parents expressed their likeness to send their daughters to the school and 68 per cent of them have not shown interest to send their daughters to the school (Subramanyam, 2003). In another study, Jha and Jhingran (2002) concluded that poverty and caste act as fundamental deterrents to education.

During the Eighth and Ninth Five-Year Plans, vocational education in tribal areas was further emphasised and additional grants were allocated, with a view to relating education to the world of work and allow students to imbibe proper skills, values, attitudes and dignity of labour. Of all the vocational courses introduced, agriculture and health and paramedical services had offered early employment than others and in both these courses, males and females secured employment immediately (Fig. 5).

Figure 5 Time Taken to Secure Employment After Studies

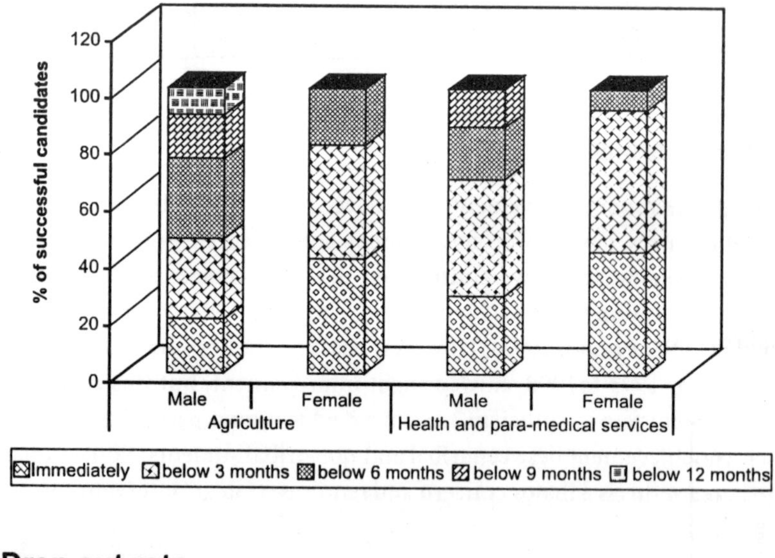

Drop-out rate

Drop-out rate, a crucial indicator in the education, needs serious concern of both general and ST students. Several schemes are implemented for retention of students in the school; still the problem persists and appears to be worst with regard to Scheduled Tribe children. Among them, the gap between general population and Scheduled Tribe students got slightly reduced, still the gap was widened between 1990–91 and 1998–99 at the secondary level, which needs immediate attention (Fig. 6).

Figure 6 Gap between STs and General Population in Drop-out rates

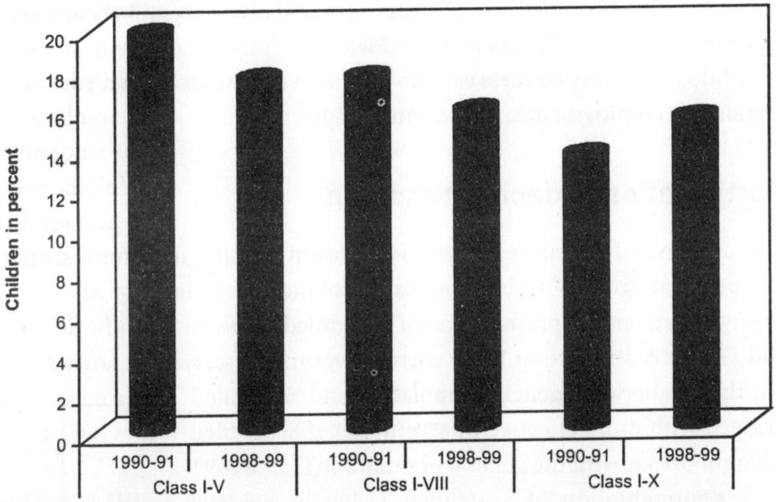

Economic status

Several employment and income generating programmes have been introduced among Scheduled Tribes to alleviate their poverty. It has been observed that such programmes have raised a large number of Scheduled Tribe fami-

Figure 7 Gap between ST & General in Population Living Below Poverty Line

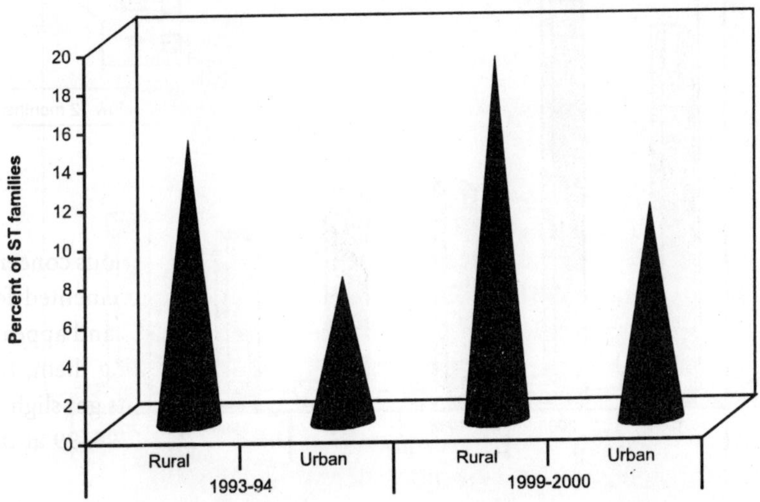

lies above the poverty line and there is a declining trend (Fig. 7). However, the rate of decline in not much appreciable and also the gap between general population and ST has increased which is because a large number of Scheduled Tribes are landless with no productive assets and with no access to sustainable employment and minimum wages.

Participation in decision-making

Participation of Scheduled Tribes in decision-making in administration and political institutions is an indication of the rise of status of Scheduled Tribes. The overall representation of Scheduled Tribes in All India Services and Group A and Group B in central government services is fairly good, but the gap between general population and Scheduled Tribes need to be bridged with more effective interventions, if Scheduled Tribes have to be brought on par with the general population(Figs. 8 & 9).

Representation of Scheduled Tribes in political decision-making institutions is also found quite impressive as they hold seats more than their due share, except in Panchayat Samitis (Figs. 10 & 11).

Figure 8 Participation in Decision-making : Administration

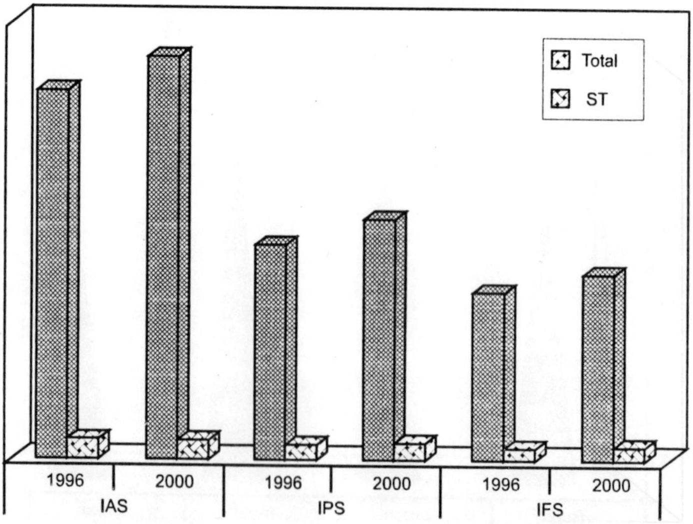

Figure 9 Participation in Decision-making: Administration

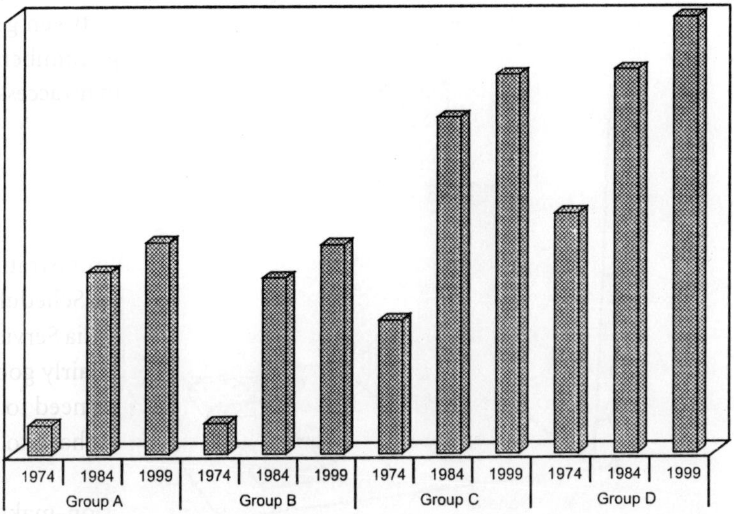

Figure 10 Participation in Decision-making : Political

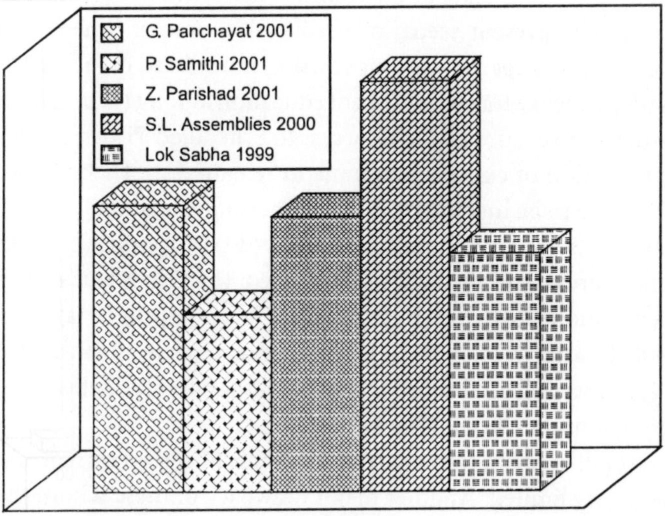

Figure 11 Participation in Decision-making: Political

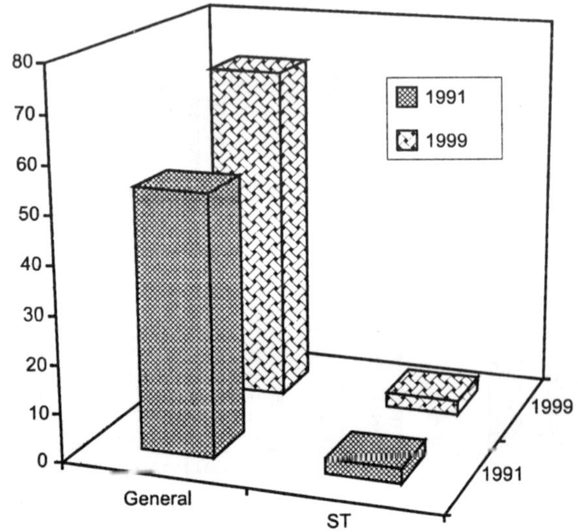

Discussion

There are 16 million Scheduled Tribe children (10.87 million in 6–11 years and 5.12 million in 11–14 years), out of the 193 million children in the age group of 6 to 14 years in the country (Selected Educational Statistics, 2000–01). The present scenario of education among Scheduled Tribes reveal a positive impact of various schemes introduced in the past 60 years after independence for promotion of education among them. The country still struggles to ensure equitable access to Scheduled Tribes; still a significant proportion of children continue to remain out of school; drop-out rate continue to be high; there is unevenness in educational participation of states; girls are far behind boys; sharp disparities exist between rural and urban areas; specific regions and Scheduled Tribes face extreme and gross educational deprivation; Scheduled Tribes appear to lag behind the Scheduled Castes in most of the larger states except the north-east.

It is now well established that expenditure per student is found to be highest in ashram schools (Fig. 12).

Overall contribution of ashram schools to spread formal education has been very limited. Another major drawback of these schools has been that 'girls did not join ashram schools because of their cultural traditions'.

Figure 12 Per-student Expenditure (in rupees)

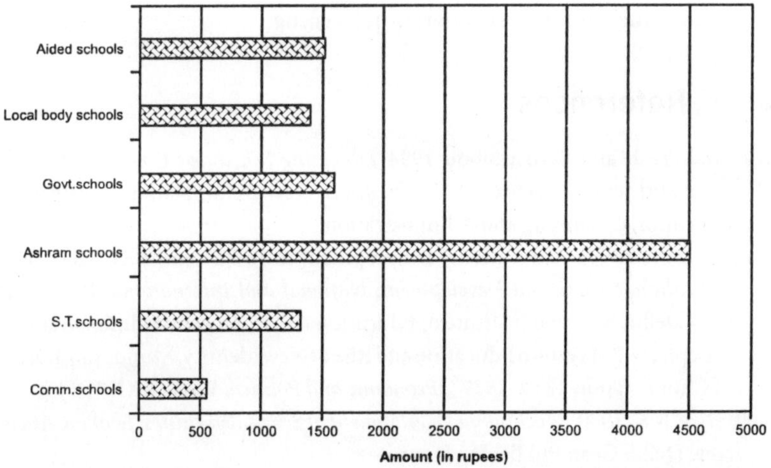

In order to improve literacy among Scheduled Tribe girls, another scheme, i.e., educational complexes was introduced in 1993–94 in those districts in the country which were having less than 10 per cent female literacy (accordingly,134 districts in 14 states were identified for implementing the scheme with full financial support from Ministry of Tribal Affairs). Majority of educational complexes (85%) are run by NGOs—a new player in the field of tribal education. An evaluation study of 27 educational complexes situated in Orissa (12); Andhra Pradesh (8); Madhya Pradesh (4); and Rajasthan (3) states reveals that (a) logistic facilities are inadequate, (b) non-coverage of Primitive Tribal Groups, (c) human resource support is also inadequate, and (d) majority (69%) are located very close to another school (which is against the norm that educational complexes may be established in those districts wherein formal schools does not exist).

In the last two decades, as the running cost of schools are increasing alarmingly, several states are planning to withdraw education from social sectors and delegate its social commitments and responsibilities to private agencies and NGOs. The ideology of the Indian New Economic Policy emphasises the pre-eminence of markets and profits. There is already enough indication that basic educational needs of the Scheduled Castes and Scheduled Tribes are getting seriously undermined under the new dispensation adversely affecting life chances of vast sections of those who have yet to make the shift to first generation learning.

References

Aggarwal, Yash and Sarika Sibou 1994 *Educating Scheduled Castes: A Study of Inter District and Inter Caste Differentials,* New Delhi: National Institute of Educational Planning and Administration.

Ahmad, Imtiaz 2003 "Educational Development in India", in J.B.G. Tilak (ed.), *Education, Society and Development: National and International Perspective,* New Delhi: National Institute of Educational Planning and Administration.

Bara, Joseph 1997 "Western Education and Rise of New Identity, Mundas and Oraon of Chotanagpur, 1839–1939", *Economic and Political Weekly,* XXXII(15).

Chatterjee, S.K. 2000 *Educational Development of Scheduled Castes: Looking Ahead,* New Delhi: Gyan Publishing House.

Chitnis, Suma 1981 *A Long Way to Go,* Bombay: Allied Publishers Private Ltd.

Desai, A.R. 1969 *Rural Sociology in India,* Bombay: Popular Prakashan.

Jha, Jyotsna and Dhir Jhingran 2002 *Elementary Education for the Poorest and Other Deprived Groups: The Real Challenge of Universalisation,* New Delhi: Centre for Policy Research.

Govinda, R and N.V. Varghese 1993 *Quality of Primary Schooling in India: A Case Study of Madhya Pradesh,* Paris: UNESCO International Institute for Educational Planning.

Govt. of India 1990 *The Report of the Commissioner for Scheduled Castes and Scheduled Tribes,* Twenty-ninth Report 1987–89, New Delhi: Govt. of India.

——. 1998 *National Commission for Scheduled Castes and Scheduled Tribes,* Fourth Report (1996–97 & 1997–98, Vol. I), New Delhi: Govt. of India.

Kamat, A.R. 1985 *Education and Social Change in India,* Bombay: Somaiya Publications.

Nambissan, Geetha B. 2000 "Identity, Exclusion and the Education of Tribal Communities", in Rekha Wazir (ed.), *Gender Gaps in Literacy and Education,* New Delhi: Sage Publications.

Pathy, J. 2000 "The End of Millennium: Liberalisation and Accentuation of the Tribal Problematique", in P.G. Jogdand (ed.), *New Economy, Policy and Dalits,* Jaipur: Rawat Publications.

Planning Commission, India 2007 *Scheme of Setting up Educational Complexes in Low Literacy Pockets for the Development of Women's Literacy* (Report), New Delhi.

Punalekar, S.P. 2000 "New Economic Policy and Tribal Reality: A Case of Gujarat", in P.G. Jogdand (ed.), op. cit.

Prasad, B.V.R. 1993 "Education, Economy and Employment: A Case Study of Chowra Island", *Vanyajati*, XLI(3): 19–21.

Sharma, B.D. 1994 *Dalits Betrayed*, New Delhi: Har-Anand Publications.

Srivastava, L.R.N. 1971 *Identification of Educational Problems of Saora of Orissa*, New Delhi: National Council of Educational Research and Training.

——. 1971 *Utilisation of Financial Assistance by Tribal Students*, New Delhi: National Council of Educational Research and Training.

——. 1971 *An Evaluative Study of Pre-metric Scholarship Scheme for SC and ST Students*, New Delhi: National Council of Educational Research and Training.

Subramanyam, V. 2003 "Role of Government for the Enhancement of Education Status among Tribes in the Integrated Tribal Development Agency Area of Paderu", *Study of Tribes and Tribals*, 1(2): 155–61.

Sundar, Nadini 2006 "Tribal Politics", in Stanley Wolpert (ed.), *Encyclopedia India*, New York: Charles Scribner's Sons.

Sujatha, K. 1987 *Education of the Forgotten Children of the Forests: A Case Study of Yennadi Tribe*, New Delhi: Konark Publications.

——. 1994 *Educational Development Among Tribes: A Study of Sub-plan Areas in Andhra Pradesh*, New Delhi: South Asian Publishers.

——. 1996 *Single Teacher-schools in Tribal Areas: A Study of Girijan Vidya Vikas Kendras in Andhra Pradesh*, New Delhi: Vikas Publishing House.

——. 1998 *Evaluation of Quality Improvement Programmes in Education: A Study in Tribal Areas of Visakhapatnam, Andhra Pradesh*, New Delhi: National Institute of Educational Planning and Administration.

——. 2002 "Education among Scheduled Tribes", in R. Govinda (ed.), *India Education Report: A Profile of Basic Education*, New Delhi: Oxford University Press.

Varghese, N.V. 1994 *School Quality and Students Learning: A Study of Primary Schooling in Kerala*, DPEP Baseline Study. New Delhi: National Institute of Educational Planning and Administration.

Velaskar, Padma 1986 Inequality in Higher Education: A Study of SC Students in Medical Colleges of Bombay (Unpublished Ph.D Thesis), Mumbai: Tata Institute of Social Sciences.

——. 1992 "Unequal Schooling as a Factor in the Reproduction of Social Inequality in India", *Sociological Bulletin*, 39 (1 & 2).

15

Medical pluralism and mainstreaming AYUSH: An anthropological analysis of health policy

P. Kalyan Reddy

Policy has become an increasingly central organising principle in the contemporary society. It is now impinging on almost all the aspects of human life which made us practically impossible to escape its shade of influence from womb to tomb. The capacity to stimulate and channel activity derives largely from the objectification of policy, through which policies acquire seemingly tangible existence and legitimacy. As Thomas Dye (1976) stated, public policy is "whatever governments choose to do or not do".

Yekezkhel Dror, the Father of Public Analysis, has advocated that policy makers should combine proven methods of systems analysis with qualitative methods and should have full awareness of special characteristics of political phenomena. This statement gives an anthropological gaze to the policy. As a cultural agent of change, policies are shaping the way we live, act and think. People are classified, shaped and ordered according to the policies but they have little consciousness of or control over the process at work. The study of policy, therefore, lead straight into the issues at the heart of anthropology, norms and institutions, ideology and consciousness, knowledge and power, rhetoric and discourse, meaning and interpretation, the global and the local, etc. (Wright and Shore, 1997). New public administration emphasising social justice and human dignity as the values of this century is particularly receptive to the participation of anthropologists (Fiske, 1979).

In this era of democratisation and universal recognition of human rights, public policy has became the prime duty of legislators and it has become their compulsion to see that a just and equitable policy is framed, focusing on increasing coverage of developmental goals. It is in this context that international bodies like UNO and WHO have codified Millennium Development Goals (MDGs), mostly related to health and education, aimed to be achieved by their member countries in a prescribed time. Health is often cited as one of the social dimensions of poverty. Good health enables each person to lead the kind of life he or she has a reason to value and capacitates to achieve true development (Sen, 2001).

Health planning is the process of estimating the number of persons and the kind of knowledge, skills and attitudes they need to achieve pre-determined health targets and ultimately health objectives. Such planning also involves specifying who is doing what, when, where, how and with what resources for what population group or individuals so that the knowledge and skills necessary for adequate performance can be available according to predetermined policies and time schedule (Hall and Meija, 1978).

The Department of Indian Systems of Medicine and Homoeopathy (ISM&H) was established in Ministry of Health and Family Welfare in March 2005 to look into the issues of dissemination of medical knowledge pertaining to these systems of medicine, delivery of services and quality management. The department was recently named as AYUSH which linguistically mean long live and the term has cultural significance in Indian rituals and blessings from well wishers. It has been actively involved in the establishment of Traditional Knowledge Digital Library (TKDL) with the cooperation of NISCAIR, Department of Science and Technology to digitise the knowledge of pharmacoepia of medical plants and herbs used in the ancient Indian medical texts of Ayurveda, Unani and Siddha. TKDL is an original proprietary database that is fully protected under national and international laws of intellectual property rights (AYUSH Newsletter, 2005). A research project called Golden Triangle Project was initiated by AYUSH in collaboration with Council for Scientific and Industrial Research (CSIR) and Indian Council of Medical Research (ICMR) for standardisation of Ayurvedic and Unani formulations and clinical trails respectively. A few Ayurvedic and Unani drugs are already inducted into reproductive and child health care programmes and kit of accredited social health activist—ASHA (India Year Book, 2007).

We have an excellent and outstanding tribal heritage in India. Each of our tribal community in India has distinct cultural knowledge of ethno-medical practices. It has already been proved beyond doubt that if sincere attempts were made much of such valuable knowledge could be brought into the use for society. The knowledge could be codified along with the medical texts of great tradition, i.e., Ayurveda, Unani, etc. At the 2002 UN sponsored world summit on sustainable development, also known as Earth Summit in Johannesburg, South Africa, the UN's first annual equator initiative prize was awarded to Kerala tribal ethnomedicine project run by *Kani* tribal people living in southern Western Ghats. By this, India has pioneered one of the first models of benefit sharing between national government and tribal people living in its boundaries (Mueller and Kani, 2004).

Why it needs to be integrated or brought into mainstream?

1. Dearth of health care professionals: It is very much clear that there are large inequalities in health care services. Many scholars have outlined that the only panacea for this is to expedite the solution through the locally existing health care resources. In this respect, the role of traditional systems of medicine is viewed as vital element as part of wholesome health package for Third World countries (Phillips, 1990). In rural India, public health services are provided through a network of integrated health and family welfare delivery system. As in 2004, an extensive network of 3,222 community health centres, 23,109 primary health centres and 1,42,655 sub-centres were in existence to provide primary health care at grassroots level (India Year Book, 2006), but most of them are having poor infrastructure and vacant posts of medical officers which along with high absenteeism are affecting the rural health care (Varatharajan, 2004).

Proper resource allocation also means equipping the first referral levels with necessary supplied, equipment and personnel, but it is a great problem in developing countries like India to establish and strengthen a strong referral network of biomedicine as about 75 per cent of health infrastructure, medical manpower and other health resources are concentrated in urban areas where 27 per cent of the population live and governments too are unable to coerce them to serve with meager salaries (Somasundaram et al., 2002; Wright and Walley, 1998).

Human resources are in very short supply in health systems in low and middle income countries compared with high income countries or with the skill requirements of a minimum package of health interventions. Equally serious concerns exist about the quality and productivity of the health workforce in low income countries (Hongoro and McPake, 2004). Studies in India focused on unnecessary health damage by traditional as well as allopathic providers concluding that unqualified allopaths often create more health hazards than their traditional counterparts (Ashraf et al., 1982).

Evidences are suggesting that there is a faulty skill mix in health care systems all over the world (Buchan and Dal Poz, 2002). So in order to rectify it is very much essential to review and perhaps to readjust with a sustained change in the system which is only possible with the induction of traditional health care services.

*2. **Patient-centred communication***: The programmes which sought to spread the benefits of western medicine to the Third World, were met with widespread non-compliance on the target populations (Leslie, 2001). The preference for folk or other traditional forms of healthcare over modern medicalcare is partly due to lesser social distance to the former (Kroeger and Franken, 1981).

Healing or treatment has two different functions: Control of sickness and producing meaning for person's experience of sickness. Modern health care performs only first function but folk and traditional health care both. In other words, modern health care can treat a problem effectively, whereas folk and traditional health care not only treats a problem but also offers a satisfying and culturally meaningful interpretation of illness. Thus, in spite of their effectiveness and curative power, modern health care services are not used widely (Gesler, 1984). The "lay therapy management group" consisting of kinsfolk, friends, associates and specialised practitioners are all well coordinated facilitating the quick mechanisms for treatment (Janzen, 1978). This highlights that alienation of medical culture from the wholesome understanding of the society will bring in imbalances and ultimately lead to misinterpretation of health care phenomena.

These systems of medicine help practitioners provide care that is in concordant with the patient values, needs and preferences and that allows patient to provide input and participate actively in decisions regarding their health and health care which ultimately lead to high quality health care (Epstein et al., 2005). It facilitates incorporating patients subjective experience of disease into clinical practice which is an essential element of good medicine (Laine and Davidoff, 1996).

3. Success strategies worldwide: The distinction between traditional and modern "opposes the changing and creative nature 2001 of modernity to an assumed stagnant and unchanging traditonalism" (Leslie, 1976). The medical institutions labelled "traditional" have undergone considerable change in the last century, far from being wholly conservative; practitioners of traditional and folk medicine have shown increasing interest in the acquisition of new skills and use of certain modern treatments and technologies in their work. Many health providers are incorporating elements of both traditional and modern medical practices into their healing methods (Cosminsky and Scrimshaw, 1980; Lock, 1980) blurring the distinction significantly. Such a syncretism approach has increasingly been delivered in the contemporary world. In essence biomedicine and traditional medicine, despite antagonistic relations between them, exhibit a great deal of overlap and even fusion.

Kanpo clinic in modern Japan is a case where *kanpo* doctors who are MD's combine biomedicine and East-Asian medicine. They tend to treat psychosomatic ailments by dietary advice based on classical theories of balancing Yin and Yang food (Lock, 1980). The same is the case with "*comadrona*" (traditional midwife) in Guatemala (Cosminsky and Scrimshaw, 1980). Her technique is not so much traditional or modern as it is the union of both the approaches; for a typical delivery she cauterises the umbilical cord with the candle flame, a traditional practice, yet afterwards she immediately applies alcohol and talcum powder, as she was taught in her modern training course. Such instances are also found in Brazil by encompassing modern science on the one hand, and aspects of the Afro-Brazilian traditions on the other (Greenfield, 1992). Alternative practitioners in *paraiso* area of California in US often exhibit therapeutic eclectism and combine different therapies depending upon the needs and desires of their clients like yoga, Alexander technique, reflexology and zone therapy (English–Lueck, 1990). There is a significant overlap between therapeutic approaches and drawing from a variety of modalities enhances the therapeutic armamentarium when working with the aged in dealing with social phobias and depression (Benzamin et al., 1987). All these cases represent successful therapeutic alliance wherever feasible.

A field of this sort of humanistic, holistic and integrative medicine needs to be upgraded in India also. A health care system that could do that successfully would bring quality of life and new ability of functioning to many people.

***4. Public choice approach*:** Nobel laureate Kenneth arrow's path breaking work, *Social Choices and Individual Values* in 1951, gave rise to a large literature examining the aggregation of individual preferences to maximise a defined set of normative criteria. Every human being tries to maximise his goals within the given number of choices and this is equally applicable to health care scenario. It all matters how well a health problem is dealt by a system of medicine, the efficacy determines its competence in the market.

In the last two decades, the whole gamma of complimentary and alternative approaches to health care has developed gaining more and more recognition. Some will go to the extreme indicating alternative medicine as the culprit in poor health outcomes, others completely deny the usefulness of biomedicine, while a third group utilises the best available methods (Ventegodt et al., 2005). People see alternative treatments offering more personal autonomy and control over health care decisions (Astin, 1998). The attraction of alternative medicine is related to power of its underlying shared beliefs and cultural assumption. The fundamental premises are on the advocacy of nature, vitalism, science and spirituality. These themes offer patients a participatory experience of empowerment, authenticity and enlarged self-identity when illness threatens their sense of intactness and connection with the world (Kaptchuk et al., 1998).

Individuals seeking care for illness are usually pragmatic, they turn to different health care systems according to their subjective assessment of problem and most suitable type of help (Leeson, 1974). In Warangal district of Andhra Pradesh, people pragmatically resort to particular systems of medicine for particular types of health problems, for example, they turn towards homoeopathy for warts and to ayurveda for piles. These medicines have become so popular that even super specialised allopathic practitioners are prescribing medications like *tuja* (homoeopathic medication for warts) and *pylon* [(ayurvedic medication for piles), (feedback from my own field work)]. As Crandon-Malamud (1991) observes all things being equal among *kuchitunas*, if one has TB one goes to the physician in a methodist clinic; if one suffers from *khan achachi* (sickness stemming from phantom) one goes to the *yatiri*, if one has upset stomach one resorts to medicine as *caseras* (home care).

*5. **Medicalisation of nature:*** Yet another aspect, although not directly linked to the health, is that many of the alternative therapies use natural compounds for treatment in contrast to the mass produced synthetic compounds of modern medicine. Alternative and holistic health movement has indirectly made people and governments too concerned about environment and biodiversity since the naturally available flora and fauna are used in medications from times immemorial. Biodiversity is the biological capital of our planet and it forms the foundation upon which human civilisation is built. The biodiversity and associated indigenous knowledge systems are two invaluable capital assets of a country like India. Tribal people who traditionally have been parts of forest ecosystems can play valuable roles in helping and maintaining such systems today.

While environmental determinism was on the wane at the beginning of the 20th century, the idea that nature and health are intricately linked has remained. The theories regarding the symbiotic relationship between the environment and health were pursued by a wide range of individuals including historians, geographers, medical physicians (Arnold, 1996). Closely associated with them is Wilson's (1984) *biophilia* hypothesis, the idea that people feel innate connectedness with the natural environment has sought to explain how contact with and appreciation of nature, contributes to a person's health and well-being. Some scholars even suggested that simple contact with nature has a restorative effect (Kaplan and Kaplan, 1989).

In a landmark paper on therapeutic landscapes, Gesler (1992: 736) identified some of the ways in which health and well-being have come to be associated with natural environment, whether this entails materials such as medicinal plants, fresh air and pure water of countryside or magnificent scenery. Contact with nature "affords a range of personal, social and health benefits" (Milligan et al., 2004). In the context of new public health, it helps us to make sense of discourse that appeals universally to valorise nature as an antidote to the stresses and strains of modern life (Brown and Brown, 2007).

India is a home to some of world's very few biodiversity hotspots, abundant with unique medicinal herbs having tremendous economic importance. These species of flora in UNESCOs world heritage sites can be saved from being entered into endangered red data list with active participation of tribals as in the case of *Kani* tribal ethnomedicine project of Kerala. Such programmes could be extended to other tribal areas too involving them in cultivation of plants of ethno-medical importance and protecting the rich biodiversity of India and at the same time reaping the potential economic benefits by earning considerable amount of foreign exchange as in the case of China which has capitalised its traditional Chinese herbal medicine by globalising and being competitive to western systems of medicine (Patwardhan et al., 2005). With these advantages in mind we shall venture into some of the approaches that proved fruitful elsewhere in the integration of traditional systems of medicine among themselves and with biomedicine in totality.

An approach to mainstream AYUSH systems of medicine

It starts with the estimation of human resources for health planning which could be a mix of the following methods (O' Brien-Pallas et al., 2001):

Method	*Description*	*Applicability to mainstream AYUSH systems of medicine*
Needs based	Projects age and gender specific service needs based on service norms and health seeking behaviour.	Estimating age and gender specific utilisation of AYUSH systems of medicine.
Utilisation based (demand based)	Estimates future requirement based on current level of service utilisation in relation to future projections of demographic profiles.	Estimating illness specific health seeking behaviours and evaluating hierarchy of resorts.

Health workforce to population ratio	Specifies desired personnel to population ratio.	Estimating the percentage of populations resorting to. AYUSH systems of medicine across different geographical regions and communities. Referrals at each level of localities and region.
Adjusted service target approach	Identifies service needs based on epidemiological and demographic profile and programmatic targets. Estimates time requirements for each intervention, based on time motion studies or expert opinion.	Continuous monitoring of the coverage and efficacy of AYUSH systems of medicine, through patient flow analysis of making effective evidence based interventions.

After the estimation of required human resources for health care, the partnership amongst them needs to be focused. Some see these partnerships as a new form of international social capital (Reich, 2000). It is aimed at creating mutually advantageous relationship which is made to be transparent, accountable with common principles of understanding, respect, trust and dignity.

Given that health promotion impact is proportional to the level of community involvement (Gillies, 1998), local community's values and perceptions towards plural medical systems are vital to the success. Partnerships for health promotion may usefully be seen to range on a continuum from networking to collaboration (Vichealth, 2004). This continuum is based on commitment, change required, risk involved and levels of interdependence, power, trust and willingness to share turf.

Issues that need attention

1. Limited knowledge of the health labour force

Accurate information of health work force is of crucial importance to health

Continuum step/stage	*Description*	*Context of mainstreaming AYUSH*
Networking	Exchange of information for mutual benefit.	Surveillance of existing epidemiological and morbidity patterns and sharing of such information.
Coordinating	Exchanging information and altering activities for a common purpose	Establishing clear lines of communication among AYUSH practitioners and between allopathic physicians.
Cooperating	Exchanging information, altering activities and sharing resources .	Strengthening referrals between and amongst AYUSH practitioners and biomedical practitioners.
Collaborating	Exchanging information altering activities, sharing resources and enhancing the capacity of other partner of mutual benefit and common purpose.	Sustainable bonding among AYUSH practitioners and with biomedical practitioners for holistic and integrative medical system.

planners and policy makers worldwide. This is because careful, informed decision-making is necessary to achieve the right balance between the supply of labour and population's health demands. Insufficient or incurable information about health labour force, for example, on the number, distribution, qualification, public/private sector employment, staff mix, age, sex, experience, etc., when combined with efforts to reduce health care spending and increase efficiency, can lead to provider shortfall or surpluses, i.e., imbalance in health care delivery (Martinez and Martineau, 1998).

The present effort under NRHM is a pre-analysed approach towards integration. An all-India survey on all aspects of health labour force along with socio-behavioural studies of utilisation of each particular system of medicine under AYUSH is needed to be conducted. Thorough and fruitful interventions could be made into primary rural health care only after a grand analysis of macro and micro level findings.

2. *Uncertainty of fiscal space*

Governments have an obligation to weigh the relative merits of spending across different sectors, since initiatives in one sphere may ultimately have crowding-out effects on others (Heller, 2006).

A permanent, sustained and predictable flow of fiscal support is essential, since it reduces the uncertainty as to whether the monetary support is simply of a one-time character and creates the potential for a scaling up of expenditure to be maintained in the future. Policy slippages by successive governments and bureaucratic processes must need to entail sufficient support. If there is a possibility that the fiscal space that allows for today's additional expenditure will not be replicated in the future, governments may find that they are forced to either under-fund the new initiative or cut back on other expenditure programmes in the future. So it is necessary to assess the scope for higher spending within the context of comprehensive and forward looking fiscal and budgetary framework (Foster, 2005).

The Government in India spends just 0.9 per cent of GDP on health care against the WHO recommendation of atleast 5 per cent; this actually translates to only 17 per cent of all health expenditure being borne by the government and the rest by the people themselves (Kapilashrani, 2005). In this backdrop, it is really a mid-day dream to believe in the sustainable support for integration of AYUSH systems of medicine into public health in the context of growing stakehold of privatisation health systems in the country.

3. *The dilemma of pharmacoepia*

The nucleus of any medical system is the pharmacoepia which alters the diseased or uncomfortable body state to a health and active state. The drugs are vital ingredients for the treatment of any illness. It is universally true with any kind of medical system. But, the traditional system of medicines uses natural compounds as it is as its medication whereas modern medicine is more towards synthetic compounds. Decrease in biodiversity has led to paucity of medicinal herbs and production of synthetic compounds on mass scale, made modern medicines really available. This has its impact on health-seeking behaviour of tribals and people in general, by which people resort to modern medicines which are at their door-step (Ghosh et al., 2007). Non-availability of traditional medicines is one reason for not using Indian systems of medicines (Singh et al., 2005).

There are other serious issues that cropped up during recent times on ayurvedic and homoeopathic medical formulations. Among those are the "lead, mercury and arsenic intoxication have been associated with the use of ayurvedic herbal medicine products" (Saper et al., 2004) and the other is questioning the therapeutic efficiency of homoeopathic medical system and concluding that it is no better than a placebo (Shang et al., 2005).

With the above concerns assuming importance it is to be noted that the institutional structure is not just the panacea for all health problems, but thorough standardisation of medical formulations and quality management in drug production should be considered in order to aver the later after effects.

4. *The institutional structures and organisational culture*

Physicians, specific knowledge allows them to play a central role in the decision making process at the health care facility. However, as health services are diverse and heterogeneous, their quality is difficult to measure, the manager cannot fully observe and evaluate physicians' input and performance. As a result, physicians are allowed plenty of discretion as to their preferred level of effort or effective time at work.

Under the NRHM, it was proposed to merge the already existing AYUSH dispensaries into primary health centres (PHCs) based on location feasibility. The existing dispensaries are already short of physicians and they are allotted to distribute and segregate their weekly schedules to work at two or more dispensaries simultaneously. This gives a wide discretion to the practitioners and their work nature becomes too diffused. There are instances where due to the dearth of AYUSH practitioners, unani doctor is allotted the responsibility of ayurveda and homoeopathy dispensary, and vice versa (feedback is from my own field work in Warangal district of Andhra Pradesh). Once the dispensaries are relocated from their original location to PHCs the dispensaries become inaccessible to the clients.

And further public hospitals showed an organisational culture that is highly permissible towards absenteeism (Cercone et al., 2000). Size increases create a work environment in which individual work performance is less noticeable (Allen, 1982). This is also true in case if PHC's become multi-practitioner centres who try to complain about each other's duties. Further, because work performance tends to go more unnoticed in large hospitals, the probability of detection and punishment is lower than in small hospitals (Jaen and Paravisini, 2001). As the number of hospital personnel increases, the exercise of supervision becomes more difficult and costly and the perceived probability of detection of absentee worker is lower (Alcazar and Andrade, 2001).

Activities such as informal payments (the so-called lanchams) and absenteeism are widespread in Indian hospitals. Among these activities absenteeism was reported to be more prevalent, with higher rates than in other public services. These dispensaries too might get infestate with such characters if merged into PHCs.

Conclusion

As the ability of states to deliver effective public health is compromised in an increasingly neo-liberal political economy (Coburn, 2000; Maskovsky, 2000) the wealthier are able to maintain access to health capital—clean water, good food, medical care, salubrious living conditions—while the vulnerability of poor increases (Bond, 2000). To improve the prevailing situation, the problem of rural health is to be addressed both at macro (national and state) and micro (district and regional) levels. This is to be done in a holistic way, with a genuine effort to bring the poorest of the population to the centre of the fiscal policies. A paradigm shift from the current 'biomedical model' to a 'socio-cultural model', which should bridge the gaps and improve quality of rural life, is the current need otherwise as rightly said by Thelma Narayan (2005) the policy of medical tourism for classes and health missions for the masses will only lead to deepening of inequalities already embedded in our health care system. The other issue that needs to be considered is before moving on to deal with prescribing integration it would be appropriate to pause for a moment or two to reflect on the issue of professional competence of each system of medicine as it is equally important however is possibility of indirect hazard due to prescribers incompetence. It is the duty of the government to see that diversity exists in medical culture also without limiting these systems of medicine to a corner in the globalised world.

Ethnography has emerged as a key research strategy not for reciting a pious liturgy on the horrors of the forms of human misery but for demonstrating the links between policy and everyday life and for carefully scrutinising the legacy of those who rightfully seek to correct conditions that are all too often beyond their control (Nguyen and Peschard, 2003).

References

Alcazar, L. and R. Andrade 2001 "Induced Demand and Sbsenteeism in Peruvian Hospitals", in R. Di Tella and W.D. Savedoff (eds), *Diagnosis Corruption: Fraud in Latin America's Public Hospitals.* Washington, DC: Inter-American Development Bank.

Allen, P.T. 1982 "Size of Work Force, Morale and Absenteeism: A Re-examination", *British Journal of Industrial Relations*, 20: 82–100.

Arnold, D. 1996 *The Problem of Nature: Environment, Culture and European Expansion*, Oxford: Blackwell.

Ashraf, A. et al. 1982 "Health, Disease and Health Care in Rural Bangladesh", *Social Science and Medicine*, 16(23): 2041–54.

Astin, J.A. 1998 "Why Patients Use Alternative Medicine: Results of a National Study", *Journal of American Medical Association*, 279: 1548–53.

AYUSH Newsletter 2005 "Digital Defence", Vol. X, MOHFF, Department of AYUSH, April–August, p. 17.

Benzamin, Z. et al. 1987 "Combined Intervention: An Electric Approach to the Treatment of Social Phobias and Depression in Elderly Long-term Care Patients", *Clinical Gerentologist*, 7(1): 51–62.

Bond, P. 2000 *Cities of Gold, Townships of Coal: Essays on South Africa's New Urban Crisis*, Trenton, NJ: Africa World Press.

Brown, Tim and Morag Brown 2007 "Off the Couch and On the Move: Global Public Health and Medicalisation of Nature", *Social Science and Medicine*, 64: 1343–54.

Buchan, J. and M.R. Dal Poz 2002 "Skill Mix in Health Care Workforce: Reviewing the Evidence", *Bulletin of World Health Organisation*, 80(7).

Cercone, J. et al. 2000 "Compromisos de gesiton, Rendicion de cuentas corruption en los hospitals de la caja, costrarricense de seguro social", Research network working paper R-418, Washington, DC: Inter-American Development Bank.

Coburn, D. 2000 "Income Inequality, Social Cohesion and Health Status of Populations: The Role of Neoliberalism", *Social Science and Medicine*, 51: 135–46.

Cosminsky, S. and M. Scrimshaw 1980 "Medical Pluralism on a Guatemalan Plantation", *Social Science and Medicine*, 14B: 267–78.

Crandon–Malamud, L. 1991 From the Fat of Our Souls: Social Change, Political Process and Medical Pluralism in Bolivia, Berkeley: University of California Press, 202–03.

Dror, Yehezkel 1967 "Policy Analyst: A New Professional Role in Government", *Public Administration Review,* 27(3): 197–203.

Dye, Thomas R. 1976 *Policy Analysis,* Alabama: University of Alabama Press.

English-Lueck, J.A. 1990 *Health in the New Age: A Study in California Health Practices,* Albuquerque: University of New Mexico Press.

Epstein, Ronald M. et al. 2005 "Measuring Patient-Centred Communication in Patient-Physician Consultations: Theoretical and Practical Issues", *Social Science and Medicine,* 61: 1516–28.

Fiske, S.J. 1979 "Anthropology and Public Administration", *Pract. Anthropol.,* 1(4): 8.

Foster, M. 2005 "Fiscal Space and Sustainability: Towards a Solution for Health Sector", *Background Paper,* Paris, 14–25. *(http//www.hlfhealthmdgs.org/documents/fiscal space towards solution. pdf)*

Gesler, M. Wilbert 1984 *Health Care in Developing Countries,* State College, PA: Association of American Geographers.

Gesler, W. 1992 "Therapuetic Landscapes: Medical Issues in the Light of New Cultural Geography", *Social Science and Medicine,* 34(7), 735–46.

Ghosh, B. et al. 2007 "Changes in Health Status of the Soliga Tribes at BRT (Biligiri Rangaswamy Temple Wildlife Sanctuary) Due to Modern Interventions", *Current Science,* 92(12), 25th June.

Gillies, P. 1998 "Effectiveness of Alliances and Partnerships for Health", *Health Promotion International,* 13(2): 99–120.

Greenfield, Sidney M. 1992 "Spirits and Spiritist Therapy in Southern Brazil: A Case Study of Innovative, Syncretic Healing Group", *Culture, Medicine and Psychiatry,* (16)1: 23–51.

Hall, T.L. and A. Meija 1978 *Health Manpower Planning: Principles, Methods, Issues,* Geneva: World Health Organization.

Heller, Peter 2006 "The Prospects of Creating Fiscal Space for Health Sector", *Health Policy and Planning,* 21(2).

Hongoro, Charles and Barbara McPake 2004 "How to Bridge the Gap in Human Resources for Health", *The Lancet,* 364: 1451–56.

India Year Book 2006

India Year Book 2007.

Jaen, M.H. and D. Paravisini 2001 "Wages, Capture and Penalties in Verezuela's Public Hospitals", in Di Tella R. and W. Savedoff (eds), op. cit.

Janzen, J.M. 1978 *The Quest for Therapy in Lower Zaire: Medical Pluralism in Lower Zaire,* Berkeley: University of California Press.

Kapilashrani, M.C. 2005 "Universal Access to Health, Rights Based Approach", *Indian Journal of Public Health,* 49(2).

Kaplan, R. and S. Kaplan 1989 *The Experience of Nature: A Psychological Perspective,* Cambridge: Cambridge University Press.

Kaptchuk, Ted J. et al. 1998 "The Persuasive Appeal of Alternative Medicine", *Annals of Internal Medicine*, 129(12): 1061–65.

Kroeger, A. and H.P. Franken 1981 "The Educational Value of Participatory Evaluation of Primary Health Care Programme: An Experience with 4 Indigenous Populations in Equador", *Social Science and Medicine*, 15B: 535–39.

Laine, C. and F. Davidoff 1996 "Patient-centred Medicine: A Professional Evolution", *Journal of American Medical Association*, 275(2): 152–56.

Leeson, J. 1974 "Social Science and Health Policy in Pre-industrial Society", *International Journal of Health Science*, 4: 429–40.

Leslie, C., ed. 1976 *Asian Medical Systems: A Comparative Study*, Berkeley: University of California Press.

Leslie, C. 2001 "Backing Into the Future", *Medical Anthropology Quarterly*, 15(4).

Lock, M. 1980 *East Asian Medicine in Urban Japan*, Berkeley: University of California Press.

Martinez, J. and T. Martineau 1998 "Rethinking Human Resources: An Agenda for the Millennium", *Health Policy and Planning*, 13: 345–58.

Maskovsky, J. 2000 "Managing the Poor: Neoliberalism, Medicaid, HMO's and Triumph of Consumerism Among the Poor", *Medical Anthropology*, 19: 121–46.

Mazumdar, D.G. 1998 "Indian Systems of Medicines, ISM and Women's Health: A Clients Perceptive", *Journal of Biosocial Science*, 39: 819–14.

Milligan, C. et al. 2004 "Cultivating Health, Therapeutic Landscapes and Older People in Northern England", *Social Science and Medicine*, 58(9): 1781–93.

Mueller, Eric and Murugan Narayanan Kani 2004 "Proceedings of First All-India Conference of Kanyakumari", Academy of Arts & Sciences, Nagarcoil: KAAS.

Nguyen, Vinh-Kim and Karine Peschard 2003 "Anthropology, Inequality and Disease: A Review", *Annual Review of Anthropology*, 32: 447–74.

NRHM 2005-2012 Draft National Rural Health Mission, Mission Document, Ministry of Health and Family Welfare, New Delhi: Government of India.

O'Brian–Pallas et al. 2001 "Integrating Workforce Planning, Human Resources and Service Planning", Proceedings of the Workshop on Global Health Workforce Strategy, held at Annecy, France, 9–12, December, 2000.

Patwardhan, B. et al. 2005 "Ayurveda and Traditional Chinese Medicine: A Comparative Overview", *Evidence-based Complimentary Alternative Medicine*, 2(4): 465–73.

Phillips, D.R. 1990 *Health and Health Care in the Third World*, Essex University, England: Longman Scientific & Technical Harlow.

Reich, M. 2000 "Public-Private Partnerships for Public Health", *Nature Medicine*, 6(6): 617–20.

Saper, Rober B. et al. 2004 "Heavy Metal Content of Ayurvedic Herbal Medicine Products", *Journal of American Medical Association*, 292(23).

Sen, A. 2001 *Development as Freedom*, New York: Oxford University Press.

Shang, A. et al. 2005 "Are the Clinical Effects of Homoeopathy Placebo Effects? Comparative Study of Placebo Controlled Trials of Homoeopathy and Allopathy", *The Lancet*, 366(9487): 726–32.

Singh, Padam et al. 2005 "Utilisation of Indigenous Systems of Medicine and Homoeopathy in India", *Indian Journal of Medical Research*, 122: 137–42.

Somasundaram, K.V. et al. 2002 "Current Health Scenario in Rural India", *Australian Journal of Rural Health*, 10(2): 129–35.

Stoner, B.P. 1986 "Understanding Medical System: Traditional, Modern and Syncretic Health Care Alternatives in Medically Pluralistic Societies", *Medical Anthropology*, 17(2): 44–48.

Thelma, Narayan 2005 "Challenges of National Rural Health Mission", *Indian Journal of Medical Ethics*, II(2): 42–43.

Tsing, A. 2000 "The Global Situation of Health". *Cultural Anthropology*, 15(3): 327–60.

Varatharajan, D. 2004 "Provision of Health Care by the Government", *Indian Journal of Medical Ethics*, 12(4).

Ventegodt, Soren et al. 2005 *Principles of Holistic Medicine: Quality of Life and Health*, Victoria, BC: Trafford Publishing, 1–2.

Vichealth 2005 Partnership Facts Sheet. Available at *http//www.vichealth.vic.gov.au.assets.content files/ Fact% 20 sheet – partnerships. pdf.*

Wilson, E. 1984 *Biophilia: The Human Bond with Other Species*, Cambridge, MA: Harvard University Press.

Wright, John and John Walley 1998 "Assessing Health Needs in Developing Countries", *British Medical Journal*, 316: 1819–23.

Wright, Susan and Cris Shore 1997 *Anthropology of Policy: Critical Perspectives on Governance and Power*, London: Routledge.

16

Indigenous medicine and its practice among the Jaunsari

S.N.H. Rizvi

Since the beginning of colonisation the imperial powers were engaged in the administration of the alien people. In this process, they encountered people who were to be controlled either by force or conciliation. The administrators coming into direct contact with these people noticed strange customs and habits among them, which were intriguing and fascinating enough to be reported as curiosities in journals and serious social science publications.

A century or more ago, anthropologists engaged in fieldwork because of the indigenous ethnographic interest, covered various aspects of human culture, including primitive medicine, witchcraft and magic. The diligence of early anthropologists, and of explorers and missionaries who gathered data on the magical beliefs and practices of the people, whom they encountered or among whom they worked, is well-illustrated by the first comparative worldwide survey of beliefs about disease causation—that cites 229 sources, a high proportion of these is ethnographic (Clements, 1932).

Migration of European people into the New World also resulted in conflict and contact with indigenous people. Typical researches undertaken as a consequence by anthropologists and other behavioural scientists are: "Anthropological data on the problem of instinct" (Mead, 1942); "Doll play of Pilaga Indian children" (Henry and Henry, 1944); "Sibling rivalry in San Pedro" (Paul, 1955); "Primitive psychiatry" (Devereux, 1940); "Elements of psychotherapy in Navaho religion" (Leighton and Leighton, 1941), etc.

Foster and Anderson (1978) note that increasing realisation of the value and usefulness of ethnomedicine has led the World Health Organization and other agencies to think of inducting non-western curers and non-western therapies in health programmes. Thus, at the more practical level, the study of ethnomedical beliefs and practices assume significance in developing and implementing culturally acceptable health care services and health education programmes.

In traditional societies similar personal decisions, as we have seen, often underlie medical careers. Herbalists and midwives, for example, frequently acquire their skills from their mothers or other close relatives. Through interest and observation, herbalists may learn about the different plants that grow nearly or that can be obtained in the sidewalk pharmacies of market towns. They may note the effects of food and herbs on patients and exchange information with other people similarly skilled. In this way, they build reputations as home curers, to be turned to, for common childhood illnesses and for diarrhoea, cold, rheumatism and the like (Foster and Anderson, 1978: 106).

The universe of study

The study relates to the Jaunsari population of Jaunsar-Bawar of Dehradun district in Uttarakhand. Jaunsar-Bawar, a homeland of the Jaunsaris is situated in the CIS-Himalayan region. It forms approximately half of the Dehradun district and located at the north-western corner of the Uttarakhand state. The area is somewhat oval in shape, it lies between latitudes 30° 31′ and 31° 33′ North and longitudes 77° 45′ and 78° 72′ East and is divided into 39 *khats* and 385 villages. River Yamuna forms its eastern boundary and separates it from Dehradun pargana. River Tons (western) forms its north-western boundary before it confluences with river Yamuna near Kalsi. Thus, the whole of the Jaunsar-Bawar is practically encircled by these two rivers. Jaunsar-Bawar is surrounded by Tehri Garhwal and Uttar Kashi districts in the east and north; Bashar, Raiengarh, Taroach, Jubbal and Sirmur in the west and Doon valley in the south.

The southern of lower portion of the region is called Jaunsar while the northern portion is called Bawar. Jaunsar is larger and triangular in shape bounded on the north by Lokhandi, on its east River Yamuna and on the west River Tons. The altitude of Jaunsar-Bawar varies from 3,000 feet to 10,075 feet above sea level. The climate of the area varies greatly from place to place according to elevation.

The Jaunsari is one of the five Scheduled Tribes of Uttarakhand, known for its institution of polyandry, which has shown signs of decline in recent years. According to 2001 census, their population is 81,375, which is about 39 per cent of the total tribal population of the state.

Discussion

The present paper deals with the manner in which problems of health and disease are solved by the Jaunsari by utilising the flora and fauna available in Himalayas. The paper has also described the indigenous system of medicine among the Jaunsari and the way it is integrated into their culture as a whole.

In Jaunsar-Bawar area, different kind of medical practitioners such as priests, magicians, exorcists and quacks abound. Many cures are affected by one or many people treating a single patient at a time or in succession. In most of the diseases recognised to have been occurred due to natural causes, specific indigenous medicine (herbs) are commonly used. Some of those are really quite effective. Jaunsaris have an extensive knowledge of herbal medicines which they have gained by bitter and successful experience. Their faith in indigenous treatments was probably strengthened with recoveries from illness, many times in succession.

In Jaunsar-Bawar, the medicine men (herbalists) acquire those skills and knowledge from their fathers. The herbalists do not tell the names of the herbs/plants, etc., to others except their son. Through interest and observation as well as in close association with their fathers, the herbalists may learn about the different plants that grow in the vicinity or in the forest of the Himalayas. They also note the effects of different food and herbs on patients; in this way they build reputations as home curers for common ailments such as cold, fever, headache, body ache, bone fracture, snake bite, dysentery and the like.

Jaunsaris, in general, are not very clear in their ideas about health, disease and treatment. They depend upon the advice of their village elders and experts. Thus, the *health care system* is an informal and undefined system, with no individual cures for many ailments. Isolation of patient and special arrangements for ill people are almost never prescribed.

In fact, most of the customs and practices with regard to health and disease, have no modern scientific basis among Jaunsaris, yet indigenous medicine is successful in this area. If the patients are cured by indigenous medicine the credit goes to the treatment applied; if it fails, is not because the treatment was wrong but that the patient was beyond help. The effectiveness of the indigenous medicine in the area depends on the following facts:

(a) A number of effective means are found in it, e.g., massage, blood letting, bone setting, and certain efficacious materia medica of floral and faunal origin.
(b) It carries with it certain psychotherapeautic qualities because treatment is a process not merely of consultation of specialists but relatives and friends, whose presence helps to cheer the diseased and invalids by removing his/her loneliness.
(c) Another important explanation for the success of indigenous medicine is that majority of those falling ill, may be cured easily because their body resistance is usually strong enough to ward off ordinary maladies, but all the same they need some treatment whether it is blowing and conjuring or wearing of charms or amulets or a decoction of some herb. Indigenous medicine gives great psychological satisfaction to the patient just as pills, capsules and injections help urban patients.

The Jaunsari remedies also, like most folk medicine, are based on trial and error experience of previous generations and have survived in the culture as a consequence of their effectiveness. The medicine man and his helpers without having even an elementary knowledge of the structure of the body (e.g., anatomy and physiology) as well as the nature of disease, are able to get remarkable success in curing disease, because they pay considerable attention to the patient's emotions, attitudes and social pressures, etc., and in such a way they made a patient better even through "unsophisticated" use of psychosocial therapeutic measures.

Correspondingly, in Jaunsar-Bawar, many people are in chronic ill health or are less healthy than they might be, because of the assault of a multiplicity of parasitic infections, viz., bouts of fever, attacks of jaundice consequent on virus infection, skin conditions of various kinds, and so on.

Many of these illnesses are or so much dramatic as debilitating, and their ultimate physical causes are beyond the capacity of indigenous medicine to discern. Their impact is often felt seasonally and irregularly, interfering for a time in the plans and purposes of the patient without actually endangering his life.

It should be reiterated, however, that the Jaunsari indigenous medicine is conspicuously unsuccessful in treating the diseases of early childhood, which causes a very high frequency of infant and child mortality.

The herbs and other household remedies which are used by the Jaunsari for certain ailments are discussed below. The plants have been called by their local names and their scientific names have been given within parenthesis. English names of some of the plants along with their local and scientific names have also been given to the extent to which it was possible.

Other ailments which necessitate the services of the 'herbalists' are listed with a brief description of the preparation and use of the medicine.

Ailments	*Treatment of ailments*
1. Fever	(i) Dried petals of *banafshah* (Viola serpens) flowers are boiled in water and the decoction is used as potion. (ii) *Podina* (Mentha arvensis) grass is boiled in water and mixed with jaggery and the content is given as potion.
2. Fever caused by cold	Tea prepared by *banafshah* (Viola serpens) is given to the patient to drink.
3. Fever caused by heat	(i) *Kheera* (Cucumber) leaves are crushed and its juice mixed with a little water is given to the patient to drink. (ii) The tea mixed with *zira* (Cuminum cyminum) seeds and *adrak* (ginger)is administered as potion. (iii) The grain of *ajwain* (Trochyspermum ammi) is boiled in water and the vapour is inhaled. (iv) *Charoita* (Swartia and Gentiana sp) is crushed, mixed with water and used as potion. (v) The tea prepared by *kachoor* (Headchium spicatum) is used as potion. (vi) *Kodhu* (Redus lasiocarpus) leaves are boiled and the content is used as potion.

	(vii) The tea prepared by *ajwain* (Trochyspermum ammi), *banafshah* (Viola serpens), *kali mirch* (Black pepper), *adrak* (ginger) and *sonth* (dry ginger) is used.
4. Heat/sun stroke	*Nilkanthi* (Chrozophora prostrata) leaves are boiled in water and the potion is used.
5. Stomach ache	(i) *Kachoor*(Hedychium spicatum) boiled in water and mixed with jaggery is used for drinking. (ii) Hot *ashes* are collected in a bowl, some water is sprinkled on the ashes, and the bowl is wrapped in a cloth and placed on the stomach. (iii) Pain below navel is cured by making the patient drink fresh cow milk mixed with *gur* (jaggery). (iv) Pain above navel is cured by making the patient drink hot *ghee* mixed with *gur* (jaggery). (v) *Pyaz* (onion), *ghee* and *gur* (jaggery) are mixed and the juice is drunk by the patient. (vi) The root of *chaamar* (Glochidion velutinum) is to be chewed.
6. Earache	Either the leaves of *nilkanthi* (Chrozophora prostrata) are rolled up and put into the ear or the juice of the same are dropped into the ear cavity.
7. Headache	(i) The pulp of ground *timour* (Zanthexylum aletum) and *chaamar* (Glochidien valutinum) leaves is applied on the forehead. (ii) *Timour* (Zanthexylum aletum) leaves are ground and mixed in bath water and same is heated. The patient is required to bathe in it. (iii) Decoction of *kali mirch* (black pepper) is used. (iv) The forehead is massaged with mustard oil.
8. Vomiting	*Podina* (Mentha arvensis) and *pyaz* (onion) are crushed and their juice is strained and used as potion.
9. Pus formation	Pulp of crushed leaves of *kushka* (Saccharum spontaneum) is applied on the affected part. This pulp kept stuck there until the patient is cured of the ailment which takes about 15 days.
10. Bronchitis	(i) *Adrak* (ginger) (Zingiber officinale): Peeled ginger is cut and stuffed with salt, covered with kneaded *manduva* flour and roasted in the fire; the patient is asked to suck it.

	(iii) The pulp of *makki* (maize) stock is burnt and powdered, then mixed with honey. It is to be licked by the patient three or four times a day.
11. Cold	(i) Egg, milk, *manduva* wine, opium and clarified butter are mixed and used as potion. (ii) Yolk of an egg is applied on the breast. (iii) *Ajwain* (Trachyspermum ammi) and *kachoor* (Hedychium spicatum) are roasted and powdered, then mixed with jaggery and given to the patient to eat. (iv) The tea prepared by *banafshha* (Viola serpens) and *zira* (Cuminum cyminum) seed is given to drink.
12. Cough	(i) The *nimbu* (lemon) is roasted among embers and is to be eaten. (ii) The shell of *anar* (pomegranate) is ground and used orally.
13. Swelling on the gums	The root of *ninai* (Arundinaria jaunsarensis) is dissolved in drinking water and this solution is applied on the gums for 7 to 10 days.
14. Swelling of the body	Dry fruits of *kachoor* (Hedychium spicatum) are powdered and mixed with jaggery or sugar and this powder is eaten twice a day.
15. Scabies	(i) The juice of *nilkanthi* (Chrozophora prostrata) leaves mixed with butter is applied. (ii) The juice of *tambaco* (tobacco) leaves is applied on the affected part.
16. Burn	A slice of *alu* (potato) is put on the burnt part.
17. Sprain	Fresh *khaida* (Chir) (Pinus roxburghii) gum is applied on the affected part.
18. Bone fracture	i) *Haldi* (turmeric) and wheat flour are fried and put on the affected part and then bark of *bimal* (Grewia oppositifolia) is placed on it and bandaged. (ii) The bark of *nona* (Annona reticulata) is powdered and boiled in water, when it curdles thick it is plastered on the affected part. (iii) The bark of *bimal* (Grewia oppositifolia) is powdered and boiled in water, when it curdles thick it is plastered on the affected part.

There are, however, a very wide variety of locally trusted 'remedies for snake bite'.

Snake bite

1. On 20th of '*Gate*' (Hill Calendar date) any person without washing his face, rinsing mouth and talking to any one else goes out alone to pick 1–2 kg of *bhang* (hemp). This *bhang* is mixed with quarter or half kilogram of *ghee.* Now the preparation is hung on the ceiling, it is believed that the *bhang* gathered on this particular day with the aforesaid precaution turns poisonous.

   Whenever, a person is bitten by snake this *bhang* is fried in ghee and every 2 to 4 hours the patient is asked to drink it. Before drinking it the affected person is given *bhang* to eat to take its poisonous quality (property) off. Then charms and other incantations are used.
2. A hooded snake is killed and its body and head are buried separately. After 8 to 10 days when the flesh is almost decomposed a very small black square frame is obtained which is known as '*Nagdhan*'. It is taken out and washed with the milk and tied in a new cloth and put away. Whenever, a person is bitten by snake this '*Nagdhan*' after being washed with the milk is placed on the spot where snake has bitten. It sucks the blood and leaves the affected part.
3. *Dhatura* (Datura stramonium) leaves are squeezed for getting juice. The juice is mixed with hot *ghee* and the affected person is made to drink it thrice or four times a day. The affected person is cured after he has vomited. The person bitten by snake is placed in a cool place, is not allowed to cross the door, house is not cleaned with broom, the corner of the women's cloth is not allowed to touch that person.
4. Water passing through the pipe of smoke hubble bubble is applied on the part bitten by snake and afterwards a small globule of onion and *ghee* mixed with this water is given to be eaten.

Scorpion bite

The mixture prepared by *Sondi* (Moringa pterygosperma) is administered orally once a day up to one month.

Dog bite

The following are the local treatments of dog bite:

(i) Chilly is powdered and the affected part is stuffed with it.
(ii) Chilly is burnt and applied on the affected part.
(iii) Chilly and salt are powdered and applied on the affected part.
(iv) Turmeric powder is applied on the affected part.

Leech infestation

During summer more often Jaunsari people drink water from streams and ponds, etc., due to which leeches enter into their nose and start sucking blood. It results in nose bleeding. For getting the leech out of the nose, the nose is covered with a wet cloth or some water is cupped in the palm and put near the nose. In this way leeches come out of the nose.

The shell of soap nut is powdered and blown into the nose through a straw pipe/pipe and this causes the leech to come out.

Wound healing

There are a number of indigenous remedies for bleeding and wound healing.

(i) *Podina* (Mentha arvensis) is crushed and its juice or paste is applied on the wound.
(ii) The root of *kachoor* (Hedychium spicatum) is dissolved in water and the prepared mixture is applied on the wound.
(iii) *Chaamar* (Glochidion velutinum) leaves are crushed and the paste/juice is applied on the wound.
(iv) *Sookha Gobar* (dry dung) is rubbed on the palm and filled in the wound.
(v) *Haldi* (turmeric), *namak* (salt) and *sarson ka tel* (mustard oil) is applied on the wound.
(vi) *Bichchu* (nettle) (Urtica dioica) leaves are crushed and the juice is applied on the wound.
(vii) The abrasion of skin is filled with clay or bandaged.
(viii) Urine of the same person is applied on the wound.

References

Clements, Forrest E. 1932 "Primitive Concept of Disease", *American Archeology and Ethnology*, 32(2): 185–252.

Devereux, George 1940 "Primitive Psychiatry", *Bulletin of the History of Medicine*, 8: 1194–213.

Foster, G.M. and B.G. Anderson 1978 *Medical Anthropology*, John Wiley, New York.

Henry, Jules and Zunia Henry 1944 "Doll Play of Pilaga Indian children", *American Orthopsychiatric Association*, Research Monograph No. 4, New York.

Leighton, Alexander H. and Dorothea C. Leighton 1941 "Elements of Psychotherapy in Navaho Religion", *Psychiatry*, 4: 515–23.

Mead, Margaret 1942 "Anthropological Data on the Problem of Instinct", *Psychosomatic Medicine*, 1: 396–97.

Paul, B.D. (ed.) 1955 *Culture and Community: Case Studies of Public Relations to Health Programmes*, Russell Sage Foundation, New York.

Rizvi, S.N.H. 1991 *Medical Anthropology of the Jaunsaris*, Northern Book Centre, New Delhi.

17

Illness and health-seeking behaviour among the Baiga tribe of Madhya Pradesh

Nilanjan Khatua

Illness and health management (healing) are fundamental to the human experience and are best understood holistically in the context of human biology and cultural diversity. Health-seeking behaviour is an important concept used in medical anthropology. The behaviour of the patient and his/her immediate kith and kin in seeking health care is studied in the context of culture. The choice of a particular therapy is studied here. Janzen (1978) has used the term "therapy management" and Chrisman (1977) has used the term "health-seeking process" to describe the same process. Majority of the health problems of the world are due to poverty, poor infrastructure, crowding and modernisation (Nichter and Sickle, 2000). These and many other factors such as availability of health care facilities of different medical systems, number of practitioners, paramedical staff and pharmaceutical drugs available in an area affect the health status of the people. Distribution of health resources in a region is also an important factor. The present study focuses on the classification and cultural meaning of illness (both somatic and mental) and the health seeking behaviour of the Baiga suffering from illness.

The present study is based on an extensive fieldwork conducted among the Baiga tribe in Baigachak of Dindori district (earlier Mandla), Madhya Pradesh in the year 1999. The Baiga is one of the three primitive tribal groups of Madhya Pradesh and dwells in the heart of thick forest. Traditionally, the Baigas were shifting cultivators, priest of Gonds, medicine men, hunters and bamboo workers but now they are compelled to practice settled cultivation. The rearing of pigs and poultry birds are their other occupations. Agricultural labour and collection of minor forest produce are their main economic subsistence activities. The casual wage labour in forest department supplement the primary occupation.

To the Baiga when a person becomes physically fit, can move freely, work without feeling tired, it is said that the person possesses good health. During illness a person takes less food and losses his/her interest to take food, blood becomes less in quantity and sometimes feels vomiting sensation and may also vomit. To the Baiga people, any kind of illness, is supposed to be caused due to wrath of deities. Whenever they face any difficulties or any kind of ill health, they start worshipping their deities at once. Intrusion of evil spirits like *bhut* (ghosts), *churelin* (female evil spirit), *raksa* (male evil spirit), and *mua* (child evil spirit) are also the causes of illness. Disease due to witchcrafts or sorcery is also prevalent among the Baiga tribal society.

To the Baiga, a very common legend used to be heard within their society "*Hindu Dhram Niyam Ke Varash, Gond Baiga Deo Ke Varash,*" says Bhola Baiga. It indicates that any kind of illness among the Baiga or Gond is supposed to be caused due to wrath of deities. It can be said that whenever the Baiga face any difficulties or any kind of ill health, they start worshipping their deities at once. On the other hand, Hindus are very particular in their way of worshipping Gods and Goddesses and they do so regularly. Some Baiga medicine men easily identify the cause of disease with the help of reading pulse-rate of the patient.

1. Quick pulse-rate (*Nari Dardarate Hai)*: It is due to ghost intrusion. The affected person cannot talk through his mouth and jaws become tight. The affected person can die in this condition.
2. Difficult to read pulse-rate (*Daba Hua Nari)*: This type of slow pulse-rate is due to wrath of ancestral spirits. The member of the particular family is affected. In such a case, there is no danger of death.
3. Slow pulse-rate and readable after certain intervals (*Nari Dabi Lekin Fit Fit Karta)*: When pulse-rate is read after certain intervals, it is believed that this is caused due to mischief of witches or male sorcerer. Sacrifices of hen, goat is offered to appease the evil spirits to get the patients cured from their ailment.

Cause of illness

To the Baiga, it is a common belief that most illness has its origin either in witchcraft or in the spontaneous and inexplicable hostility of unseen beings. Elwin (1986) quoted: "Disease", says Hothu family, "is not caused by dirt or bad water or food. It is always the work of witches or evil spirits". The causes of illness are described below:

Illness due to natural causes

The Baiga has no conception of natural infection or contagion. Elwin (1986: 360) said that the rough and inaccurate character of Baiga physiology and anatomy is of very little importance in their general medical theory, which considers that hardly any diseases are due to natural causes. They have no fear of contact with a leper, and will unhesitatingly have intercourse with a woman suffering from an acute vaginal discharge. The Baiga has some conception that in the old days the Baiga never suffered from cholera. It was only when they started visiting the villages in the plains that they brought it back with them. For example, they believe that when *Naksurki Mata* came into a village, she was not content with one victim, but went round giving cold to everybody. The Baiga do, however, in some cases admit a possibly natural cause for disease. Thus, fever may sometimes be caused "by drinking a lot of water when you are cold". Headache may be due "to hot breeze blowing into a man's nose and ears". Itch comes from lying naked on the earth or by laughing when a horse breaks wind. Veneral disease, specially, is apt "to come from our own bodies".

Elwin (1986: 361) mentioned that the Baiga have developed a fairly elaborate theory of veneral disease. To the Baiga, all venereal disease is one infection. A man first catches *thanki* (gonorrhoea); if untreated, this develops into *garmi* (syphilis); the next stage is variously described as *parmi*, *sujag* or *dhat* (various forms of chronic gonorrhoea including gleets). At last comes *patthari* or stricture, when the mouth of the penis is shut and all the urine flows back into the stomach. It swells and swells—the man dies in agony.

Arthritis, however, is sometimes related to gonorrhoea. Leprosy and yaws are correctly regarded as distinct diseases. "Syphilis", says Lahakat, "lives in a woman's vagina, and by going to her, you get it. Woman is a real danger, and brings these sores upon us". Gonorrhoea is sometimes induced by excessive intercourse. Jethu agreed that syphilis came from connection with infected women, but it might also be caused by eating hot things and by drinking too much *mahua* liquor. The Baiga do not suffer very greatly from syphilis; their special scourge is gonorrhoea. This is not caused by sexual intercourse except in one special case. "You don't get gonorrhoea by going to a girl," said Jethu, "but through drinking hot water and going out in the hot sun. Then the urine turns yellow and it burns us. When a man goes every day in the sun he gets fever and this turns into gonorrhoea. *Thanki* (gonorrhoea) gets its name because when a man urinates, he is in intense agony and says, "*Than Than Than*". Another way of catching gonorrhoea is to step over a place where someone has urinated, "you can also get it from a witch. Who puts *Samduria Deo* on the stone where they wash clothes; then even if 36 families wash clothes there, every one of them will get it" (In the tradition of that region thirty-six has a special significance. Besides it being a manner of speaking, it means plenty or beyond any doubt).

Illness due to wrath of supernatural beings

According to Elwin (1986: 362), "There is hardly a God or spirit in the entire Baiga pantheon who may not sometimes be moved to send disease upon mankind. Even *Bhagavan*, the creator may do so. Perhaps this is not surprising when we consider the way he tricked the first Baiga and sent death into the world. It is hard to explain the widespread belief that *Bhagavan* himself sends worms into a wound. This idea is common all over the central provinces, though it may well have originated with the Baiga, and it is very moving to see the horror and despair with which the discovery of this complication is greeted. The whole family is excommunicated. They are shunned by men; the curse of God is upon them. There is no remedy. Only an expensive tribal dinner will free them of the deed".

The Baiga believe firmly in the activities of the *Mata* (deity). Elwin mentions that there are in all twenty-one sisters who give disease to men. They are the sisters who dance by night in the *gunia's supa*, whom only *gunia* can see. A list of deities or spirits are given below along with their disastrous results and appeasing offerings.

Spirits/Deities	*Illness*	*Offerings given*
Chilkin piri	Pains in stomach	Black pig, three chickens, coconut and incense.
Hardahin Bai	Yellow vomit	Sacrifice of pig.
Dispiri mata	Syphilis	The ears of a buffalo.
Mirgi Devi	The bringer of epilepsy	Tongue of a horse must be cut out for sacrifice.
Naikin Bai	Attacks the bullocks	A black goat.
Hadphoran Marhi	Small pox	Black bangles, rosary, a *bandan* such as is tied round the head and a *likli.*
Kairadeshahi	Still birth	Speckled she-goat. On the goat they must put *likli, sarria, bandan,* and black bangles and let it go free in the jungle.
Durpatta Mata	Prevents a child born	
Maura Mata	Children fits	Black chicken and coconut.
Ghatchindan	Attack cattle by the throat	Black chicken and coconut.
Baihi and Bauri bai	Drive men mad	Spotted goat, a black she-goat
Kapni Piri	Ague	A coconut.
Chingan Mata	Man's hand and feet with rheumatism	Chickens of five different colours, a pig, coconuts and liquor.
Dhahu Dhukan	Pain in the chest	A black chicken and coconut.
Gala Devi	Mumps, swelling of the neck and cheeks	Black she-goat.
Churelin Mata	Making the young men impotent after robbing them of their seed	Black chicken with a black bangle and red *sarria* bangle and red *sarria*

Rahabasin Mata	Makes the people ill with fear	Black chicken.
Pharka Undharan Mata	Opens the door and comes into the house, and makes all the vessels rattle	Tie two little gourds over the door.
Phoki Mata	Cattle with dysentery	A goat and a pig.
Jappi Mata	Is the sleeping disease	Ghee and a little *gur* (jaggery).
Raksin Mata	Itches with large sores	Chicken of seven different colours.

Among the *Devata, Narayan Deo* is apt to catch a man by the throat and prevent him swallowing. When this occurs a *Laru* pig must be dedicated to the deity and sacrificed. *Baghesur pat* is lord of the jungle; he often takes the form of a tiger, and punishes those who have failed to implement their promises when praying for a good crop. *Chitawar Deo* is another dangerous godling, who lives in the *Chhindi* palms of Bilaspur, and when annoyed or incited, by a witch, assumes the form of a snake, and bites his enemy (Elwin, 1986: 366).

The Bhut (Ghosts)

In Baiga usage, the word *bhut* may cover jealous ancestors, the ghosts of women dying in childbirth, the spirits of unmarried men, the whirlwind and such familiar demons as the *mua* and *massan.* These ghosts are equally dangerous to mankind. To the Baiga, they are no more than the possibly dangerous ghosts of the departed. The whirlwind is also a *bhut,* and no one should ever use a piece of cloth that has been carried by it up into the air. *Marki* is another very troublesome *bhut,* recognised by ripples on a stream, who causes vomiting and dysentery. *Bhut* lives mostly in tamarind trees and pipal trees, and it is dangerous to sit beneath them at night. When a *bhut* catches a person, *gunia* (spiritist) can detect the *bhut* and bind the *bhut.* The person can be recovered only when proper offerings were made.

The Churelin

The *churelin* is the female dangerous spirit of the other world. The *churelin* is the ghost of a woman who had died in pregnancy or child-birth. She takes the form and size of a peahen, with her feet turned backwards. Elwin (1986: 367) narrated that there are two kinds of *churelin*, the *papi churelin* and the *dharmi churelin*. When the *dharmi churelin* comes to a village, the sick recovers, the children are born without pain. But when the *papi churelin*, like a black vulture, comes and cries *kai o! kai o!*, all the sick die, and parturient women cannot deliver.

The *churelin* is thus not necessarily malicious, but she is always dangerous. She provides young men with exquisite and thrilling experiences, though they may also bring death. It is the *churelin*'s habit to seek lonely men. When she finds one, she takes the form of a beautiful girl, naked, alluring, and lies down beside him in his empty hut. "She comes in the shape of his mother, sister, aunt, sometimes his lover, and sleeps with him." But when a man dreams that he is with someone he knows, it is generally assumed that this is not a *churelin*, but a girl who is making love-magic for him. "Men grow very weak through this. To drive her away, a man prepares parched rice and scatters down to eat the rice and forgets all about him", as per Dhan Singh's account.

The Raksa

The *raksa* is a much more unpleasant being. He is the ghost of a man who has never experienced coitus. His face red and burning, his body covered with thick black hair, he lives in a *semur* tree, waiting for an unwary village maiden to pass his way. "He comes and presses a girl while she is asleep; she can neither move nor speak while he is covering her; he takes her like a husband and cries *ai ai ai* and goes away". Dhan Singh, a *Dewar*, however has tamed a *raksa* and this affable familiar ghost now lives in his house and guards his grain-bins, but makes himself troublesome to any young woman visiting the house.

The mua and massan

The *mua* and *massan* are the two mischievous spirits and the *massan* often acts as the familiar of witches. The *mua* is the ghost of a child who has died before learning to talk. To Hindus, *massan* belongs to the *smasana* or burial ground. He causes wasting diseases such as tuberculosis in children. Sometimes he takes the form of a bear and wanders in the hills. The Baiga do not connect him with the burial ground, but locate him under stones by the road side or behind trees in the *bewar*, where he may suddenly pop out and steal the peasants food. *Mua* and *massan* may be sent by witches to catch or possess a man and may give him almost any disease.

Illness due to witchcraft or sorcery

The Baiga's life is heavily overshadowed by the dark cloud of witchcraft. Elwin (1986: 370) reported that although many diseases and disasters are caused by the hostality of the unseen *devata* and *bhut*, probably the majority of evils are due to witchcraft. If a man is killed by a tiger, or bitten by a snake, if a mother cannot be delivered of her child, if a boy's limbs wither and he goes lame, if a storm destroys the crops, if the milk curdles or the meat goes bad, the Baiga immediately look round for a witch or sorcerer who might have reason for their harm.

In the words of Evans-Pritchard (1937, 68), "we shall give a false account of Zande philosophy; if we say that they believe witchcraft to be the sole cause of phenomena. This proposition is not contained in Zande patterns of thought, which only asserts that witchcraft brings a man into relation with events in such a way that he sustains injury". This would be equally true of the Baiga mind.

The Baiga witch differs from the European in being solitary. The Baiga witch is unutterably lonely, practising her art in secrecy and terror. Nor are there any special marks by which a witch may be known, except that possibly her eyes may shine red in the dark. Elwin mentioned that he has been unable to find any trace of a tradition of polymastia (extra breasts) or polithelia (additional nipples). Elwin (1986) reported that how does the Baiga witch set about her business. She may injure her enemy in many different ways; she may affect him directly and immediately by the power of her eye, she may destroy him by a curse; she may invoke the aid of the *bhut* or *devata* to bring disease to his house; she may send a snake to bite him or a tiger to kill him; she may herself come by night and drink his blood; she may send her magic flying through the air on a leaf, a pebble or a bat.

Elwin (1986: 371) cited an example of witchcraft. "A Baiga couple were living in the village. He was a *gunia*, she a witch. They had three sons and two daughters. She had had five husbands; one by one she had killed them all. She married this man, not knowing that he was a *gunia*. One day he went to his *bewar* (shifting cultivation) to cut the trees. She put her magic (*jadu*) in a leaf, and ordered it to go to the *bewar* and kill this man also. Unseen by anyone, the leaf flew through the jungle; it hit her husband on the chest; he fell down. But he was a magician; he had already seen the wickedness of his wife. He had nothing with him, only some cotton to make fire to light his pipe, and the hollow bamboo—*thondhi.* He took his wife's magic and put it on the cotton, he stuffed the cotton into the bamboo; he pointed it towards his wife, where he thought she was; she sent it away from him. Soon he was well again and came home with a bundle of roots on his head. But his wife had been struck by the returning magic and was hiding in terror in the house, for she knew that now she had a master who was a stronger magician than herself".

The witch commonly makes a snake out of the dirt of her body and sends it to kill someone. The witch once killed a person in this way. The witch also sends tigers. She calls *Baghesur Pat* (lord of the jungle) and persuades him to take the form of a tiger and kill her enemies. "The tiger that killed two people at Bohi was sent by a witch, who was so powerful that the *dewar* (magician) could not properly perform the rites that would bind the creature's mouth" (Elwin, 1986: 373). The direct curse of a witch is very powerful. The witches had so much poison in their eyes that when they looked at a tree it immediately withered away. The Baiga dread the evil eye in much the same fashion as the rest of India.

It is also believed that a witch may take some dust from her own left heel and put it on her left eye. When she wants to injure someone she flicks a little of it towards him with a curse. When a witch dies, her *jiv* (soul) goes to Bhagawan. He refuses to let her be reborn in any human being, holding that she has done enough harm already; instead he lets her soul take possession of the feeble body of an owl. But even then her capacity for mischief, though limited, is not ended. If she can sit, in the form of an owl, on a house where a child has just been born the parents—if they are foolish—may throw stones or sticks at her. The owl picks up the missile and dips it in the nearest stream, then puts it in the sun to dry. Then as the stone or sticks dries, the child's body will also wither with the wasting disease that they call *sukhi.* If you do want to throw anything at an owl, it is safer to use clods of earth, as these will either break at once or at least melt when dipped in the water.

Illness as a punishment for breach of tribal law

The Baiga consider the breach of tribal law as a punishment—the cause of disease. For example incest may bring leprosy, blindness or worms to devour the hands and feet. The Baiga have no fear or horror of leprosy and do not segregate lepers in any way. In a village there are three brothers, all of whom had been born dumb. This was ascribed as their parents' incest, and in this case it was found that the boys were regarded with distaste as something monstrous.

Breaches of the rules of exogamy are supposed to have the same effect. Another fruitful cause of disease is plough cultivation. It is noted that one's children have always been weak and sickly on account of using the plough.

Elwin (1986: 375) mentions that to ride on a horse, or even to wear shoes is dangerous. "In the old days, Bhagavan told Nanga Baiga that he and his children were not to plough, nor ride on horseback, nor touch horse-dung, nor wear shoes. Now we do all these things and they have brought poverty and sickness upon us", says Jethu.

Mistakes in ritual and the failure to implement promises made to *bhut* or *mata* may also bring disease. Once a Baiga had a severe attack of fever as a result of offering cock of the wrong colour to *Dharti Mata.* Blindness may be caused by eating the first mouthful from the hands of an excommunicated person. Itch comes as a result of laughing when a horse or cow breaks wind. No penalty seems to attach to a giggle when a human being does so. To the Baiga, all animals and snakes as well as many spirits, are purely neutral in character. They generally never do harm unless they are incited thereto by a witch or unless their victim is standing on *papi dharti* (in a state of mortal sin).

Disease distribution

"In the contemporary world the ecological approach is basic to the study of epidemiological problems" (Foster and Anderson, 1978). This is examined in different ecological zones, inhabited by the tribes. And the Baiga is living in hilly and forest area. Here attempt is made to highlight the disease distribution among the Baiga of Madhya Pradesh.

List of Diseases (among Baiga)

Local name	*English version*
Tapan	Fever
Barati	Ricket
Dama	Asthama
Khasi	Cough and cold
Prihi	Jaundice
Patt Jathe	Loose motion
Mur Dukhai	Headache
Sukha	Tuberculosis (T.B.)
Khajri	Scabies
Biskuti	Karbankle
Kod	Leprosy
Fulni	Body swelling
Garmi	Syphilis
Parmi	Chronic gonorrhoea
Dhat	Gleet (Leucorrhoea)
Bahari Bimari	Malaria
Ulti Dast	Diarrhoea
Khoon-ulti	Dysentery

The deficiency of hygienic drinking water leads to a number of water borne diseases and health hazards. Falciparum malaria is also common due to heavy rain of this hilly and forest areas. Malnutrition is the chief factor which causes affliction of various diseases like dysentery, thyroid, goitre, ricket, etc. Unhygienic living condition is also responsible for their various types of skin diseases. Premarital sex and sexual relation with more than one individual also leads to suffering from venereal diseases like gonorrhoea, syphilis, etc.

Diagnosis by health specialists

The symptoms of the diseases are to be diagnosed first by the village medicine man when he is called by a sick person. For the diagnosis and detection, the classic methods are the *bahari-khari*, and *supa-tuma*.

The *bahari-kari* is the method used for the detection of cause of the disease. When using the *kari*— two pieces of straw, the magician asks it a number of questions, to which it answers "yes" or "no" by altering its length. The length of this straw is breadth of twelve fingers. "It is held in the hands and first pointed down to the ground to the accompaniment of a *mantra.* Then the question is asked, and it is measured by the hand, four fingers at a time. If its length increase‿ to the breadth of thirteen fingers, the answer is affirmative and favourable; if it decreases to eleven, the answer is negative and dangerous" (Elwin, 1986: 377. The *bahari-kari* is generally used for matters of less importance, to detect minor crime of theft, to decide whether the day is favourable for an enterprise. The *gunia* tries to discover through his *kari* whether or not it will be safe for him to start on the cure of the sick man, or whether he too will be caught by the prevailing evil. He also asks whether he is likely to be successful. If the *kari* gives a favourable reply by elongating itself, the magician proceeds.

Supa-tuma

In this method all that is needed is the *supa,* the winnowing fan and a *tuma,* a dried gourd with a long handle, a little of fire, the gum of *sarai* which is used as incense, and some rice or *kodon.* The magician goes to the sick man's house with a sympathetic person who will act as his "control" and sits down in a corner of the room. He takes the rice with an open hand —the hand must not be clenched over the ground or winnowing fan—and going to the sick man, waves the rice over him from head to foot. He returns to his place, puts the rice in the *supa* and the gourd on top of the rice, and makes the usual offerings of *sarai* gum and fire before them. The disciple or *tumihar* as he is called, washes his feet and comes to sit in the front of the *gunia.* Then the *gunia* removes the gourd from the winnowing fan and the *tumihar* takes it in his hand. He places the handle on the ground and sits silently. The *gunia* picks up a few grains of rice and throws them at the gourd. This has the effect of sending a *mata* into the gourd and making it vocal. Then with a mantra he binds any witch who might try to interface with the proceedings.

Now the *gunia,* taking the *supa* in his left hand, begins to rub the rice round and round with his right hand, at the same time reciting long strings of mantra in a curiously soothing sing-song tone. The *gunia* begins with "*sirseti pat*", then he takes the names of all the gods, and sends them out to search for whoever is causing trouble. The gods go out and search everywhere. The *tumihar* replies by shaking the *tuma* in his hands in different ways. When an affirmative answer is given, he shakes his gourd vigorously backwards and forwards. When the gods answer no, he shakes it to and fro. There is a little rice in the gourd, which makes a sudden startling rattling noise.

Diagnosis by Ban-bati and Pidha-Ghumana

The Bhaina Baiga employs the *ban-bati* method of divination. The disciple places a small earthen lamp in a network of string and holds it up before the *dewar* (magician). The *dewar* repeats a mantra and proceeds in the same way as in the *bahari-kari.* The only difference is that there the answers were given by the varying length of a bit of straw, and here they are given by the waving of a light lamp. When the answer to the *dewar's* question is an affirmative, the lamp swings towards him; when it is negative, it swings to and fro. When the real culprit or cause of the disease is named, the lamp swings with great vigour. If it goes out, it means that a witch has interfered with the rite.

The Dudh Bhaina practise *pidha-ghumana* (a method of divination). They put a little *kodai* on the ground, on that a drinking pot, on that a flat wooden seat called *pidha.* On this the disciple or "control" is seated. The *dewar* sits in front of him with a *kari* or a lighted lamp. The control leans forward with his hands on the ground, and as the *dewar* put his questions he is whirled round and round by the spirits. If the answer is yes, he goes anti-clockwise, if no, he goes clockwise.

Diagnosis by the barua and the dham

Among the Baiga there is another important type of divination where the god speaks directly, through the mouth of a man or woman who has passed into a state of dissociation. Elwin reported that there are a number of people, known as *barua* in every village, those on whom "the god can ride". During most religious ceremonies, these persons are liable to fall into a sort of frenzy—they throw themselves on the ground, they wag their heads desperately to and fro (this is called *jhupna*), they beat themselves with iron scourges, they thrust iron spikes through tongue or cheeks. It is believed that the god is riding upon them. At such moments, they often reveal secrets that have not been discovered by the ordinary methods of *gunia.*

Some magicians *(panda)* trust this as their usual methods of divination. They fix a day when their clients are to visit them and regularly fall into trances and prophecy. This is known as *dham.* The *dham* requires a certain amount of apparatus. The *panda* builds a little *madhia* (shrine) for himself, and erects a couple of poles before it. He may furnish it with a wooden ladder, with a *jhula* (swing), a *barahi* (a rope studded with iron spikes), a *gurud* (an iron chain spiked, having a knob at the end), a *pidha* (a flat board studded with spikes) and a pair of spiked shoes. When the god rides upon the *panda*, he may rush up the ladder—not touching it with his hands, he may beat himself with the chains, sit on the *pidha*, swing violently in his *jhula*, or walk about on the spiked shoes. He does undoubtedly achieve a certain degree of anesthesia. Then from spiked seat he utters his oracle with great authority. Sometimes, the magician can diagnose witchcraft, which is too powerful for him to go further.

Treatment of illness

Treatment by making the appropriate offerings

When the nature and cause of the disease from which the patient is suffering is diagnosed by the *gunia*, he must proceed to take the proper remedies to ensure his recovery. If he diagnoses a definitely supernatural cause, he asks the sick man to make the offerings prescribed by long customs for every separate spirit of disease; if the sickness is due to *Narayan Deo*, he fixes a day for the dedication of the *laru* (small pig), sometimes even the promise of an offering later on, when times are better, is sufficient. Here is a list showing the different offerings for different deities.

Deities	*Offerings*
Dulha Deo	Red hen, coconut, nut
Holi Rai	White or black hen
Khermai	Goat (reddish)
Budi-Dai	Goat (black)
Satbahi Debi	Black hen
Pani harin	Chick (black), coconut
Narayan Deo	Laru (Small pig)

If the offerings are supposed to be late or anything being dismissed to not to sacrifice in promised time then the deities are believed to do something of disastrous result. Even a great epidemic occurs in the village, which is impossible to be controlled by the hospital doctors also.

Treatment by driving the disease away

Elwin reports that where witchcraft is the cause of any sickness, and the witch is known, she herself is forced to remove the evil and send it out of the village. This is done in various ways. The most common method is to place the disease or the evil spirit who brought it on a goat or hen, and drive it into the jungle. Three other rites are associated with this policy of direct action, *jhat puja*, *jua puja* and the making of a *thua*. In this case, after the *gunia* has discovered that a witch has sent the disease whose origin he has been asked to investigate, he proceeds, not to offer sacrifice but to direct and drastic punishment of witch, and to a form of sympathetic magic which is expected to remove the evil influence from the victim.

Jua puja is apparently quite as effective as *jhat puja*. "Once a witch killed her own eldest son by her magic. The father, who was *gunia*, came home and tried every kind of offering, but his child lay still and cold. Then at last he started *jua puja*. He took lice from the boy's hair and taking the creature in his hand, nipped off its head between his nails. He put a fire there and he let a drop of its blood fall on the fire. Then he wrapped its body in a leaf and carried it to the nearest stream and threw it in. The magic that had killed the child, had entered the body of the louse, and it was carried away by the water. When the father returned he found his son breathing and next day he was well again".

Treatment by the use of mantra

The simple recitation of mantra is common to all tribal communities for the treatment of various kind of illness. The power of mantra is often effective to defeat the nefarious activities of witches, to drive away troublesome ghost, to save a man from snake or scorpion bite. Elwin (1986: 389) recorded some specimens of *mantra* used to bind or banish *bhut* and other evil spirits, in order to bring the poison down of scorpion bite, snake bite, to staunch the flow of blood they use *mantras* to get immediate results.

Treatment by herbal medicines

The Baiga are famous as the medicine men. Besides the magico-religious treatment of the diseases, treatment by medicinal plants is very much popular among the Baigas for curing the various diseases. The *dewar* is village medicine man who prescribes various herbal medicines when he is called for treatment of diseases.

Local Name	*English equivalent of the disease*	*Indigenous medicine used*
Garmi	Syphilis	Roots of *ban semar* (*Galactia tenuiflora*), *hasiya daphar* (*Baliospermum axillare*). Grind these up together and make the powder into pills with *gur*. Give one every morning for 21 days. Some black pepper, fruit of *bel* (*Aegle marnelos*), bark of *dudhia* (*Holarrhena antidysenterica*), seeds of *ghol* (*Portulaca oleracea*). Dry, grind and mix together. Put in milk and drink.
Thanki	Gonorrhoea	Steep the rhizorne of Kurkoti (*Pachystoma senile*) for a night in water. Add sugar and black pepper. Root of bhawarsal (*Hymendictyon excelsum*), the ripe fruit of *dhan–baker* (*cassia fistula*). Crush them together; mix the expressed juice with water. Roots of ramdatan (*Smilax macrosphylla*), seeds of *lalphatta* (*Panicum crus-galli*). Grind together, boil in water. Cool and drink for three days.
Dhat Parmi	Gleet and Chronic gonorrhoea	Bark of *dudhia* (*holarrhena antidysenterica*), root of *Khamer* (*gmelina arborea*). Grind and give to drink in milk. Bark of bahera (*Terminalia belerica*), *tendu* (*Diospyros melanoxylon*), a little plant called *muhmundi* (*thespesia lampas*) that grows in swamps. Mix, dry, grind and makes pills with *gur*.
Ulti-dast	Diarrhoea	Bark of *saja* (*Terminalia tomentosa*), *tinsa* (*ougeinia dalbergioides*), *karar* (*Bauhinia purpurea*). Pound up together with water.

		Let it stand all day. Drink in evening. Chew the bark of *karikorai* (*Holarrhena antidysenterica*).
	Sleepiness	Take and use a twig of *pipal (Ficus religiosa)*. Then as the leaves of the *pipal* tremble without wind, the patient will be alert and awake always.
	Impotence	Tuber of black *musri* (*curculigo orchioides*). Give to eat on an empty stomach. The liver of a sparrow or other small bird, eaten daily.
Ankh fulni	Sore eyes	Fruit of *aonla* (Emblica officinalis). Grind it up and make a poultice for application to the eyes.
Khasi	For cough	The expressed juice of *harra* fruit (*Ferminalia chebula*).
Mur dukhai	Headache	Leaves of *amli* (*Bauhinia malabarica*). Grind, mix in cold water and apply to forehead. Leaves of *jhunjhuria* (*Phoenix acaulis*). Crush the leaves and make a poultice for the head.
Haddi tutna	Broken bones	Take the creeper called *harsingri* (*Nyctanthes arbor-tristis*) and apply it to the fractured part, tying it on firmly. Also give a little of it to eat.
Chingran bad	Paralysis	Bees' wax, fruit of the *pipal* (*ficus religiosa*), fruit of the *karaiyu* (*miliusa jelutina*). Mix and grind. Make an ointment with *ramtilla* oil (*guzotia abyssinica*).
	Fever	Bhimka roots and *karela* (*Momordica charantia*). Dry, mix, grind. Make into pills with *ramtilla* oil, and give five a day for three days.
Bukher	Scorpion bite	Take the leaves of the gurbel creeper (T*inospora cordifolia*), pound them, and

	boil them in water. Bathe the patient in this and also give a little to drink. Grind up the root of *tikur* (*curcuma angustifolia*). Make poultice and apply to head. Ground flowers of *mahua* (*bassia latifolia*) applied as a poultice, and some *mahua* liquor taken internally.

Conclusions

The lack of hygienic drinking water leads to a number of waterborne disease and health hazards. Falciparum malaria is common due to heavy rain of these hilly forest areas. Malnutrition is the chief factor, which causes affliction of various diseases like desentery, thyroid, goitre, rickets, etc. Unhygienic health habits and living condition are also responsible for their various type of skin disease. Premarital sex and sexual relation with more than one individual also leads them suffering from venereal diseases like gonorrhea, syphilis, etc. Infant mortality rate (IMR) shows a higher trend among the Baiga, i.e., 125 per 1,000 live births as compared with the national average of 80 (1991–92 census). Maternal mortality rate is found high, i.e., 2 per 408 live births among the Baiga, which is much more than that of national average (4 to 5 per 1,000 live births). Common health problems found among the children of the Baiga tribe are diarrhoea, simple cough and cold, skin infections like scabies, boils, jaundice, disease related to malnutrition. Treatment through magico-religious practices and treatment by the use of herbal medicine are popular among the Baiga healing practices. The herbal medicines are prescribed by the village medicine man (*dewar*).

References

Basu, S. 1994 *Tribal Health in India* (edited volume), Manak Publications Pvt. Ltd., New Delhi.

Bhasin, V. and V.K. Srivastava 1991 "Medical Anthropology: A Review", *Journal of Human Ecology*, No. 1, Special Issue, Patiala.

Chauhan, D. and Sangita Kamdar 1997 "Social Sector and Development: Focus on Health Care", *Yojana*, Vol. 41, No. 4, New Delhi.

Chrisman, N.J. 1977. "The Health Seeking Process: An Approach to the Natural History of Illness", *Culture, Medicine and Psychiatry,* 1: 351–377.

Elwin, V. 1986 *The Baiga,* Gain Publishing House, New Delhi.

Ebrahim, G.J. 1991 *Practical Mother and Child Health in Developing Countries,* Macmillan Education Ltd., London.

Evans-Pritchard, E.E. 1937 *Witchcraft, Oracles and Magic among the Azande,* Oxford University Press, Oxford, 68.

Foster, G.M. and B.G. Anderson 1978 *Medical Anthropology,* John Wiley, New York.

Gopal, K. Rani 1987 *Economics of Health and Nutrition: Some Aspects of Growth and Welfare,* Chugh Publications, Allahabad.

Janzen, J.M. 1978 "The Comparative Study of Medical Systems as Changing Social System", *Social Science and Medicine,* B12, 121–129.

Joshi, P.C. 1988 "Traditional Medical System in the Central Himalayas", *Eastern Anthropologist,* Vol. 41, No. 1, 77–96.

Kalla, A.K. and K.S. Singh (eds) 1986 *Anthropology, Developments and Nation Building,* Concept Publishing, Delhi.

Laubscher, B.J.F. 1937 "Sex, Custom and Psycho Pathology", *Archives of General Psychiatry,* London, 811.

Mukherjee, B.M. and N. Khatua 1998 "Exchange and Reciprocity in the Kamar Tribe", *Man in India,* Vol. 78, Nos. 3&4, 349–54.

Niéhter, M. and Sickle, D. (2000) The Challenges of India's Health and Health Care Transition, in A.A. Ayres, *India Briefing: Quickening the Pace of Change* (p.37). Armonk, New York USA: Asia Society Publication.

Pandey, B.N. et al. 1999 "Impact of Industrialisation in Socio-cultural and Health Aspects of Tribal Group of South Bihar, India", *Jr. of Human Ecology,* Vol. 10, No. 1, 15–28.

Park, J.E. 1974 *Textbook of Preventive and Social Medicine,* Banarasidas Bhanot Publishers, Jabalpur, MP.

United Nations 1994 *Report of the International Conference on Population and Development,* Cairo, Egypt, September (Preliminary version), UN, New York, 25–54.

World Health Organization 1994 Health Population and Development, WHO Position Paper for International Conference on Population and Development, Cairo, WHO, Geneva.

18

Coping with cataract blindness among tribal patients: Some case studies from Mysore district, Karnataka

C.K. Kantharaju and H.K. Bhat

Blindness, the loss of eyesight, is one of the most serious misfortune in human life. Apart from loss of functional ability and self-esteem, blindness and other related visual impairments have considerable economic significance. They lead to a greater loss of productivity, income and social dependence on others and require rehabilitative and supportive measures.

Cataract accounts for approximately 16 million cases of blindness worldwide. In most of the developing countries like India and China, it accounts for approximately half of all blindness. A cataract results from a change of transparency of the normal crystalline lens in the eye. When the lens becomes opaque, it prevents the light from entering the eye. This condition causes gradual loss of vision and blindness. Cataract may have different origins; some children may be born with it and in some cases cataracts develop after eye injuries. However, cataracts are largely related to the ageing process.

The problem of blindness and its magnitude is much higher in India. Of the 31 million, India alone has 9 million blind people, which comes to more than one-third of the total blind in the world. According to a Health Ministry survey, prevalence of cataract is higher among women, tribal population and in rural areas, in contrast to industrial countries where it typically afflicts the elderly. Some 40 per cent of the cases in India are within the productive age of 40–50 years. Bulk of curable cataract blinds resides in rural areas and is beyond the reach of the existing urban-based facilities. The reasons, which are responsible for higher prevalence of blindness in India, include, lack of adequate ophthalmic personnel, lack of availability of services and lack of sources of information on eye care services. Underutilization of available manpower, imbalance in availability of eye care services in rural/urban areas, lack of knowledge and concern about malnutrition, man-made blindness due to quack practice and home remedies also add to the problems in improving the conditions of the people.

The study

The present study mainly focuses on the problems of low uptake of eye care services and concept of blindness among Scheduled Tribes population in Mysore district. The study also aims to identify the various barriers (physical, economic, social and cultural to low uptake of eye care services) with special reference to cataract blindness and its treatment.

Based on the objectives of the study, an interview guide was prepared and the information was gathered by residing in the tribal settlements (*hadis*) and involving in the daily activities of the people. The idea was to supplement the data collected through interviews by systematic observation. In addition, the information was also collected by informal discussion and conversations, genealogical technique, formal and informal interview and case study methods were employed.

The study was conducted in the rural areas of Mysore district, especially in the HD Kote Taluk, the most backward taluk in the district. Ten tribal settlements known as *hadis* were selected for the study. These settlements are located in the fringe area of Rajiv Gandhi National Park, Nagarahole and a few settlements are located inside the national park. These settlements are selected based on the following criteria: urban influence, accessibility of eye care services, external influences were considered while selection of tribal settlements.

The three major Scheduled Tribes covered in the study are Jenukurubas, Bettakurubas and Yeravas. These Scheduled Tribes were basically food gatherers and hunters. Food gathering and hunting was the first adaptation of humankind ever made. The lifestyles of the Scheduled Tribes are gradually changing owing to exposure to various cultures. Change in their economy, material culture, dress pattern and use of consumer goods can be easily seen. In spite of all these changes, the members of Scheduled Tribes of the region have been able to maintain their identity. Each Scheduled Tribe has its own council, which regulates its internal affairs. However, it is noticed that previously elders of the tribe known as *Yejamanas* took most of the decisions regarding their own group, but nowadays, any able-bodied man who strives for the welfare of his people can be considered as a *Yejamana*. Nowadays, women are also taking active part in the affairs of their community and they appear to fight for their rights. Many women among them insisted that they were the main decision-makers in their settlements today. In other words, the ancient forest dwellers are undergoing a process of transformation.

Results and discussions

The complete household census was conducted in all selected tribal settlements and 342 households were visited. The census data was analysed for different variables like sex-wise composition of population, level of education, etc.

There were 47.38 per cent literates and 52.62 per cent illiterates in the sample. Among literates, 40.32 per cent and 48.78 per cent have received primary and higher primary level of education, respectively. There were only 3.08 per cent who have completed SSLC in tribal settlements.

The present study uncovers the people's perception towards blindness, their beliefs associated with cataract blindness in particular, accessibility of eye care services and various barriers to low uptake of eye care services among Scheduled Tribe population. In all, 160 members of Scheduled Tribes consisting of 80 males and 80 females were interviewed.

There are only 12 informants aged less than 30 years and majority of the informants are aged more than 50 years. Since the study is focused on cataract problem and it is associated with age, the informant's age was also considered at the time of interview.

The informants were classified based on their vision status into four categories; cataract blind, operated, caretaker and others. Out of 160 informants, 59 were suffering from cataract blindness and only 7 were operated. All of them are economically very backward and they derived their livelihood from wage labour. The socio-economic conditions of these informants are very poor.

The purpose of the study is to uncover the cultural mode of behaviour among members of Scheduled Tribes regarding attitudes, beliefs and various misgivings about cataract blindness and various barriers attached to uptake of eye care services in the district. The informants were asked to answer each research question with detail (one or more responses). In addition, several supplementary questions were also put to the informants to elicit more information. This technique of interview in which a number of responses are recorded is known as free listing technique. The basic idea of the researcher is that the most frequently mentioned responses by the informants were the most significant indicators for the community. They may also indicate the cultural traits of the community. The data collected were triangulated with data collected by observation, focus group discussion, informal interviews and case study methods.

Blindness: Emic definition

Majority of the informants described blindness as "not able to see properly" (126), "defect in vision" (42), "both the eyes are closed" (22), "no light in both the eyes" (16) and "not able to see due to *pore* (curtain) on eyes" (13). This clearly shows the culturally significant emic definitions of blindness.

Cataract blindness: Signs and symptoms

The most common and culturally significant responses regarding signs and symptoms are "foggy vision" (99), "abnormal muscular growth over the eyes" (62), "blurred vision" (32), "watering of eyes" (28), "not able to identify" (25) and "development of a curtain *(pore)* over the eyes" (25). The less frequently mentioned responses are "burning of eyes", "multiple vision", "not able to identify cows/cattle in the field", "not able to insert thread into the needle", "not able to move without the help of others", "headache", "watering of eyes during cooking", "not able to stitch old cloth".

Causes of blindness

(a) Congenital blindness

Congenital blindness was attributed to a number of causes, the most significant were "curse of deity" (83), "sin committed in the previous birth" (59) and "heredity" (44). The less frequently mentioned responses are eye injuries during the collection of minor forest produces, agricultural work or any other activities resulting in permanent visual disability and eye exposure to the hot sun or viewing solar eclipse.

(b) Cataract blindness

Cataract blindness was attributed to a number of causes and the responses mentioned are more than ten. The most frequently mentioned responses are "carrying heavy load of fire wood on head" (59), "ageing" (47), "not oiling the hair regularly" (46) and "chewing tobacco, betel nut, gutka, jarda, pan", etc. (44).

Following are some of the responses recorded during the fieldwork which are illustrative of the cultural significance of the cataract blindness.

Bolaiah, a 65-year-old man belonging to Scheduled Tribe, having lower class income, belonging to Seegooruhadi with cataract blind vision status said "I am having fear that they will spoil my eyes, so 1 don't need operation and according to my horoscope, I will die if I go to the hospital for surgery".

Annaiah, a 68-year-old man belonging to Scheduled Tribe, having lower class income, belonging to Seegooruhadi with cataract blind vision status said, "I am very poor, I don't have enough money and even I have problem to run my family. If I stay in bed for two to three days due to illness or some injuries, my family members have to borrow money from our landlords even for food. So this leads to debt under landlords. If I have to spend Rs. 500 to Rs. 600 to go to hospital our family will face debt in future".

Kalaiah, a 70-year-old man belonging to Yerava Scheduled Tribe, having lower class income, belonging to Udbooruhadi with cataract blind vision status said, "If I wish to be operated, I need money for transport, money to get admitted at the hospital, money for food to myself and my assistance during operation and after operation I can't work as before, due to weakness and even I have to take more than 50 days for recovery of my health".

Mallamma, a 65-year-old woman belonging to Yerava Scheduled Tribe, having lower class income, belonging to Udbooruhadi with cataract blind vision status said, "I am old, I don't want operation at this age, I want to die like this only".

Rama, a 68-year-old man belonging to Bettakuruba Scheduled Tribe, having lower class income, belonging to Hunsekuppehadi with cataract blind vision status said, "See, I am counting my days, what will be the use of having an operation at this age?"

Puttaiah, a 71-year-old man belonging to Jenukuruba Scheduled Tribe, having lower class income, belonging to Malada hadi with cataract blind vision status said, "At this age, my present eyesight is enough, I don't have any ambitions or work to do at this age, this is God's wish so how can I go to the hospital?".

Gowramma, a 71-year-old woman belonging to Scheduled Tribe, having lower class income, belonging to Maladahadi with cataract blind vision status said, "I have an eye problem, because God has desired me to live this way".

Kenchaiah, a 49-year-old man belonging to Scheduled Tribe, having lower class income, belonging to Karapurahadi with normal vision status said about his father, "what is the use of making him to see when he is going to die?".

Putti, a 45-year-old woman belonging to Scheduled Tribe, having lower class income, belonging to Maranahadi with normal vision status said about her mother-in-law, "she has become very old and giving lot of problem, what is the use of taking her to the camp and doing the surgery?".

Sallamma, a 43-year-old woman belonging to Scheduled Tribe, having lower class income, belonging to Maranahadi with normal vision status said about her father-in-law, "he has become very old and so I thought that it would be of no use if I take him for treatment, he has become a burden at this old age, we think it would be better if he dies soon".

Barriers to use of eye care services

The most common response for not using the existing eye care services is "lack of money" (137). The study was conducted among members of

Scheduled Tribes. They were economically backward sections of the society, this was the expected answer. Other culturally most significant responses were "fear of surgery or treatment" (79), "lack of information on eye care services" (61) and "lack of family members who are willing to help blinds to get treatment" (51).

Conclusion

In all, data were collected from 160 informants comprising 80 males and 80 females from ten rural tribal settlements known as *hadis*. A majority of them are socially, educationally and economically very backward. These members of Scheduled Tribes were living in unhygienic conditions. These settlements are located in remote areas, even some of them do not have proper roads. There were 59 informants suffering from cataract blindness. There is a need of surgery for these people according to our observation. But the cataract blindness persons are unable to utilize the available services. The major constraints are their poor economic status and fear of surgery and treatment. In addition to this, lack of transportation facilities, lack of proper information on eye care services, etc. act as barriers.

To overcome the problem of cataract blindness in tribal settlements the anthropological interventions are essential. If an anthropologist acts as a facilitator, who can help those people in old age to resolve the barriers which inhibit the utilization of modern eye care services, they can regain their vision and lessen the dependence on others. An anthropologist can convince the service providers to arrange eye screening and surgery camps in rural areas where bulk of cataract patients reside. He can also initiate a dialogue with cataract blind individuals and motivate them to regain their vision.

References

Abou Gareeb, I. et al. 2001 "Gender and Blindness: A Meta-analysis of Population-based Prevalence Surveys", *Ophthalmic Epidemiol*, Vol. 8, No. 1, Feb, 39–56.

Barnard, Alan 2000 *History and Theory in Anthropology*, Cambridge: Cambridge University Press.

Beals, Ralph et al. 1977 *Introduction to Anthropology*, 5th Edition, New York: Macmillan Publishing Co. Inc.

Bernard, H. Russell 1994 *Research Methods in Anthropology: Qualitative and Quantitative Approaches*, New Delhi: Sage Publications.

Bhat, H.K. 2000 "Community Diagnosis and Its Relevance for Voluntary Action in Primary Health Care", *Man and Life*, Vol. 26, Nos. 1&2 (Jan–June).

Dandona, L., R. Dandona and R.K. John 2001 "Estimation of Blindness in India from 2000 through 2020: Implications for the Blindness Control Policy", *Natl Med J India*, Vol. 14, No. 16 (Nov–Dec), 327–34.

Foster, G.M. and B.G. Anderson, (1978.). *Medical Anthropology*, New York: John Wiley.

Limburg, Hans 1997 "Rapid Assessment for Cataract Blindness in Persons of 50 Years and Older", District level survey conducted in all districts of Karnataka in 1995, DANPCB, New Delhi.

Nichter, M. 1982 "Project Community Diagnosis: Participatory Research as a First Step Toward Community Involvement in Primary Health Care", Paper presented at A.A. Society Meetings, Washington DC, December 4–7.

Pelto, Pertti J. and Gretel H. Pelto 1978 *Anthropological Research*, Cambridge: Cambridge University Press.

WHO-UNICEF 1978 "Primary Health Care", Report of the International Conference on Primary Health Care, Alma Ata, USSR, Geneva.

List of contributors

S.N. Ratha, Dean, M.G. National Institute of Research and Social Action, Hyderabad. Also, former Professor of Anthropology, Sambalpur University, Sambalpur, Orrissa.

P.K. Misra, E–583, J.P. Nagar, 1st Stage, 17th Main, Mysore.

P.R.G. Mathur, Director and Secretary, Ananthakrishna International Centre for Anthropological Studies, Palakkad, Kerala.

T.B. Subba, Professor, Department of Anthropology, North-Eastern Hill University, Shillong, Meghalaya.

P. Ishwara Bhat, Vice Chancellor, National University of Judicial Sciences, Salt Lake City, Kolkata, West Bengal.

R.K. Kar, Ashit Nagar (Begchipara), Diburgarh, Assam.

V.R. Rao, Professor, Department of Anthropology, University of Delhi, Delhi.

A. Chandrasekar, Research Associate, Anthropological Survey of India, Southern Regional Centre, Bogadi, Mysore.

R.S. Negi, 29-A, Circular Road, Dehradun, Uttarakhand.

Sanjib Ganguly, Department of Anthropology, Vidyasagar University, Midnapore, West Bengal.

Argina Khatun, Research Scholar, Department of Anthropology, Vidyasagar University, Midnapore, West Bengal.

Samiran Bisai, Research Scholar, Department of Anthropology, Vidyasagar University, Midnapore, West Bengal.

Subal Das, Research Scholar, Department of Anthropology, Vidyasagar University, Midnapore, West Bengal.

Kaushik Bose, Professor, Department of Anthropology, Vidyasagar University, Midnapore, West Bengal.

Ajay Kumar Gharami, Associate Professor, Department of Anthropology H.S. Gour University, Sagar, Madhya Pradesh.

Udita Rathi, Research Scholar, Department of Anthropology, University of Hyderabad, Hyderabad.

B.V. Sharma, Associate Professor, Department of Anthropology, University of Hyderabad, Hyderabad.

B.R. Vijayendra, Assistant Anthropologist, Anthropological Survey of India, Southern Regional Centre, Bogadi, Mysore.

S.A.A. Saheb, Superintending Anthropologist, Anthropological Survey of India, North-West Region, Dehradun, Uttarakhand.

B.V. Raviprasad, Research Associate, Anthropological Survey of India, Southern Regional Centre, Bogadi, Mysore.

P. Kalyan Reddy, Assistant Director, TCR and TI , Hyderabad.

S.N.H. Rizvi, Anthropologist, Anthropological Survey of India, North-West Region, Dehradun, Uttarakhand.

Nilanjan Khatua, Museum Keeper, Anthropological Survey of India, Southern Regional Centre, Bogadi, Mysore.

C.K. Kantharaju, Programme Manager, Vivekananda Girijan Kalyana Kendra, Technology Resource Centre, Mysore.

H.K. Bhat, 771, 5th Cross, Roopnagar, Bogadi, Mysore.

Index

Adak, D.K., 93
Aggarwal, Yash and Sarika Sibou, 187
Ahmad, Imtiaz, 185
Alcazar, L. and R. Andrade, 210
Allen, P.T., 209
alternative development, 30
applied anthropologists
    role of, in planning and evaluation, 44–46
applied anthropology, 42
    theory of, historical context of, 40–43
Arnold, D., 204
Ashraf, A. et al., 201
Astin, J.A., 203

Bamshad, M.J., Kivisild, T., et al., 106, 112
Bamshad, M.J., Watkins, W.S., et al., 106
Bara, Joseph, 105
Basu, A.R., 6, 7
Basu, S.K., 136
Behura, N.K., 94
Belshaw, C., 7
Benzamin, Z. et al., 203
Beteille, Andre, 63, 65
Bhatt, V., 6
Bhattacharyya, N.P., Basu, P., et al., 106
Bhushan, Bharat, 96, 97
Binford, Lewis R., 10
blindness, 244, 247
    in India, 244–45, reasons for, 245
Bond, P., 210
Brittenham, G., B. Lozoff and J.W. Harris, 123
Brown, Tim and Morag Brown, 204
Buchan, J. and M.R. Dal Poz, 201

cataract blindness, 247
    causes of, 248
    signs/symptoms of, 247–48
Cercone, J. et al., 209
Chambers, Robert, 7
Chandrasekar, A. et al., 106
Chandrasekar, A., Saheb, S.Y., et al., 111

Chatterjee, S.K., 186, 187
Chaudhury, S.S., 9
Chitnis, Suma, 187
Chrisman, N.J., 225
Clements, Forrest E., 215
Coburn, D., 210
congenital blindness, 248
  causes of, 248
Cordaux, R., Saha, N., et al., 108
Cosminsky, S. and M. Scrimshaw, 202

Das Gupta, Biplab, 92
Das, G. 95, 98
Das, T., 19
Desai, A.R., 185
development
  origin of, 93–94
  process/concept/idea of, 7–8, 96
Devereux, George, 216
disability, 151
  among STs, educational and employment challenges for, 154–56
Dye, Thomas R., 198

Eckholm, E., 21
eco-tourism, 99
Elwin, V., 9, 19, 33, 66, 67, 69, 227, 228, 230, 232, 234
Embree, John, 43
English-Lueck, J.A., 202
Epstein, Ronald M. et al., 202
Esman, M.J., 8
Evans-Pritchard, E.E., 10, 42, 43, 232

farmer suicides
  in India, 35–36

Firth, Raymond, 10
Fiske, S.J., 199
Flannery, T.F. and Peter Schouten, 21
Forde, C.D., 10, 12
forest dwelling STs, 82
  forest rights of, 82–83
Foster, G.M. and B.G. Anderson, 216, 234
Foster, M., 208
Friedl, John, 10
Furtado, Celso, 93

genetic structure
  of India, 105, components of, 105
Gesler, M. Wilbert, 201
Gesler, W., 204
Ghosh, B. et al., 208
Ghurye, G.S., 69
Gillies, P., 206
good health, 199
Goulet, D., 7
Govinda, R and N.V. Varghese, 189
grass roots democracy, 86
Greenfield, Sidney M., 202
Gubhaju, B., K. Streatfield and A. Majumdar, 136
Guha, Ramachandra, 93
Gulliver, Philip, 42
Gupta, Abhik, 98

Haimendorf, C.F., 95
Hall, T.L. and A. Meija, 199
Headland, T.N., K.L. Pike and M. Harris, 67
health care system, 218
health planning, 199

health-seeking behaviour, 225
  among tribes, 227–42
health-seeking process, 225
Heller, Peter, 208
Henry, Jules and Zunia Henryh, 216
Higham, C., 108
Hongoro, Charles and Barbara McPake, 201
human body, 102
human
  origin of, 162–63

Indian Constitution, 75, 92
Indian society
  during the colonial period, 1–2
  in ancient times, 1
Indian Y chromosome
  topology of, 111–12
indigenous medicine system
  among tribes, 217–23

Jaen, M.H. and D. Paravisini, 210
Janzen, J.M., 201, 225
Jha, Jyotsna and Dhir Jhingran, 190

Kamat, A.R., 186
Kapilashrani, M.C., 208
Kaplan, R. and S. Kaplan, 204
Kaptchuk, Ted J. et al., 203
Kar, R.K., 95, 96
Kivisild, T., Kaldma, K., et al., 106
Kivisild, T., Rootsi, S., et al., 111
Kivislid, T., Bamshad, M.J., et al., 106, 107
Kluckhohn, Clyde, 43, 44
Kroeger, A. and H.P. Franken, 201
Kumar, S., Padmanabham, P.B., et al., 106, 109

Lahr, M.M. and R.A. Foley, 109
Laine, C. and F. Davidoff, 202
Lee, Richard B. and Irven DeVore, 10
Lee, Richard B., 10
Leeson, J., 203
Lehman, H. and M. Cutbush, 117
Leighton, Alexander H. and Dorothea C. Leighton, 216
Leslie, C., 201, 202
Linton, Ralph, 25
Lock, M., 202

Mahadevan, K., 135
Mahana, R.K., 30
Malinowski, B., 25, 41
Mandelbaum, David G., 8
Martinez, J. and T. Martineau, 207
Maskovsky, J., 210
Mazumdar, D.N., 33
McElreavey, K. and Quintana-Murci, L., 109
MDGs, 199
Mead, Margaret, 43, 215
Metspalu, M. et al., 106, 108
Milligan, C. et al., 204
Misra, P.K., 32, 63
mitochondrial DNA, 102
  role of, in human evolution, 102–3
Mohapatra, Ajay, 11
Mountain, J.L., Hebert, J.M., et al., 106
mtDNA haplogroups
  in India, topology of, 106–9
  in the world, 104–5

Mueller, Eric and Murugan Narayanan Kani, 200

Nambissan, Geetha B., 187
Nandy, A., 93
Nanjundayya, H.V. and L.K.A. Iyer, 163, 164
Narayanan, V.N., 96, 97
National Policy on Education, 186
objectives of, 186
New Economic Policy, 195
Nguyen, Vinh-Kim and Karine Peschard, 211
Nichter, M. and D.l Sickle, 225
Norstrom, Christer, 32
north-east India, 95–96
tribal development in, 97–99
other traditional forest dwellers (OTFDs), 82
forest rights of, 82–83

Palanychamy, M.G. et al., 106
Pandey, C.D., Arvind Verma and R.S. Tiwary, 136
Pathy, J., 185
Patil, Suresh and Ramji Gupta, 162
Patwardhan, B. et al., 205
Paul, B.D., 216
Phillips, D.R., 200
Prasad, B.V.R., 189
Primitive Tribal Groups (PTGs), 3
in India, 3, status of, 32–33
public policy, 198
Punalekar, S.P., 185

Qamar, R., Ayub, Q., et al., 108
Quintana-Murci, L., et al., 106

Ratha, S.N., M.C. Goswami and F. Nesha, 11
Reddy, N. Subba, 34
Reich, M., 206
Richards, M., Rengo, C., et al., 106
Risley, H.H., 2
Robertson, A.F.,7
Rosenhan, D.L.,64
Roy Burman, B.K., 4, 5–6, 30, 63
Roy, S.C., 11, 19
Roychoudhury, S., Roy, S., et al., 106

Sachs, Worlfand, 94
Sahlins, Marshall D., 2
Sanders, Irwin T., 8
Sandhwar, A.N., 11
Sandhya, S., 136
Saper, Rober B. et al., 209
Scheduled Tribe(s), 92
economic status of, 191
education of, role of Christian missionaries in spreading, 185; present status of, 185–86
emergence of the term, 2–3
in Andrha Pradesh, disability among the, 152–54; welfare policies for, 156–58
in India, welfare of, 5–7; population of, 135, 170, 184
literacy among, trends in, 187–91
Scheff, T., 64
Schneider, Harold K., 7
Seers, D., 94
Sen, A., 199
Service, Elman R., 2
Shang, A. et al., 209

Sharma, B.D., 6, 94, 185
Sharma, K.K.N., 136
shyness of culture, 66
Singh, J., B.A. Rao and S.P. Ram Krishnan, 123
Singh, K.S., 4, 33, 164
Sinha, A.C., 63, 67, 69
Sinha, Surajit and B.D. Sharma, 32
Somasundaram, K.V. et al., 201
Srivastava, L.R.N., 186
Srivatsava, V.K., 33
Steward, Julian H., 2
Steward, Lieut R., 95
Subba, T.B., 68, 70
Subramanyam, V., 190
Sujatha, K., 187, 189
Sundar, Nadini, 184, 185
Sutton, F.F., 96
Syngai, D., 98

Talwar, P.P., 136
Tambets, K., Kivisild, T., et al. , 106
Tax, Sol, 9
Thangaraj, K., Chaubay, G., et al. , 108
Thangaraj, K., Singh, L., et al., 111
Thelma, Narayan, 210
therapy managements, 225
Thoits, P.A., 64
Thurston, E., 171
Todaro, M., 7
Todaro, M.P., 94
tribal culture(s)
    of India, 25
tribal development, 8, 93
    in India, 93, 94
    in north-east India, 97-99
Tribal Sub-Plan (TSP) strategy in India, 6, 34, 93
tribe(s), 63, 68
    and evolution, 69–70
    as reciprocal people, 70–72
    classification of, 185
    concept of, in Indian context, 4, 62–63, 67–68, 69, 70, 92
    defining a, politics in, 63–65
    emergence of the term, 2–3
    in India, 92, state of, 31–34
    scheduling of, 184
Tylor, E.B., 25

Underhill, P.A., Passarino, G., et al., 111

Varatharajan, D., 200
Varghese, N.V., 189
varnasrama system, 1
    in ancient Indian society, 1
Velaskar, Padma, 186
Ventegodt, Soren et al., 203
Vidyarthi, L.P. and B.K. Rai, 95
Vidyarthi, L.P., 95

Wilson, E., 204
Wisenfild, S.L., 118
withcrafting
    among tribes, 232–33, 239
Wolfe, Marshall, 93
Wright, John and John Walley, 201
Wright, Susan and Cris Shore, 199

Xaxa, Virginius, 63

Y chromosome lineages, 111
Y chromosome, 110
Yadav, H., 6